New Directions
in Austrian Economics

New Directions in Austrian Economics

Edited by Louis M. Spadaro

SHEED ANDREWS AND McMEEL, INC.
Subsidiary of Universal Press Syndicate
Kansas City

This edition is published in cooperation with the programs of the Institute for Humane Studies, Inc.,
Menlo Park, California; and Cato Institute, San Francisco, California.

New Directions in Austrian Economics
Copyright © 1978 by the Institute for Humane Studies.

Jacket and cover design copyright © 1978 Cato Institute, San Francisco, California.

Library of Congress Cataloging in Publication Data

Main entry under title:

New directions in Austrian economics.

    (Studies in economic theory)
    Includes bibliographical references.
    Papers sponsored by the Institute for Humane Studies
and presented at a symposium held at Windsor Castle
Sept. 1976.
    1. Austrian school of economists—Congresses.
I. Spadaro, Louis M. II. Institute for Humane
Studies. III. Series.
HB98.N48   330.15'7   77-28611
ISBN 0-8362-5104-0
ISBN 0-8362-5103-2 pbk.

CONTENTS

EDITOR'S PREFACE

Because the approach of the bicentennial of both the American Revolution and the publication of Adam Smith's famous *Wealth of Nations* tended to overshadow another milestone—the passing of a hundred years since the occurrence of the "marginalist" revolution in economic theory—the observance of the latter has been left mostly to economists.

Even among this relatively small company, whatever celebration there was tended to be further subdivided owing to the fact that the economic revolution of the 1870s arose independently in three different places and took implicitly different forms. Two of them—the English and the French variants—soon merged either with pre-existing analysis or with subsequent formulations and so have lost some of their specificity and identity.

The third—the Austrian—branch not only represented, from the outset, a more daring departure from received doctrine, but remained, in the intervening century, more independent and distinctive in its essential insights, its analytical method, and its implications for economic and social policy.

Thus it was that early in September of 1976, a small group of Austrian economists (most of them returning from a sentimental journey to Smith's birthplace) met for a few days in historic Windsor Castle to celebrate their own special anniversary. A number of papers prepared for the occasion were presented there and are here offered to a wider audience. The participants at the Symposium also engaged in a great deal of formal and informal discussion of the papers, which it was not possible to include in the present volume.

The arrangement of the articles here follows the order and purpose of their presentation at the symposium. The first and last are, respectively, a retrospective and a prospective for Austrian economic theory; the rest deal in their various ways with a number of significant points at the leading edge of Austrian analysis, where it interfaces or takes issue with contemporary economic thinking.

Thus, Professor Lachmann's paper is a thoughtful assessment of the present state of Austrian theory and a lucid statement of its essential distinguishing features. This provides the basis for a provocative critical examination of some of the implications of that theory and for a number of imaginative suggestions for its future extension.

Professor Egger attempts to locate and explain some of the critical points on which Austrian theory differs significantly from currently received doctrines. His discussion of these "differentia" offers a valuable bridging service to a potentially wide audience who would otherwise find it difficult to perceive and evaluate important Austrian insights on substance and method.

The methodological divergence between currently prevailing economic analysis and Austrianism is explored in depth in the paper by Mario Rizzo. By juxtaposing econometric and praxeological approaches, Dr. Rizzo provides a useful framework for critical examination of the claims and validity of the positivism that implicitly pervades so much contemporary theorizing.

The contribution by Kirzner complements and extends the distinctively Austrian insight into the role of information in the economic process to which Hayek called attention in a well-known article some forty years ago. In the present article, Professor Kirzner analyzes the function of error in economic decision-making as well as its relationship to information and to the nature of entrepreneurship.

Professor Littlechild addresses himself to the problem of social cost—a concept that not only pervades much of modern welfare economics, but also constitutes a major point of contention between Austrians and conventional theorists. Littlechild examines the validity of the concept itself as well as some attempts to deal with social cost from a subjectivist perspective.

Still another focus of disagreement between Austrians and the prevailing orthodoxy is monopoly theory and the concept of competition on which it rests, whether explicitly or not. Professor Armentano's paper is a critical examination of the conventional approach as well as of several variants of the Austrian view.

The essay by Professor O'Driscoll takes up a question that has divided economists for a very long time: whether there exists in a market economy an order not externally imposed upon it. In the course of his analysis, O'Driscoll argues that a number of problems in economic analysis that appear to be separate from this question as well as from one another are ultimately reducible to it.

Professor Rothbard examines the conventional definitions of the money supply and argues that the consistent application of an Austrian approach requires expansion of the meaning of the supply of money to include a number of important components currently excluded. Rothbard points out, moreover, that different components of the money-supply may have very different business cycle effects—a source of error that is systematically overlooked by the usual aggregative treatments of the subject.

Professor Moss calls into question the claim made by some Austrian economists that the subjective concept of time preference as developed by Mises implies that a positive rate of pure interest would necessarily appear even in a pure exchange economy (i.e., one with no production). Moss attempts a pure exchange model in which the emergence of such interest would necessarily depend on the presence of certain objective conditions.

Professor Garrison undertakes the considerable task of depicting macro-economic relationships diagrammatically and in a manner consistent with the Austrian insistence that valid explanations of economic relationships must ultimately refer to individual choices rather than rest on the facile assumption that aggregates interact directly. His graphics are applied to production, exchange, and other relationships in an attempt to establish a better and wider appreciation of Austrian analysis.

The last paper, by this writer, attempts to discern, in the light of the successes and failures of the past and present, some general guidelines for the future development of Austrian economics. It tentatively concludes that such development will most probably need to involve a much wider range of methods, disciplines, and professions.

Finally, it is the editor's pleasant duty to express a few acknowledgements on behalf of all the participants. We are grateful to Professor Arthur Shenfield for agreeing to act as chairman for the conference meetings and for his patience and wit in the discharge of a sometimes difficult task. The presence of Professor Friedrich von Hayek at the meetings was inspiring to the scholars participating, and his contributions to the discussions added insight and wisdom. Sincere thanks are also due Admiral D. H. Mason and the staff of St. George's House, Windsor Castle, for all their hospitality and help. Lastly, a very special word of thanks is extended to the University College at Buckingham and to the Institute for Humane Studies for sponsoring the Symposium—and to Koch Industries, Inc. without whose moral and material support neither the conference nor this book would have been possible.

Louis M. Spadaro
Fordham University
July, 1977

An Austrian Stocktaking: Unsettled Questions and Tentative Answers

Ludwig M. Lachmann
New York University
and University of Witwatersrand (South Africa)

I

In a decade in which the neoclassical consensus no longer holds sway, many economists are looking for new paradigms, less exacting to our credulity and more in conformity with what common experience teaches us about the daily flow of knowledge from man to man and our inability to know the future. Here Austrian economics presents three distinct features by which it may be distinguished from other contemporary schools of economic thought.

The first, and most prominent, feature of Austrian economics is a radical subjectivism, today no longer confined to human preferences but extended to expectations. It found its perfect expression many years ago in Hayek's statement, "It is probably no exaggeration to say that every important advance in economic theory during the last hundred years was a further step in the consistent application of subjectivism."[1]

Secondly, Austrian economics displays an acute awareness of the many facets of time that are involved in the complex network of interindividual relations. Time, as the dimension of the interval between input and output, is important, but it is not all-important. Menger's rejection of Böhm-Bawerk's theory of capi-

1

tal[2] was largely, if not solely, prompted by the latter's disregard of all those economically relevant aspects of time that do not fall under the headings "time preference" and "period of production." To Menger, time was, in the first place, the dimension in which the complex network of interindividual relations presents itself to us. Austrian economics has retained and cultivated this Mengerian perspective. Time is the dimension of all change. It is impossible for time to elapse without the constellation of knowledge changing. But knowledge shapes action, and action shapes the observable human world. Hence it is impossible for us to predict any future state of this world.

The third feature of Austrian economics, a corollary of subjectivism and awareness of the protean character of time, is a distrust of all those formalizations of economic experience that do not have an identifiable source in the mind of an economic actor. Such distrust naturally engenders skepticism about macroeconomic aggregates. To Austrians, all economic thought is thought within the context of means and ends implying choice. Austrian economics is certainly more than "a pure logic of choice." At some stage, we have to introduce "subsidiary assumptions." Expectations are a good example, the granting of credit is another. But Austrians will not accept formalizations of economic experience that altogether defy the category "means and ends," concepts that are nothing but formalizations of records of statistical observations in which the events recorded appear devoid of their historical character and meaning.

In what follows, the implications of these three features will be explored by applying them to a number of problems with which Austrian economists have good reason to concern themselves. But, quite apart from the three features, the Austrians, being such stout defenders of the market economy, are naturally involved in every attack on it. An argument currently in fashion among the would-be sophisticated says that the existence of so few forward markets in the real world proves that the effectiveness of the market process in coordinating economic plans and action is gravely hampered. In the climate of our time, the implication that here is a promising field of government intervention into all kinds of markets is almost a foregone conclusion. The argument thus calls for an answer. In the final section we shall have to address ourselves to the general question of what, from the Austrian point of view, economic science can hope to accomplish, and what it cannot.

II

Classical economics saw in value, its central concept, a property inherent in all economic goods, derived from the technical processes of production giving rise to them, a kind of economic gene. In the subjective revolution of the 1870s, the first step in the direction of subjectivism was taken when it was realized that value, so far from being inherent in goods, constitutes a relationship between an appraising mind and the object of its appraisal. The value of a garment depends in the first place on how many people want to wear it, and the strength of such desire in each individual, and only in the second place on technical processes of production.

In this century, expectations present themselves as obvious aims for our next step in the direction of subjectivism. Their significance for economic dynamics is evident: all economic action is, in the first place, shaped by plans dependent on expectations. So much is common cause.

In the real world human expectations always diverge. This divergence of our expectations is no less a natural feature of the economic landscape than the divergence of our tastes, the subjectivism of expectations no less essential an ingredient of the subjectivist paradigm than the subjectivism of tastes. The future is unknowable, though not unimaginable. Since all economic action is concerned with the future, it is not surprising that individual differences of the human imagination find their expression in plans of action. A good deal follows from this simple observation.

First of all, expectations are more important in asset markets than in the markets for products. In some of the latter, to be sure (e.g., in the markets for agricultural products and for fashion goods), expectations play a prominent part. But it is of some significance that whatever scope there is for the expression of expectations in such markets is in general commensurate with what scope there is for the holding and variability of commodity stocks. In a pure flow market, in which no stocks can be held, expectations can find little expression, except in consumers' decisions to defer purchases. In product markets in general, in which both flows and stocks are traded, the influence of expectations is proportionate to the share of stock transactions in total transactions.

It is thus by no means surprising that in asset markets, such as the Stock Exchange, being pure "stock markets," expectations are paramount. Without divergent expectations, without "bulls" and "bears," such markets evidently could not exist. It is important to understand that the notorious volatility of Stock Exchange prices is, in the first place, due to the ease with which in a pure stock market it is possible to move from one side of the market to the other, to be a buyer in the morning and a seller in the afternoon, or vice versa if one holds stock. In the potato market, by contrast, most participants are firmly wedded to one side, being either producers or consumers, while only the merchants, holding stocks, are able to change sides.

In the second place, short-run stability of the potato market has to be sustained by "a given taste for potatoes" on the one hand and stability of agricultural technology, area of acreage, and wage rates on the other, while the markets for securities are sustained by no such forces since there is no cost of production or consumer demand for them. Here stability is not inconceivable. But it is impossible for expectations about a certain event at a future date to remain constant while this date is moving nearer. The daily flow of the news will affect some of the divergent expectations. Some bulls will turn bears or vice versa. This, as Professor Shackle has shown with such vigour, is the major reason for the well-known volatility of asset markets.

Austrian economists, face to face with these facts, have to ask what they imply. Their first implication, in our view, is that we should abandon all concern with a "dynamic equilibrium" in the sense of a state of affairs in which all expectations are consistent. Such a state of affairs is not merely an unrealistic assumption to make, it is (literally) "humanly impossible." A market economy without asset markets cannot exist, and all asset markets have the attributes we described. Even the assertion of a "tendency" towards such a state of affairs has to be qualified by adding that it is one among others.

The second implication of these facts is that, though they destroy such notions as the "steady state equilibrium" of neoclassical growth theory, they permit us to see what use might be made of the notion of market-day equilibrium in asset markets. This is a matter that should be of great interest to Austrian economists as devoted exponents of the market process.

The market, of course, cannot make divergent expectations converge any more than it can forecast the unknowable future. What it does accomplish, however, is remarkable enough: it imparts to an aggregate of subjective, divergent, expectations what we might call a measure of "social objectivity" by striking a balance of them. It divides bulls and bears into two equal halves, thus producing a "balance." The price reflecting this balance is the market-day equilibrium price. The shareholder, actual or potential, who finds this price in the list learns something that must be of interest to him: how the market as a whole "changed its mind" between yesterday and today, whether bulls turned bear or vice versa. This need not move him to change his own expectation, of course, but it enables him to pit his own view against "the market view." An asset market equilibrium resting on divergent expectations thus has its uses. Of course, owing to the volatility of expectations, it cannot last. Tomorrow will see a new balance of expectations and a new equilibrium price. This is how the market process operates in the asset markets, which are such essential organs of the market economy.

A final implication of the volatility of asset markets, though obvious to any observer of the scene and well known even to novelists, has been strangely neglected by economists. The daily fluctuations of asset prices, an everyday feature of life in a

market economy, mean capital gains and losses to asset holders
and cause a daily redistribution of wealth. In fact, it is hardly an
exaggeration to say that the mode of distribution of wealth in a
market economy is largely, though not solely, the cumulative
effect of the capital gains made and losses suffered in the past.
This should be a sobering thought to all those who contemplate
other forms of the redistribution of wealth, e.g., by taxation, and
in particular to those who are ready "to accept the market
economy but only after a redistribution of the existing wealth."
As long as asset markets are open, the process of redistribution
of wealth must continue. If the government redistributes wealth
at the end of September, the mode of its distribution in October
will not last. By November, the market will have modified it, by
December even more so. This process is a prominent feature of
the market economy, an inevitable concomitant of the market
process, and ultimately a consequence of the divergence of expectations.

III

To acting man time is no continuum. The future is uncertain,
the past alone known, or at least knowable. "We cannot have
experience of actuality at two distinct 'moments'. The moment of
actuality, the moment in being, 'the present', is solitary. Extended time, beyond the moment, appears in this light, as a
figment, a product of thought."[3] As time is continuously flowing
across the threshold of the present, it is undergoing a change of
quality. With regard to our knowledge, then, time is
heterogeneous, comprising the unknowable and the knowable.
Hence Austrian economists, compelled by their commitment to
subjectivism to view all problems in the perspective of the actor,
cannot but look askance at all theories employing the mathematical notion of time as a continuum and will cast a suspicious eye
on expressions such as dY/dt. To acting man, time means something different.

All our knowledge belongs to the past. It is therefore, in
principle, possible to classify all items of knowledge by a time

index of their acquisition, and this, of course, is what historians of science are doing. But the relationships among various items of knowledge may assume various forms, and mere dating may tell us little about what we want to know.

To simple minds, all knowledge presently acquired is additive to prior knowledge. Mankind is piling up an ever-growing store of knowledge, a veritable treasure house of the mind from which not a single item is ever removed. Austrian economists, put on their guard by their experience in the theory of capital, know that it may not be so: some old knowledge is rendered obsolete by new knowledge. The intertemporal relationship between items of knowledge may be substitutive, not additive. Or it may be complementary, where the new knowledge enhances the compass of the old and opens new fields for the combined application of both.

In our "kaleidic" society, the obsolescence of old knowledge is a fact of fundamental importance. Its consequences are ubiquitous. Even where technical progress is slow, our knowledge of the market, i.e., other actors, is soon out of date. Time cannot elapse without changes in the constellation of knowledge accompanied by capital gains and losses.

Austrian economists, laying stress on the coordinating function of the market, face a problem here: If the market coordinates existing knowledge, what happens when knowledge changes while the process is taking place, when people acquire knowledge of which it is possible that tomorrow it may have become obsolete? Leaving this question open, we must now turn to looking at the problem of time and knowledge in a different perspective.

Similarly, as is the case with Böhm-Bawerk's structure of production, we may look at the relationship between various items of knowledge either diachronically or synchronically. The first we have already done, and concluded that the intertemporal relation between items of knowledge may be additive, substitutive, or complementary. But the same, of course, applies synchronically.

In a market economy, the plans of competing firms may be

inconsistent. The same applies to the innovations introduced to serve the implementation of the plans. Where these are additive, however, firms will soon learn them from each other. Where they are complementary, profitable arrangements for their joint exploitation will be made in the usual way. But where they are substitutive, the plans of competing firms derive additional doses of inconsistency from this very fact. The market as the final arbiter will determine which of these innovations survive and become part of the social body of technical knowledge.

From the Austrian point of view, the time aspect as well as the relevance of consumers' wants to the economic significance of new knowledge need emphasis. Not all technical change is technical progress. At the moment at which new knowledge becomes available, nobody can tell *ex ante* which of the items of which it is composed will *ex post* make for economic success. Only years of experience in the workshops and in the market can tell that. We must not treat as social fact what, at the moment at which the relevant decisions have to be taken, cannot be more than subjective opinion.

The relevance of all this to current discussions on the "social rate of return to investment in information," alleged to be in excess of the "private rate," is obvious enough. We might add that our argument will also cast new light on "product differentiation," so often described as a monopolistic device practised by wily producers on an unsuspecting public. Can anybody imagine how the airplanes, gramophones, or fountain pens of 60 years ago could have evolved into their present-day shapes without continuous product differentiation? Time has more aspects of economic relevance than are dreamt of in neoclassical theory.

IV

The last 30 years saw the ascent of macroeconomics and a temporary eclipse of Austrian thought. What attitude should Austrian economists adopt today towards macroeconomic aggregates? We spoke above of skepticism engendered by a distrust of all formalizations of economic experience which do not have an identifiable source in the mind of an economic actor. But a more positive attitude is called for. Austrian economists must attempt, wherever possible, to impart a measure of subjectivism to the products of macroeconomic thought.

We may note that Austrian aversion does not pertain to these aggregates as such. Austrian economists, after all, did discuss the balance of payments of the Habsburg Empire. It pertains to the construction of an economic model in which these aggregates move, undergo change, and influence each other in accordance with laws which are devoid of any visible reference to individual choice. Like the bodies of a planetary system, each aggregate is affected by changes in other aggregates, but never, it appears, by changes taking place within itself. It is this conception of the mode of relationships among aggregates, rather than the existence of the aggregates themselves, which defies subjectivism.

At first sight it seems futile to attempt to change this state of affairs by splitting large aggregates into smaller aggregates. But where it is possible to show that movements of the smaller aggregates are responsive to changes which constitute effects of individual choices, while the movements of the larger aggregate are not, such an attempt might be promising.

In *Prices and Production*, Professor Hayek rejects the Fisherian notion of the price level and substitutes the price levels of capital goods and consumption goods for it. One might think that one is as macroeconomic as the other. But the whole point of the operation consists in the fact that the two price levels are tied to the saving-consumption decisions of income earners, while the Fisherian price level is not.

Such an evolution towards subjectivism by means of the disaggregation of macroaggregates has actually taken place in the theory of money over the last 60 years. It cannot surprise us that the textbook industry has ignored it. It is perhaps more remarkable that economic thinkers, even some who took a prominent part in it, appear to be unaware of it. But it is surprising indeed that Austrian economists, of all people, should have taken no notice of "this further step in the consistent application of subjectivism."

As late as in 1911, in Fisher's *Purchasing Power of Money*, the framework of monetary relations presented in the famous Quantity Equation consisted entirely of macroeconomic entities, either aggregates like M and T or averages of aggregates like V and P. Within this context, the Quantity Theory proper asserted a relationship between M and P.

The following year, Mises took the first step in the direction of subjectivism by stressing the important role of individual cash balances. In Cambridge, Pigou tried to subjectivize the rigors of the Quantity Equation by means of the "Cambridge k."[4] The discovery of the variability of bank credit played its part. While commodity money "exists" in a physical form, the creation and maintenance of a volume of credit requires acts of choice. An element of subjectivism entered into the supply of money.

In 1930 Keynes, in the *Treatise*,[5] introduced the distinction between the industrial and the financial circulation, later called active and idle money. We have here a clear case of a dissolution of a macroaggregate (M) into smaller aggregates amenable to choice, the choice between money to use and money to hold. And in 1934, for a fleeting moment, a few economists even became aware of what was happening, viz. that night in November 1934 when young Dr. Hicks read his paper, "A Suggestion for Simplifying the Theory of Money,"[6] with its emphasis on subjectivism, to a baffled London Economic Club most of whose members felt that something important had been said, but could not quite make out what.

Even in the ranks of the Quantity theorists, subjectivism today makes its influence felt. We find Professor Friedman, whom nobody would regard as a subjectivist, telling us that while the old Quantity Theory emphasized the supply of money, the new Quantity Theory (domicile: Chicago) prefers to put its emphasis on the demand for it. This demand, as has been noted by many, has a remarkably Keynesian flavor. In the theory of money subjectivism appears triumphant.

In the theory of capital I made an attempt to move in the direction of subjectivism in my book, *Capital and Its Structure* (London, 1956). There I tried to dissolve the capital structure into the capital combinations of the various firms and to show how these are amenable to, indeed the expression of, individual plans. Perhaps the attempt was premature.

How far attempts to infuse subjectivism into other fields of macroeconomics will succeed, only the future can show. It seems fairly obvious, however, that the time for some steps in this direction has come. Austrian economists should be best able to take such steps.

V

Futures markets? They can reconcile, just conceivably, our PRESENT ideas, based on our PRESENT knowledge. What of tomorrow's new knowledge destroying the old or rendering it obsolete, what of tomorrow's choices and decisions, tomorrow's discoveries, tomorrow's inventions, work of imagination? . . .

We are not omniscient, assured masters of known circumstance via reason, but the prisoners of time.

　　　　　　　　　　　G. L. S. Shackle
　　　　　　　　　　Journal of Economic Literature
　　　　　　　　　　June 1973, p. 519.

The market economy has never been without its critics and enemies. Those who feel threatened by the market; those who, however unwisely, feel they could do better without it; economists with little imagination; those, like the devotees of Pareto optima, with only too much of it; those who find most entrepreneurs disgusting characters; those attracted by the romantic charm of a feudal order in which they never had to live; social thinkers offended by the raucous tone of modern advertising; and social thinkers who know only too well how to exploit envy and greed in the service of anticapitalistic movements—all these make a formidable array of opponents.

On the other hand, the market economy has been able to draw support from a 200-year-old tradition of economic thought. Here Austrian economists, side by side with non-Austrians, have taken a prominent part in supporting it. In this century, outstanding thinkers like Cassel, Hayek, Mises, and Pareto have defended the market economy against many misunderstandings and fallacies.

But of late the wind appears to have turned, and the heirs of Cassel and Pareto have changed sides. Leading thinkers of the neoclassical school have launched an attack on the market economy, charging it with inadequacy in a field in which, many of us would have thought, some of its most impressive achievements are to be found: in the provision of facilities for intertemporal trading.

To our knowledge, Professor Koopmans first launched the attack in 1957, criticising what he called "the overextended belief of the liberalist school of economic thought in the efficiency of competitive markets as a means of allocating resources in a world full of uncertainty." He continued, "To my knowledge no formal model of resource allocation through competitive markets has been developed, which recognizes ignorance about all decision makers' future actions, preferences, or states of technological information as the main source of uncertainty confronting each individual decision maker, and which at the same time acknowledges the fact that forward markets on which anticipations and intentions could be tested and adjusted do not exist in sufficient variety and with a sufficient span of foresight to make presently developed theory regarding the efficiency of competitive markets applicable. . . . In particular, the economics profession is not ready to speak with anything approaching scientific authority on the economic aspects of the issue of individual versus collective enterprise which divides mankind in our time."[7]

In a similar vein Professor Arrow, in a recent Presidential Address to the A.E.A., told his listeners, "Even as a graduate student I was somewhat surprised at the emphasis on static allocative efficiency by market socialists, when the nonexistence of markets for future goods under capitalism seemed to me a much more obvious target."[8]

In February 1973, Professor Hahn, in his well-known Inaugural Lecture in Cambridge,[9] employed the same argument to show that general equilibrium theory has its practical uses in providing a sophisticated critique of the market economy. "The argument will here turn on the absence of futures markets and contingent futures markets and on the inadequate treatment of time and uncertainty." He continued, "Practical men and ill-trained theorists everywhere in the world do not understand what they are claiming to be the case when they claim a beneficent and coherent role for the invisible hand" (p. 14).

This critique of the market economy calls for an answer. In the first place, it is perhaps obvious that no existing state of affairs can be effectively criticised by comparing it with a purely imaginary one, such as the general equilibrium model in its most up-to-date and sophisticated form. The critics fail to tell us how a world with perfect intertemporal markets for everything is to be brought into existence. Nor are we given any hint as to how a socialist economy would or could provide a substitute for it.

Second, the critics appear to share an altogether exaggerated notion of what forward markets can achieve. They can provide "cover" against some contingencies, they coordinate expectations, "bullish" and "bearish." But they cannot make the uncertain future certain, they cannot prevent plans from being upset by events nobody could have foreseen, they cannot eliminate the difference between *ex ante* and *ex post*. Shackle has expressed this so well in the quotation at the top of this section that no further comment seems called for.

Third, this entire argument rests upon a confusion between *actual* and *potential* markets. No practical conclusions can be drawn from the mere fact that certain transactions which are possible do not actually take place. There are today no markets for ostrich feathers or top hats, but there probably would be if fashion were to turn.

Our inability to observe certain transactions does not permit us to infer that they are impossible. They may not be profitable in given circumstances. In a society full of risk-averters, risk-capital may be so scarce that it can be provided for only a few markets. Many potential markets never become actual because transaction costs are too high, and all transaction costs are, certainly to Austrians, opportunity costs. Have our critics ever considered what immense precautionary (and variable) money balances would have to be carried against forward commitments in the world they are envisaging?

Arrow actually goes into "the causes for the absence of markets for future goods" (p. 7). "It seems to me there are two basic causal factors. One is that contracts are not enforceable without cost and forward contracts are more costly to enforce than contemporaneous contracts; the other is that because of the many uncertainties about the future, neither buyers nor sellers are willing to make commitments which completely define their future actions" (p. 8).

It is doubtful whether either of these can provide a *general reason*. The cost of enforcing contracts is low in law-abiding societies, high in others. Moreover, as Arrow admits, the market may provide its own sanction by excluding defaulters from further trading. The second reason should lead to a general discussion of the limits of forward markets in the spirit of Shackle's remarks, but it does not. We are told instead, "As Hicks showed a long time ago, complementarity and substitution can occur over time as well as simultaneously. If . . . uncertainty can tend to destroy markets, then we can conclude that the absence of some markets for future goods may cause others to fail" (p. 9).

As far as one can judge, this means that we are facing an "externality" here, according to modern welfare economics a source of "market failure." If so, the answer is that external economies invite joint exploitation by potential beneficiaries. The second reason seems no better than the first.

Finally, and for us most important, this criticism of the market economy illuminates the limitations of the neoclassical mind rather than the shortcomings of the market. This mind, incapable of conceiving of "the market" otherwise than in terms of a system of markets in general equilibrium, is helpless when confronted with a real world in which not all potential markets are actually in operation. Not knowing that those whose view of the market they criticise conceive of it in terms very different from their own, our critics tacitly assume that everybody, like their well-trained disciples, identifies the market economy with their general equilibrium model. To Austrians, by contrast, the market, as Hayek taught, is a process rather than a state of affairs, a process which comes to an end when equilibrium is reached. During the course of this process it happens all the time that some potential markets become actual and some actual markets potential, though nobody, of course, could say for how long. Some economists who are critics of the market appear to suffer from a lack of imagination.

Needless to say, the circumstances in which intertemporal markets come into existence provide an important subject for empirical study, a most significant aspect of the market process. It is to be hoped that Austrian economists will take their full share in its pursuit. It is not obvious why a model in which all obstacles to the birth of intertemporal markets are assumed away should be of much help to us in pursuing such a study.

VI

In the recent development of economics, there is much Austrian economists cannot but disapprove of. We already mentioned macroaggregates and what might be done with them. But what positive contributions do they have to offer for the future of economic science?

Following what was said above, we have to distinguish between the unknowable future and the knowable past. In neoclassical thought this problem does not arise, since one is ostensibly engaged in finding "laws" applying as much to the one as to the other. But there are the well-known puzzles among which the problem of *ceteris paribus*, our inability to specify all the conditions under which the laws are to hold, takes prominence. Austrians simply have to face the fact that the autonomy of the mind precludes determinism: If knowledge shapes action and action shapes the human world, the future is unpredictable. "But if theory pretends only to give an account of particular, peculiar and special moments (such as may be scarcely ever attained in fact) and repudiates any hope of connecting them by any intelligible, permanent mechanism allowing prognosis, then the theory ought explicitly to be a classificatory one, putting situations in this box or that according to what *can happen* as a sequel to it. Theories which tell us what *will* happen are claiming too much."[10]

In other words, insofar as the future is concerned, economics will have to become far more a descriptive discipline than it is at present, giving an intelligible account of a number of future possibilities inherent in present situations, unable to rely on the strict necessity of determinism or even of numerical probability. Economists will have to acquire new skills, the skills required for description and comparison of large numbers of possible situations. Remembering how much time and effort have of late been invested in mathematical skills, the skills of symbolic precision reflecting necessity and determinism, we cannot but feel uneasy about the concomitant circumstances of such a change of paradigm.

What promise does the knowable past hold for the future of economics? Here we encounter the problem of the relationships between economics and history. According to a view widely held today, it is the task of the analytical social sciences to produce "covering laws" which the historians will then apply to concrete cases. But the economist can offer the historian only laws valid *ceteris paribus*, unlikely to be of much use to the latter without specification.

Yet it remains true that the past is the great storehouse of facts, offering us a vast stock of material for empirical generalizations, interesting in themselves provided we do not pretend that they are universal laws. Here we are able to compare *ex ante* with *ex post* since we know, or in principle are able to know, what happened to plans. We might find out how much capital was malinvested in a certain decade. We can ascertain economic growth patterns of the past without having to rely on "steady state" models. We might even trace the multiple sources from which technical progress flowed in the past. The fact that most generalizations we might draw from this material will be limited in time need not, after all we said, discourage us. Nor need we be afraid lest we trespass on the field of the historians who may welcome such help as we are able to offer. Whenever a complex of relationships persists for a period of time, it constitutes both an analytical and a historical subject. The finances of the Habsburg Empire under Böhm-Bawerk or the political structure of the Republic of Venice are obvious examples. They are historical and analytical subjects.

Above all, Austrian economists will want to trace market processes of the past. To identify economic history with the evolution of the market economy is a bold idea at the application of which Sir John Hicks tried his hand a few years ago.[11] A good deal might be done within this framework.

As the heirs of Menger, Austrian economists will take a particular interest in how the market evolves those "organic institutions" it needs.[12] But the degeneration of these institutions is a subject that no less deserves our attention. It might be worth our while to attempt to find out when exactly, and in what circumstances, the downward inflexibility of money wage rates became the prominent feature of the Western world it today unfortunately is. It would be even more interesting to link it to the evolution of the institutions of collective bargaining. History offers many instances of institutions which, created for one purpose, came to serve another. The parallel with malinvestment is obvious.

Statistical time series are records of the past. Impossible as it is to derive empirical laws by correlating them, such correlations may nevertheless cast some light on the events of the time of their origin. How much information these time series will disclose depends on our ability to ask meaningful questions of them. Subjectivism asserts itself here in that different social scientists will ask different questions. How large the proportion of persons in "tertiary occupations" was in a given society during a certain period may be of interest to one social scientist. Austrian economists, by contrast, might prefer to know how many of them were independent agents, active middlemen and dealers, since the operation of imperfect markets depends so largely on agents of this type. Asking meaningful questions is a skill that has to be acquired.

It is to be hoped that economic science will in the future, as it has done in the past, though not in the recent past, offer scope for many diverse skills and talents. At the moment, this must seem a sanguine hope. Austrian economists are perhaps in a better position than anybody else to make a contribution towards this end.

REFERENCES

1. F. A. Hayek, *The Counter-Revolution of Science* (Glencoe, 1952), p. 31.

2. J. A. Schumpeter, *History of Economic Analysis* (1954), p. 847, footnote 8.

3. G. L. S. Shackle, *Epistemics and Economics* (Cambridge, 1972), p. 245.

4. A. C. Pigou, "The Value of Money," *Quarterly Journal of Economics* (November 1917), pp. 42–43.

5. J. M. Keynes, *A Treatise on Money* (1930), Volume I, Chapter 15.

6. John Hicks, *Critical Essays in Monetary Theory* (Oxford, 1967), pp. 61–82.

7. Tjalling C. Koopmans, *Three Essays on the State of Economic Science* (McGraw-Hill, 1957), pp. 146–47.

8. K. J. Arrow, "Limited Knowledge and Economic Analysis," *American Economic Review* (March 1974), pp. 1–10.

9. F. H. Hahn, *On the Notion of Equilibrium in Economics* (Cambridge, 1973).

10. Shackle, *op. cit.*, p. 72.

11. John Hicks, *A Theory of Economic History* (Oxford, 1969).

12. Carl Menger, *Problems of Economics and Sociology* (Urbana, 1963), pp. 151–59.

The Austrian Method

John B. Egger
Goucher College

There has been a renewal of interest in the Austrian School of economics in recent years. Good public relations deserve part of the credit: the 1974 Nobel award to F. A. Hayek and the series of seminars sponsored by the Institute for Humane Studies have had some effect. But beneath these lies the substance: economists are learning that information has a great deal to do with human behavior—and they are learning that the Austrian School long has focused on the broad and narrow behavioral implications of fragmented information.

Recognizing that the Austrian School is different or novel or even better is easier than recognizing exactly what makes it different. Sometimes the span between the recognition and the identification of the difference is long and difficult. Making it shorter and easier is the goal of this paper. It does not particularly advance the frontiers of Austrian methodology, but aims at presenting the basic differences between the Austrian School and the neoclassical orthodoxy[1] in terms likely to be clear to students of the latter. The paper's target reader is perhaps the graduate student who studies to the point of memorizing statements like "The Austrian School studies purposive human action" and yet is still unable to see how this relates to what he finds in his microtheory course.[2]

DOES A PRIORISM DIFFERENTIATE AUSTRIANISM?

Murray Rothbard and Ludwig von Mises, two of the great

19

Austrian School economists, strongly defend the proposition that economics is *a priori*.[3] The primary question for my thesis is: does this position differentiate the Austrian writers from other economists? While arguing that the laws of economics are independent of the specifics of human experience, Mises stood opposed to historical and institutional approaches which held even the very *theory* of economics valid only in particular historical or institutional settings. Of course a theory whose most basic principles change over time is no theory at all; Mises was thus defending the very possibility of a science of economics.

But it was never his intent, in his statements of *a priorism*, to differentiate his and his followers' method from that of the neoclassical economists. Their "constrained maximization" technique is every bit as independent of historical circumstance as is the technique of spinning out implications from the "action axiom."[4] Because *a priorism* does not differentiate the Austrian School, it is not a defining characteristic of the School.

EQUILIBRIA, STATIC AND DYNAMIC

One of the avenues by which the nature of the "Austrian differentia" can be approached is an examination of two meanings of "equilibrium."[5]

In the conventional sense (which I term "static"), "equilibrium" refers simply to a state in which prices of the various goods result in zero excess demand for each of them. The term "static" is often taken to mean "timeless" and is indicated by the absence of time parameters in the supply and demand functions, but the essentially static nature of this conception of equilibrium is not violated even if some of the goods among which the individuals choose are "future goods."

Consider as a typical example the interactions among three individuals, each with an endowment of goods and a specific utility function. Under certain reasonable assumptions about the forms of these utility functions, some set of relative prices among these goods will be consistent with the preferences and initial endowments of the three individuals. The market's, and each individual's, excess demand for each good will be zero at this set of relative prices. The nature of this equilibrium is not at all changed if some of the goods are promises of future delivery of others—based upon knowledge, let us say, of a regular Sunday night manna delivery. Each individual independently considers his present and future preferences, and the individuals' interaction determines a mutually consistent (present and future) price vector.

This is certainly *an* equilibrium. In the context of the particular moment's valuations and expectations, any further changes in any of the prices would cause some net excess demands to become nonzero. But it is a *static* equilibrium in this sense: it does not differentiate between future expectations which are consistent among the individuals and those which are inconsistent.[6] Even though a unique price vector of "future goods" is determined, we have no assurance that the plans on which the individuals based their future valuations are consistent. In the simplest case—that of divergent expectations about physical data—an equilibrium relative price between beach umbrellas and rain umbrellas may be determined under circumstances in which one individual thinks it will rain tomorrow while the other two believe it will be a pleasant day for swimming. But even if expectations about physical data coincide, expectations about each other's action plans may be contradictory: each individual may base his demand for, say, "tomorrow's automobile services" on the expectation that he alone plans to drive on a certain narrow, dusty mountain road. In either of these cases, a unique static equilibrium price vector may be determined, but the passage of time will reveal the inconsistency of the individuals' expectations and hence require the determination of a new price vector. This equilibrium is static because it is built upon inconsistencies of which the individuals will learn in attempting to follow their plans. Only a dynamic equilibrium incorporates consistent future plans, and hence is not disturbed "endogenously"—by the very act of following one's plans.

The Hayekian dynamic equilibrium,[7] in short, consists of a market-clearing price vector based upon interpersonally consistent expectations; the static equilibrium discussed above consists of a vector of market-clearing prices based upon plans which the individuals may *or may not* be able to carry out.

Two quite different perspectives on the economic problem are implied by these two viewpoints on the nature of "equilibrium." I claimed at the start of this section that these perspectives will illuminate the distinction between the Austrian School and the neoclassical microapproach. There is just a bit more groundwork.

The analysis characterized above as static concentrates upon the existence of a price vector consistent with the momentary relative valuations of the individuals. The conditions of the world expected by these individuals—which include the actions of other individuals—remain in the shadows; the only relevant issue is the subjective rate of substitution among the commodities, and there is no way to judge whether or not the subjective rates of substitution determined by the different individuals are based upon contradictory future expectations. Static analysis begins at a point at which expectations and marginal utilities (or preference orderings) have already been formed and allows us to determine the existence and uniqueness of a price vector (which may include future goods) consistent with these preferences. Whether the preferences themselves are based upon consistent expectations is simply beyond the pale of this approach. I have thus come to believe that it is not quite accurate to argue that the (static) analysis of equilibrium conditions "assumes away" the problem of inconsistent expectations:[8] it simply has nothing to say on that issue.

Such an approach may be considered "timeless," in a sense, whether or not there are "future goods" in the commodity bundles. For the passage of time would reveal whether the individuals' expectations were interpersonally consistent or not, and this would transform the problem into something quite different from that with which static analysis deals. It would, to be specific, shift us into the realm of the dynamic equilibrium or disequilibrium nature of the static conditions we have derived.

The difference between a market-clearing price vector corresponding to a static and one relating to a dynamic equilibrium is that the latter necessarily incorporates interpersonally consistent expectations. The process of deriving, by logical deduction, the distribution of goods and relative prices under *this* sort of equilibrium presupposes that the premises on which the deduction is based—the preferences *and plans* of the individuals—are, themselves, logically consistent. Thus the application of our static tools to dynamic questions requires a great deal more in the way of assumption: that each individual foresee exactly those actions which the others plan to take.[9] This interpersonal consistency of expectations must be presupposed before the specific pattern of prices and distribution can be logically deduced.

THE "AUSTRIAN DIFFERENTIA"

In his seminal "Economics and Knowledge" Hayek made a statement which for some time I found puzzling:

> ... since equilibrium is a relationship between actions, and since the actions of one person must necessarily take place successively in time, it is obvious that the passage of time is essential to give the concept of equilibrium any meaning. This deserves mention, since many economists appear to have been unable to find a place for time in equilibrium analysis and consequently have suggested that equilibrium must be conceived as timeless. This seems to me to be a meaningless statement.[10]

Why could not this great economist understand what I knew: that all we had to do was leave t out of our equations?

The answer is provided in the above section. Whether or not there are "future goods" (or t's in the demand functions),[11] the search for a logically consistent set of preferences (i.e., a market-clearing price vector) does not necessarily present us with a logically consistent set of *plans*.[12] Although the price vector determination completes the job of the auctioneer, the matter of interest to the individuals participating in the mar-

ketplace is whether or not their actions will achieve the expected
results—which most assuredly will not be the case if their expectations are logically inconsistent.

Questions concerning the existence, uniqueness, and stability
of a price vector which is mutually consistent with the *preferences*
of many different individuals are, in short, of an entirely different character from the questions and problems which arise when
one investigates the existence, uniqueness, and stability of the set
of expectations or *plans* which is interpersonally consistent.

Concentration upon this latter set of issues constitutes the
Austrian *differentia*. The distinction cannot be appreciated from
a simple statement removed from the context of the above remarks, but it appears correct to argue that: whereas most contemporary microtheory focuses upon the abstract logic of preferences, the Austrian School focuses upon *action*.[13]

MAN, THE ENTREPRENEUR

The above comments may help to clarify some of the claims
made by the Austrian School writers:[14] although the "abstract
logic of preferences" can employ the technique of mutual determination via the solution of sets of simultaneous equations, an
analysis of the plans underlying these preferences and how plans
are modified must incorporate the concepts of purpose and
learning. "Purpose" in this sense cannot refer simply to the *a
prioristic* universal goal of "utility maximization"; it refers to
some *specific* goal the individual wishes to achieve and consequently to how his actions and plans are likely to be modified
when he learns that the economic environment is going to be
different from that which he anticipated when he developed his
initial plans. Simultaneous determination may govern the logical
analysis of preferences, but the "older concept of cause-and-
effect"[15] is the only technique appropriate to the study of learning and the modification of inconsistent plans. The "cause," of
course, is the individual's subjective perception of an opportunity to improve his situation, and the "effect" is a change in his
way of acting, or in his plans.

This process of the revision of inconsistent plans requires that the individual be able to recognize those features of his original plans which caused the inconsistency and that he recognize also the changes in his plans which tend to eliminate that inconsistency. Such abilities constitute at least part of what economists call "entrepreneurship." (The popular notion of "creating a new product or service" is simply a special case in which a businessman thinks he perceives the desirability of a change in his own plans and hopes that the resulting plan inconsistency [he plans to get rich but potential customers have yet to learn of his new product, so they don't plan to buy any] will be resolved by a subsequent revision of his potential customers' plans rather than of his own.) It is precisely the relation among entrepreneurship, plan revision, and action which explains the irrelevance of entrepreneurship to neoclassical microeconomic theory which takes preferences as axiomatic and does not concern itself with the possibility of carrying out their underlying plans.

Professor Kirzner's important work refers to the "alertness to information" as entrepreneurship.[16] But the importance of the Austrian viewpoint is more clear if we realize that this ability is precisely what differentiates man from other living beings, that "entrepreneurship" in general is indistinguishable from use of the rational faculty, from the ability to conceptualize, from thinking.[17]

Concept formation requires differentiation and integration: differentiation among the infinite variety of attributes of certain items or situations, isolation of a specific attribute common to the items, and integration of the different items or situations into a concept according to whether or not they possess the chosen common attribute. The process is one of grouping into classes, or classification, and is common to all thought. A decision is a classification, and decision is the goal of all thought.

How is this process of classification related to action? An individual's action hinges upon the comparison: "What will things be like if I don't act," versus "What will they be like if I do?" To make such a decision the individual must construct hypothetical states of the future, one conditional on the individual's act and the other on its absence. Once the concretes of the situation are perceived, the process of conceptualization consists of the isolation of certain characteristics common to this and to other situations. These other situations may be historical instances the individual remembers or an imaginary case in which he envisions himself in the role of another person and considers how *he* would behave in that role. In either case the function of the isolation of certain features is to eliminate unessential clutter: specific details of the scene which are not thought to be "important." It is the ability to isolate correctly the relevant—causal—aspects of a situation or an ongoing process, and hence to accurately predict its future in both the absence and presence of one's own action, which constitutes successful entrepreneurship. And it is the attempt to do so which constitutes entrepreneurship, successful or not.

But all thought is exactly of this form. Whether one is trying to think through the causal forces behind the Industrial Revolution or to analyze a Frost poem, the technique is to hypothesize alternatives and to isolate particular causal elements, characteristics which appear to make the crucial difference between what *is* and what might have been. The only difference between such contemplative thought and the popular view of entrepreneurship is that the historian or poet has at his command the data needed to test his hypothesis, while the fledgling businessman must wait and see whether customers come. But during the interval of time between the development of the counterfactual hypothesis and its test (e.g., "perhaps X caused the Industrial Revolution . . . but that would imply a certain pattern of relative prices which did not, in fact, occur," or "why didn't Frost write 'The woods are owned by Mayor Jones, whose wife sells pickled cabbage at the fair' instead of 'whose woods these are I think I know'? . . . but that would eliminate the degree of generality Frost is trying to convey in the rest of the poem . . . ."), the test lies as much in the future as that facing the businessman.

To be able to speak of "entrepreneurship" and "thought" as different concepts is useful, to be sure. But this analysis suggests that the entrepreneur is anyone acting in accordance with his specifically human nature. A school of economics which, because of its focus and method, can accord a central role to the entrepreneur is simply respecting the nature of man. Surely this is an important aspect of the Austrian differentia.

METHOD: MATHEMATICS AS AN ANALYTICAL TOOL IN ECONOMICS

If we are to analyze the function of mathematical terminology in economics, we must analyze it at its best. The difficulties associated with the use of differential and integral calculus are well-known (e.g., the requirements that products and factors be infinitely divisible, that individuals consider infinitesimal changes relevant, that all preference orderings be representable by a total utility function and production relations by a total product function), so analyses using differentiable and integrable objective functions are no longer at the frontiers of mathematical economics, except perhaps in the study of uncertainty. The more general approach of set theory has been developed largely since Debreu (1959),[18] and it is a real and significant improvement over differential calculus in economics. Those who wish to criticize mathematical economics must take on its best.

Bertrand Russell contends that "pure mathematics is the class of all propositions of the form 'p implies q'. . . ."[19] The claim of equivalence between pure logic and pure mathematics is sometimes attributed to Russell and Whitehead's *Principia Mathematica* (1910–13), but the same idea is presented forcefully in the first few pages of Russell's 1903 work. Russell was led to this conclusion by the discovery that numbers are sets,[20] that ordinary algebra is therefore an application of set theory, and that any statement of implication can be rewritten in set-theoretic terms: e.g., "p implies q" is identical to "q is a subset of p." Venn diagrams even give us pictures.[21]

Jevons felt that economics was by nature mathematical be-

cause it deals with numbers.[22] Modern mathematicians prefer to
identify the roots of their subject with the theory of sets. A set is a
collection of undefined "elements," which may represent any
property we wish to attribute to them, and the theory of sets
consists of the logical relations among them. Because of the
completely general nature of these sets and elements, we can
embrace a much wider view of the nature of mathematics than
can those who restrict themselves to, say, functional notation;
James R. Newman's cursory sampling of a few modern
mathematicians' views of their own subject indeed suggests that
the boundary between logic and mathematics is becoming increasingly blurred.[23]

Furthermore, either logical relations or mathematics—
whatever the distinction may be—is capable of expression in
either verbal or abstract symbolic terms. Jevons was correct in
this regard: one cannot identify the basically mathematical or
nonmathematical nature of a discipline according to whether or
not it is expressed verbally.[24]

From this viewpoint it appears as if Austrian School writers'
criticisms of mathematics in general—rather than of crude
mathematics, or of symbolic mathematics—are, in essence, criticisms of pure logic, which is not always (sometimes, perhaps, but
not always) what they intend. The real issue is: are there advantages to be gained from the substitution of *symbols* for *words* in
economics?[25]

The advantages claimed for this substitution include
economy, precision, and rigor.[26] The economy arises simply
from the fact that a symbol (e.g., x) is more brief than the set of
words it denotes (e.g., "the number of oranges he buys per
week"). The precision and rigor follow from the abstract nature
of symbols: once a set of symbols is appropriately defined (i.e.,
related verbally to the problem of interest) the entire corpus of
the formal theory of relations among these symbols becomes
applicable to one's problem. The ability to draw on the pure,
abstract theory of logic (or mathematics) provides the rigor, and
the exactness required in the definition of symbols forces the
precision.

It is clear enough that representation with symbols is always possible: by defining $f()$ and x appropriately we can represent "absence makes the heart grow fonder" by "$f^1(x)>0$."[27] The question is, why bother? What advantages might such symbolism offer? There will be advantages—economy, precision, rigor—only if the symbols will be used repeatedly in the course of some logical analysis.

The economy is achieved by omitting repeated verbal identification of the symbols. The form in which this generally occurs is: verbal definition of symbols, a (perhaps long) process of deduction from the initial postulates with a symbolic conclusion, and a statement in words of the meaning of the conclusion (obtained by reference to the symbols' initial definitions). Mathematical symbolism is indeed economical in this case, if only the final deduced proposition is held to be important. If the problem were analyzed in verbal terms, much unnecessary and redundant restatement of the symbols' definitions would occur. Many academic journal articles are precisely of this form: a few words at the beginning and end, pages of symbolic mathematics in the middle.

To evaluate the process of symbolic analysis outlined above, we must consider the epistemological significance of language. Words are concrete audiovisual representations of the abstractions called concepts, in which form all knowledge is retained.[28] As a consequence, any mathematically derived symbolic propositions which are to be meaningful must be translated into words. (If they are merely translatable then they are merely potentially meaningful.) Thus, the long sequence of intermediate steps in a logical derivation must be expressed verbally if it is to be related to human experience. But without subsidiary hypotheses about how people learn, these intermediate steps are *not* meaningful as guides to the comprehension of behavior and cannot be related directly to human experience. Only the conclusion can, in the sense that it describes an "equilibrium" state toward which actions are headed. Equilibrium theorists who make extensive use of mathematical symbolism are, in fact, saving a great deal of paper and time. The fact that causality is lost is irrelevant to one concerned only with descriptions of equilibria.

Those who perceive economic theory as a set of propositions which are logically implied by initially hypothesized preference sets and production possibilities understandably find symbolic logic and mathematics a powerful tool: economical, precise, rigorous. But the analysis of the conditions specific to an equilibrium presupposes that the conditions necessary for equilibrium exist. This is hardly much to ask if one restricts his viewpoint to *static* conditions, in the sense discussed earlier in this paper—that is, to search for a price vector logically consistent with the individuals' preferences at a specific moment. If one sees the central purpose of economics as the analysis of action, however, the relevant equilibrium is the *dynamic* one, and its preconditions—interpersonally consistent future plans or expectations—cannot be merely hypothesized. One must attempt to examine the ways in which this interpersonal consistency of expectations can be brought about. This requires the introduction into one's analysis of empirical (nondeduced) statements about what reactions individuals are likely to have when confronted with unexpected developments.[29] If these reactions were implicit in the initial propositions and therefore could be logically derived from them using their symbolism, they would not be reactions to unexpected developments at all: they would simply be preprogrammed behavioral changes in accordance with perfectly foreseen changes in data and would be empty of learning.

The introduction amidstream of unexpected developments thus requires the use of *words*. Symbolism is economical only when one can draw on it for a long time. Process analysis, however, by requiring the continual specification of nondeduced empirical hypotheses about learning and expectation revision, and hence about causality, can make little use of this economy.

Of course, if one looks upon the process of plan revision and movement toward a dynamic equilibrium as a series of discrete jumps, one can associate a static equilibrium price vector with each discrete set of preferences as they emerge throughout the process. This would seem to enhance the role of pure logical deduction and symbolic technique, rather than to minimize it. But the meaning of these sets of price vectors is not clear. They are still unrelated to the consistency of the expectations on which the preferences supporting them are based.

Those who are firmly wedded to the symbolic analysis characteristic of so much of modern economics may prefer to contend that their work alone is theory, that the introduction of non-deduced hypotheses about reactions to unexpected changes converts one's study into applied work. But I should point out that logic is common to all fields of study, and it is only the introduction of specific empirical characteristics that makes an engineer's analysis of a nonlinear control system at all different from an economist's study of business cycles. The logic used by physicists is the same as that used by biologists and by economists. What differentiates physics from biology from economics is the nature of the empirical links between the objects studied and the abstract logical rules the analyst employs.

UNCERTAINTY AND MATHEMATICS IN ECONOMIC ANALYSIS

I cannot undertake here a systematic examination of recent trends in "the economics of uncertainty." It deserves mention, however, because it may seem to reconcile the "imperfect information" of the dynamic disequilibrium and the use of mathematical symbolism. In what sense does "uncertainty economics" incorporate imperfect information and learning?

The relative-frequency concept of probability[30] is not applicable to human action with its unique events.[31] For discussion I will simply assume here something which I am by no means convinced is legitimate: that there is an appropriate subjective probability concept according to which future states can be ordered by cardinal degrees of belief.

Modern analyses using this approach are, like their deterministic counterparts, inevitably *static*. Even the most sophisticated of the techniques, that of "stochastic dominance," which permits the entire subjective distribution (rather than only its mean and variance) to be considered,[32] necessarily involves the reduction of an alternative to a "certainty equivalent," an ordinal which can be value ranked against other alternatives. Essentially, a hypothetical and certain alternative is manufactured—one which has the same *value* as the uncertain state—and preferences are constructed on the basis of this hypothetical alternative. For example, a man may be indifferent to the choice between $40 and a 50-50 chance at $100 or nothing. In determining preferences he will act as if $40 were actually the alternative; market prices of lottery tickets, for example, will be determined in this manner.

When we consider the individual's plans, rather than his preferences, we see at once that the state of winning $40 with certainty cannot have been expected and planned for. It is simply not one of the possible outcomes. As a consequence, the uncertainty models are by their nature static: perfectly sufficient for the analysis of market-clearing prices, but no more capable of incorporating learning and the removal of plan inconsistency than the deterministic static analyses. When the individual discovers that he has—or has not—won the $100, he no longer acts and plans as if he were certain to receive $40. Static uncertainty analysis has contributed to our understanding of price determination under uncertainty, but it does not permit us to analyze a process of action and learning.

THE AUSTRIAN METHOD

What implications do the foregoing comments have for methodology? How are propositions about economics to be developed? The formal study of patterns of consistent preferences—which I have called the "abstract logic of preference"—may employ the techniques of formal logic and mathematics, particularly set theory. The study of consistent plans, and how inconsistencies in interpersonal expectations are eliminated through learning, requires a technique (if it may be so called) different from the abstract symbolism of mathematics. It requires that specific nondeduced hypotheses be advanced about how an individual's plans and preferences change when he is confronted with unexpected events. The fact that these propositions about learning cannot be logically derived from other accepted statements may make the analysis appear unscientific, because of course it renders the conclusions dependent upon the accuracy of the empirical hypotheses. But if one accepts Popper's terminology,[33] the possibility of falsification is precisely that which makes a proposition scientific rather than unscientific.

In fact, it may not be the empirical elements themselves which give Austrian work an "unscientific" appearance, but instead the way in which they are introduced. Rather than being simply empirical assertions presented as part of the statement of a problem from which logical implications are then deduced (e.g., "such-and-such an elasticity is greater than one"), these propositions about learning must be introduced in the middle of the analytical process. One is not allowed to follow through with his logic: the smooth workings of the logical derivation are interrupted by the discovery and revision of inconsistent plans.

But this introduction of nondeduced hypotheses does not imply that "anything goes"; the nature of these hypotheses is governed by the introspective and experiential evidence that people learn from experience; that when confronted with plan inconsistencies they tend to revise their plans in the direction of consistency.[34] The development of an "Austrian process analysis" consists largely of an examination of how individuals are likely to interpret market or nonmarket changes as evidence that their own expectations must be revised. If different inconsistencies are brought to light when they proceed to act on these revised expectations, some further changes in plans (perhaps, this time, the plans of the other people) will be required. It is always possible to advance some reasonable hypothesis about the nature of the plan changes.

The role of symbolic mathematical analysis consists of the determination of the specific conditions which would exist under plan consistency. Whether there "really are" such consistent plans implicit in current expectations but somehow unrecognized, deep below the level of awareness,[35] or whether (as is far more likely) current expectations *are* fundamentally inconsistent so that some hypothesis must be invented about what plans would be like if they *were* consistent, this state of plan consistency is the benchmark, the goal providing a general direction to entrepreneurial activity. But the process by which it is approached must be analyzed with unfailing sensitivity to what the acting individual finds in the course of his actions and how he is likely to revise his expectations when he learns these things.

As an example of what difference all this makes, we could consider literally any process in time, especially a process we could consider evolutionary. The monetary theory of Menger and Mises[36] provides an excellent example because Mises' conclusion—the regression theorem—provides the solution to the so-called monetary-value theory dichotomy still challenging today's monetary theorists.

Starting with a set of preferences based upon use values alone (although of course it is irrelevant to the mathematics what they are based upon), we can logically derive a consistent static set of relative prices. Now suppose one individual learns or guesses that he can use a certain good as a trading medium and thereby acquire goods he could not otherwise have obtained. His preference for this "trading good" rises above its pure use value. Once again we can logically derive a new static price vector, based this time on his higher valuation (the cause of which, once again, is irrelevant). Now we can hypothesize that others observe this intermediate trading, or get the same idea independently, or observe that our initial individual is now more willing to accept the trade good than before, so their valuations of it rise for this reason. Once again, we can derive a new static price vector, this one revealing again the higher relative price of the traded good. As the learning process proceeds, the good becomes *money*. Its relative price ("the price level") is tied by the gradual process of learning to the barter relative price of the good from which it developed.

The whole approach, which provides such fruitful insight into monetary evolution, is rooted in the question: why do individuals pay more for a good than its use value? The answer is: they have learned, through observation and experience, of its acceptability in trade. However rigorous symbolic logical deduction may be, it can tell us very little about such everyday evolutionary processes.

CONCLUSIONS

The *differentia* of the Austrian School is its focus upon the plans—the action-relevant plans—of the individual rather than upon his preferences. Preferences can be treated in an abstract fashion, as the preponderance of contemporary economic theory demonstrates, and such analyses make correct and beneficial use of mathematical symbolism. But the study of plans and how they are brought into interpersonal consistency requires a much more sensitive reading of the nature of human thought and action. Hypotheses about learning and changes in expectations can be based only upon such introspective philosophizing as the attributing of one's own thought processes to others and guessing, again based upon one's own personal experiences and hypothetical behavior in similar circumstances, about the specific *purpose* of the other's behavior.[37]

What of the big issues on which the School seems to offer special insight? It is tempting, at first, to try to "define" the School by simply listing them: time preference, opportunity cost, business-cycle theory, monetary theory, imperfect information, entrepreneurship, capital theory, the role of time, analysis without symbolic mathematics. Time preference and opportunity cost are now part of conventional economics.[38] But the others are still special to Austrians, and the particular Austrian outlook arises—in each of these cases—from the approach I have outlined here: emphasis upon action (not preferences), recognition that action takes time and that because plans may be inconsistent the results of actions are uncertain, and willingness to adopt a method appropriate to this outlook.

A price is paid for all of these insights, and that price is the purely deductive method. This technique, the approach of today's mathematical economists, is superbly suited to analysis of the conditions under which known, given preferences are consistent—my static equilibrium—but only to that. Since Austrians are not willing to restrict their viewpoint to the abstract logic of preferences, they must be willing to admit nondeduced hypotheses about plan revision into their analyses.

So which is better—neoclassical and mathematical economic theory, or Austrianism? It is simply not true that all of the advantages are on one side: mathematical symbolism offers decided advantages when the problem is one of pure and complex logical deduction, but the Austrian approach must be used when the problems are not of this sort. And they never are, in any real application—business cycles, planning, monetary policy, they are all *dynamic* issues, swept under a rug in contemporary economics by a methodological bias for pure deduction and against any hypotheses having to do with thinking.

Hayek pinpointed the differences in 1942 when he noted that:

... the most marked tendency of the development of scientific thought in modern times. . . . has been correctly described as one toward the progressive elimination of all "anthropomorphic" explanations from the physical sciences. Does this really mean that we must refrain from treating man "anthropomorphically"—or is it not rather obvious, as soon as we put it in this way, that such an extrapolation of past tendencies is absurd?[39]

The difference between physical and social sciences is not that the former is "inductive" and the latter "deductive." It is that the physical sciences can use pure deduction because their objects cannot plan and learn. Neoclassical and mathematical economists use the same method by restricting their analyses to "men" who cannot plan or learn any more than can a frictionless plane, whereas the Austrian School builds its entire system and method around these distinctively human potentials—thinking, planning, learning. Which is better? Each of us must answer. But we must answer first: to what extent is economics a study of man?

NOTES

1. By "neoclassical orthodoxy," I refer to the approach taken in C. E. Ferguson, *The Neoclassical Theory of Production and Distribution* (London: Cambridge University Press, 1969) and dozens of intermediate microeconomic theory textbooks.

2. Works taken to represent the Austrian School include especially: F. A. Hayek, *Individualism and Economic Order* (Chicago: Univ. of Chicago Press, 1948); Ludwig von Mises, *Human Action* (Chicago: Regnery, 1966); Israel M. Kirzner, *Competition and Entrepreneurship* (Chicago: Univ. of Chicago Press, 1973); Ludwig M. Lachmann, *Capital and Its Structure* (London: LSE, 1956); Murray N. Rothbard, *Man, Economy, and State* (Los Angeles: Nash, 1962).

3. Mises, *op. cit.*, pp. 32–36; Rothbard, *op. cit.*, pp. 63–66; also, Mises, *Epistemological Problems of Economics* (Princeton: Van Nostrand, 1962), pp. 12–13.

4. Rothbard, *op. cit.*, pp. 1, 63.

5. On the many ways in which this word has been used, see Fritz Machlup, "Equilibrium and Disequilibrium: Misplaced Concreteness and Disguised Politics," in *Essays in Economic Semantics* (New York: Norton, 1967).

6. On this issue, see F. A. Hayek, "Economics and Knowledge," reprinted in *Individualism and Economic Order*, p. 40, *passim*.

7. "The state of equilibrium as here understood is a state of complete compatibility of *ex ante* plans . . ." (F. A. Hayek, *The Pure Theory of Capital* [Chicago: Univ. of Chicago Press, 1941], p. 23).

8. I do not know if this has ever been said of my static conception, but it certainly (and rightly) has been said of the dynamic equilibrium. It is important that we appreciate the distinction.

9. F. A. Hayek, "Economics and Knowledge," p. 45; also his "The Use of Knowledge in Society," in *Individualism and Economic Order*, p. 91.

10. "Economics and Knowledge," pp. 36–7.

11. "The introduction of time parameters into the equations is no solution" (Mises, *Human Action*, p. 356).

12. In a comment on an earlier draft of this paper, Professor Israel M. Kirzner observed that the very clearing of a market implies that the participants' *short-run* plans are brought into consistency even while the outcome permits inconsistencies in *long-run* plans (which I simply call

"plans") to remain. I accept Kirzner's point, but it does not seem to invalidate what follows.

13. My phrase "abstract logic of preference" is obviously modelled after Hayek's "Pure Logic of Choice," but fits my purpose better.

14. See especially: Mises, *Human Action*, pp. 350–57; Rothbard, *Man, Economy, and State*, pp. 277–80.

15. George Stigler, *Production and Distribution Theories* (New York: Macmillan, 1946), p. 181.

16. Kirzner, *Competition and Entrepreneurship*, p. 68.

17. Some of the following is based upon Ayn Rand, "Introduction to Objectivist Epistemology," which appeared in various issues of *The Objectivist* between July 1966 and February 1967.

18. Gerard Debreu, *Theory of Value* (New York: Wiley, 1959).

19. Bertrand Russell, *Principles of Mathematics* (New York: Norton, n.c.d.), p. 3. Originally published in 1903.

20. Morris R. Cohen, *A Preface to Logic* (New York: Holt, 1944), pp. 9–11.

21. I have been informed both by a philosopher and by a mathematician that Russell failed in his lifelong attempt to prove the identity between logic and mathematics.

22. W. Stanley Jevons, *The Theory of Political Economy*, 5th ed. (New York: Kelley & Millman, Inc., 1957), p. 3.

23. James R. Newman, *The World of Mathematics*, 4 vols. (New York: Simon and Schuster, 1956), III, p. 1830.

24. Jevons, *op. cit.*, pp. 4–5.

25. Several critics of this paper have pointed out that words *are* symbols which represent concepts. Of course I accept this, and urge that my "symbols" in the following be interpreted as "second-order symbols," standing for words.

26. One or more of these advantages have been claimed by many economists. For one example, see Josef Hadar, *Mathematical Theory of Economic Behavior* (Reading, Mass.: Addison-Wesley, 1971), pp. 5–7.

27. Mr. Roger Garrison points out that the verbal phrase expresses causality while the symbolic expression does not. His observation is absolutely correct, and it strengthens all of my subsequent points about the relative natures of mathematical and verbal analyses.

28. Rand, *op. cit.*, *passim*.

29. Hayek, "Economics and Knowledge," p. 33, *passim*.

30. Richard von Mises, *Probability Statistics and Truth* (London: George Allen and Unwin Ltd., 1961), first published in 1928.

31. See Mises, *Human Action*, *op. cit.*, pp. 105–18; also, G. L. S. Shackle, *Expectation in Economics* (Cambridge: University Press, 1952), pp. 5, 109–27.

32. See, for example, J. Hadar and W. R. Russell, "Rules for Order-

ing Uncertain Prospects," *American Economic Review*, LIX, No. 1 (1969), pp. 25–34.

33. Karl Popper, *The Logic of Scientific Discovery* (New York: Harper and Row, 1968), p. 40.

34. Hayek, "Economics and Knowledge," p. 44, *passim*.

35. It seems to me as if those who argue that entrepreneurship is always moving toward and never away from an equilibrium must adopt this viewpoint.

36. Carl Menger, *Principles of Economics* (Glencoe: The Free Press, 1950), pp. 257–71; Ludwig von Mises, *The Theory of Money and Credit* (Irvington-on-Hudson, NY: Foundation for Economic Education, 1971), pp. 97–123. See also Philip H. Wicksteed, *The Common Sense of Political Economy*, 2 vols. (London: Routledge & Kegan Paul, 1967), I, pp. 136–37.

37. See F. A. Hayek, "The Facts of the Social Sciences," in *Individualism and Economic Order*, p. 66.

38. It has been pointed out to me that although these terms are now in common use, they are often not applied in the consistently subjectivist Austrian manner.

39. Hayek, "The Facts of the Social Sciences," pp. 64–65.

Praxeology
and Econometrics:
A Critique
of Positivist Economics

Mario J. Rizzo
New York University

The ultimate goal of a positive science is the development of a "theory" or "hypothesis" that yields valid and meaningful (*i.e.*, not truistic) predictions about phenomena not yet observed.[1]

Although written a quarter of a century ago, Milton Friedman's "The Methodology of Positive Economics" remains the immediate philosophical justification for much of the contemporary approach to economics research. Nevertheless, the general points raised in that essay were not new even at the time, but were an ingenious adaptation of some of the positivist arguments of the 1930s, and the somewhat revisionist work of Sir Kàrl Popper.[2] Today, thoroughgoing positivism is clearly in retreat, if not already defeated, in philosophical circles, but a variant of it remains quite vibrant in many of the social sciences, particularly economics. It is the task of this essay to present a critique of "positive economics" and, at least, some indications of a viable alternative.

I. PREDICTION AS THE GOAL

From the positivist epistemological viewpoint, is the opening quotation to be taken as an *a priori* or an empirical statement?

If *a priori,* then it is a statement about how we shall use the term "positive science" and is merely a linguistic stipulation. As such, one might equally well choose to stipulate some other meaning.

If empirical (*i.e.*, a statement about what people have in fact considered positive science), then, of course, it does not express a necessary truth and *could* be otherwise. But then for a long time the Darwinian theory of evolution yielded no predictions and yet was considered scientifically acceptable.[3]

Furthermore, Friedman makes no attempt to survey what has been considered economic science to find out whether "prediction" has indeed been the defining characteristic. In fact, there are many theoretical frameworks which generate no testable predictions but are, nonetheless, considered part of economics. For example, it is frequently unclear what (predictive) relevance discussions on the existence and stability of equilibrium under many special assumptions (the empirical significance of which is unknown) have for a world which is never actually *in* equilibrium. Of course, one might claim that this is *bad* economics, and so the demarcation is really between "good" and "bad" science. There is, however, no escape here, for it merely leaves unanswered the question: Why is nonpredictive economics bad science?

Another possible escape might be to claim that, while nonpredictive theories may be scientific, they do not qualify as *positive* science. To this we are justified in merely replying: "So what?" What advantage is being claimed for positive science except that its ultimate goal is prediction? In that case, we are back where we started: Why *must* prediction be our goal?

The goal of prediction might well obscure what has in fact been considered a worthwhile aim of science: the explication and apprehension of *necessary* connections. Purely predictive "theory" is little more than a mnemonic device designed to relate *x* to *y*. But the *nature* of that relation may be unknown. The Babylonian astronomical forecasting techniques, which were merely trial-and-error arithmetic calculations, are an example of this kind of "black box" framework.[4] The principle of explanation remains unknown in the sense that the connection between the initial and marginal conditions (x_1, x_2, x_3, etc.) and the consequence (*y*) is not apprehended as necessary. The relation is characterized by an arbitrary givenness.

But while it may be true that prediction cannot be considered a *sufficient* attribute for "scientific" theory, it still might be a necessary one. However, we have already implicitly refuted this assertion by showing that within a positivist epistemological framework such necessity can be derived only from an essentially arbitrary prior stipulation.

II. FALSIFIABILITY AS THE CRITERION OF MEANING

The emphasis on prediction as *the* aim of science has its roots in a positivist criterion for the meaningfulness of a statement. To be meaningful, it has been said, a statement must be in a form such that it is *in principle* falsifiable by any observer.[5]

For example, let us take "the hypothesis that a substantial increase in the quantity of money within a relatively short period is accompanied by a substantial increase in prices."[6] Aside from problems concerning data availability and the skills of the particular investigator, is this hypothesis falsifiable? For now, let us say it is. Hence, the positivist would claim that this is a genuinely scientific statement. In fact, the meaning of a hypothesis is identified with the relevant test of its veracity. As Moritz Schlick tells us, "the meaning of a statement can be given only by indicating the way in which the truth of the statement is to be tested."[7] Of course, this cannot be literally true. If meaning is identified with the test, then what is being tested? But, if there is a meaning independent of the test, then the positivist criterion falls in on itself, and unfalsifiable statements can be meaningful. If we are not to take Schlick's statement literally, then it seems difficult to find any coherent interpretation of it.

But, of course, the whole concept of a unitary criterion for meaning is somewhat strange when viewed from within a positivist framework. Once again: Is the proposition *a priori* or empirical? A stipulated definition of "meaning" to include falsifiability is not in itself impressive: One could have stipulated otherwise. Viewed empirically, the criterion is immediately refuted by two thousand years of Western philosophy which claims that metaphysics and ontology are meaningful pursuits.

Aside from these issues, the falsifiability criterion loses much of its initial plausibility when the contradictory of a falsifiable statement is examined.[8] If we admit as falsifiable that all inflations are caused by increases in the money supply, then the contradictory,[9] some inflations are not caused by increases in the money supply, is *not* falsifiable. If the latter hypothesis is meant to apply to the future as well as to the past, one could always claim that the inflation not caused by money supply increases will appear if you just search long and hard enough. No example of money-supply-induced inflation refutes the proposition, and with a future, as well as a past, time horizon one has an *infinite* pool of inflations within which to search for the complete absence of nonmonetary inflations.

Consequently, the falsifiability criterion involves a major transformation in our system of logic: Although a given statement may be meaningful (or scientific), the negation of that statement is meaningless (or unscientific).[10]

A possible route of escape from this argument might appear to be the claim that while, strictly speaking, the statement that some inflations are not caused by increases in the money supply is not falsifiable, evidence could be accumulated which would render it more or less "probable." Alas, this is no escape either. The truth or falsity of any statement is not a random variable like tosses of a coin, and hence a frequential interpretation of the "probability" concept is impossible here. So the meaning of the term "probable" can only involve a *subjective* degree of belief. This amounts to a radical transformation of the whole positivist framework. The criterion now becomes: Any statement which could be rendered more or less "probable" by reference to empirical evidence is a meaningful statement. But then this is a psychological—rather than a logical—criterion. Any proposition for which our subjective degree of belief could be increased or decreased by "evidence" is meaningful. Worse still, what kinds of statements does this criterion exclude? Probably none. It would seem that human beings are not imaginative enough to conceive of propositions that have no relationship *at all* to the world. Hence, for any nontautologous (in the narrowest sense) statement, it is possible to find empirical "evidence" that has *some* bearing on its truth or falsity. Hence, all statements are meaningful. If this is so, then the original intent of the positivist criterion crumbles.

Any statement of degree-of-belief probability does not fit comfortably within the positivist framework. Statements such as "that some inflations are not monetarily induced is 'probable' " are, of course, neither verifiable nor falsifiable in principle. More importantly, they do not carry with them any element of intersubjective testability (which was such an important goal). A stipulation that certain kinds of evidence will be interpreted as making a statement "probable" is no real solution. This makes the criterion of meaningfulness (or the demarcation between science and non-science) purely conventional.

III. CRITIQUE OF ECONOMETRICS[11]

Ceteris paribus prediction is prediction of "stylized facts": *x* leads to *y if* other factors are held constant. But since, in general, they aren't, we are not predicting a "real-world" event. Rather, we are predicting a hypothetical consequence.

To subject the hypothesis to potential falsification, we must control for the other relevant variables. Suppose we try to do this by using multiple regression analysis. Then:

1. How do we know when we have adequately controlled for extra-economic factors? (There is no *a priori* assurance that economic factors are the only ones that matter in a given situation.) This would require a theory of the interaction

between economic and non-economic variables. How do we go about subjecting this to falsifying tests?

2. How do we test the theory which enables us to determine the other economic factors that must be held constant in order to isolate the effect of x?

From the positivist framework the problem is crucial. How could we ever know that the (auxiliary) hypothesis, *i.e.*, all other relevant factors have been held constant, has been falsified? We obviously cannot claim that it has been refuted if x does not result in y because it is *that* very relationship which is undergoing testing in the first place. It is clear that, unless we have additional hypotheses about the effects of each of the to-be-held-constant variables on y, we shall not be able to subject the crucial *ceteris paribus* clause to refutation. Furthermore, these auxiliary hypotheses (or perhaps a single hypothesis since it is their total effect with which we are concerned) must be independent of the central one in the sense that the falsification of the former must be independent of the falsification of the latter. Now, if we claim that we really don't care if the *ceteris paribus* clause is "true" because all that counts is the predictive ability of the central hypothesis, then we have gotten ourselves into a new quagmire. First, why have *ceteris paribus* clauses at all? Second, what are we falsifying if, in fact, x does not result in y? Certainly not the hypothesis as stated. Suppose the "evidence" fails to refute our hypothesis; then what have we corroborated? Again, not the original hypothesis because the apparent consistency of the data with the framework may be illusory, being entirely due to the "proper" variation of the factors which were supposed to be constant. Third, this whole viewpoint reinstates the "black box" approach to science and hence vitiates the aim of rational explanation.

It is quite possible to claim that, although the central hypothesis must be falsifiable in order to be meaningful or scientific, the *ceteris paribus* clause need not be. All that is needed in the latter case—it might be asserted—is a kind of educated judgment or *verstehen*. While this might be permissible within other epistemological frameworks, it will not be adequate to support the claims of positivism. If we can say that "all other relevant factors have been held constant" without falsifiability and still can be making a meaningful empirical statement, why can't we do the same in the case of "*x* causes *y*," the central hypothesis? If we can (which seems likely given the initial admission), then once again the criterion of positive science crumbles.

IV. MAXIMIZATION

Under the influence of the "marginalist revolution," economics has become a discipline devoted in major part to the finding of functional maxima and minima. The individual consumer or producer is assumed to maximize or minimize something and, from this postulated behavior, testable implications are drawn. It is important to keep in mind that the maximization behavior itself is not subject to falsification, because it serves not as a substantive hypothesis but as a superstructure which gives rational coherence to the falsifiable implications.

Any particular instance of concrete behavior may be "explained" or rationalized in terms of maximization (or minimization) of some appropriate quantity (*e.g.*, utility, wealth, etc.). Since maximization is fundamentally a characteristic of intention (this the positivists won't admit), any concrete behavior may be viewed *as if* it were the maximization of *something*. This has serious implications.

Suppose we wish to test not the applicability of a specific economic hypothesis to a given area of human behavior (say, marriage), but, rather, the validity of viewing this kind of behavior as an instance of economic or maximizing activity *per se*. In other words, we don't care whether a particular maximizing model is appropriate, but we ask whether this is an example of maximizing behavior at all.

It might be claimed that this formulation of the problem makes no sense. After all, we are never testing economics or maximizing behavior as such, but only specific hypotheses of whatever kind. This, of course, misses the crucial point of the need to decide upon a research framework in advance of specific cases.

Is the statement "this is an example or instance of maximizing behavior" a meaningful and scientific one? Clearly not. Since the set of possible falsifiers is empty, any behavior can be "explained" in terms of maximizing something.[12] But the hypothesis, "this is an instance of maximizing sales," can be refuted by appropriate behavior, and so is a meaningful statement. This produces a curious paradox. The more general statement about maximization is meaningless (or unscientific), but the more particularized version of it constitutes a positive scientific hypothesis.

Some authors have tried to escape this problem by claiming that the (maximizing) framework *can* be refuted by comparison to an empirically richer and more general alternative framework. Indeed, Lakatos has gone so far as to say, "There is no falsification before the emergence of a better theory."[13] This means, in effect, that if two hypotheses—one maximizing and the other non-maximizing—both equally well "explain" a particular case of economic behavior, then the one which is part of a more general approach, the specific applications of which have been corroborated in other cases, is to be preferred. This, however, introduces a subtle and important change in the falsifiability criterion. No longer is a statement meaningful or scientific by virtue of *its* empirical content but, rather, by the overall corroborated empirical content of other statements to which it is in some sense related. It is hard to recognize this as an epistemological criterion rather than as an aesthetic one.[14] Nevertheless, by some inexplicable train of thought, a statement becomes meaningful because of its relation to other similar statements which, having been corroborated, are themselves meaningful by virtue of their relation to, say, the former hypothesis. (Apparently, there is some kind of "simultaneous determination of meaning" argument underlying all of this.)

Let us look at this problem in a slightly different manner. The maximizing framework "proves" its worth, we might say, by predicting everything that the alternative framework does, plus a little more.[15] Hence, it acts, in a sense, as a falsifier of the alternative perspective.

This formulation does not seem very convincing. In economics, at least, it would be surprising if, say, the maximizing framework predicted literally all of the facts predicted by the alternative. Normally, I suspect, the "better" framework would predict *some* of these facts, and some additional ones. Furthermore, competing frameworks frequently do not even ask the same questions. Why, then, should they be judged on whether they give the same answers (plus a little more)?

All this aside, it is hard to see why, from a purely positivist epistemological perspective, considerations of the framework's success in other particular instances should affect the meaningfulness or scientific character of a hypothesis in any given specific case.

V. EVIDENCE

Until this point, we have implicitly considered as self-evident the answer to the question: "What shall count as evidence for and against a hypothesis?" How do we recognize a falsifying or corroborating result? The answer is, indeed, far from self-evident. In fact, this issue poses some crucial problems for the positivist approach, which, we shall contend, it is incapable of handling.

A hypothesis relates a variable x to a variable y, *ceteris paribus*. Let us assume that the *ceteris paribus* clause has been corroborated adequately; then what would amount to falsification of the hypothesis? To be more specific, hypothesize "that a substantial increase in the quantity of money . . . is accompanied by a substantial increase in prices."[16] In order to test this statement, we must have some criteria by which we can relate the theoretical terms "money" and "prices" with their empirical counterparts. This is the crux of the problem.[17]

Something must point the way from theory to the relevant "facts"; we need what shall be called "referential statements." In our illustration, examples of referential statements might be: "The empirical counterpart of theoretical 'money' is M_1"; or, "by 'prices' is meant the consumer price index." The need for referential statements in applied economics is not restricted to the positivist variant of the science. What is peculiar to positivist economics, however, is a problem arising out of the epistemological status of such statements. If they are to be considered *a priori*, then (from a positivist viewpoint) we are merely talking about how we use words, and no link between the theoretical constructs and "empirical reality" is established. Then it must be established via falsifiable hypotheses. Yet this is an impossibility. (Referential statements make no predictions; they do not say, for example, that an increase in x results in an increase in y. Hence no predictions can be falsified.)

Now it is possible to recast the referential statements in such a way that they will be refutable: "If the criteria of applying the theoretical construct 'money' are, in fact, applied, then M_1 will be found to be the appropriate empirical counterpart." Clearly, this won't work because it requires that we know the criteria *prior* to the testing procedure which was to establish (or at least corroborate) these criteria in the first place.

Testing the referential statements is impossible unless we already know the criteria of applying the theoretical terms. If we already know these (in any meaningful way), then testing is unnecessary. But, from a positivist perspective, it is clearly impossible to have any meaningful knowledge about the real world which is given *a priori*.

One might attempt to obviate these difficulties by choosing empirical variables so as to present the particular hypothesis in its best light. (Choosing a definition of the money supply so as to best predict GNP is an example of this.) Unless one is attempting to insulate a hypothesis from refutation, there seems to be no clear reason for doing this. If empirical variables were chosen so as to present the hypothesis in its *worst* light, and it still remained unrefuted, would we not then have more fully corroborated it? In any event, the outcome of a potential test should not be the determining factor in whether it is performed.

VI. THE LOGICAL CHARACTER OF PRAXEOLOGY

The epistemological status of praxeology (which is identical to economics very broadly conceived) is a subject of considerable misunderstanding and confusion. Within a positivist framework the claims of praxeology make no sense. Knowledge is either *a priori* and certain but not pertaining to "reality," or it is empirical and uncertain but clearly embedded in the "real" world. An examination of the logical character of praxeology reveals these categories to be totally inappropriate. Praxeology claims to present knowledge which is at once both absolutely certain and empirical. This is the paradox which we shall have to explain.

Praxeological theorems or deductions are based upon the fundamental self-evident axiom, *i.e.,* man acts or, what is the same, engages in purposeful behavior. The question at issue, then, is: In what precise sense is this axiom "self-evident," and what does it say about the world?

The action axiom is empirical in the sense that it is derived from inner experience or immediate introspection. It is *scientifically* empirical because it passes the intersubjectivity test: The experience is universal and hence, in principle, can be assented to by the observers and the observed alike. Hence, the fact that the axiom is based on introspection cannot open the praxeologist to the charge that his deductions are of a purely personal and unscientific character. We are dealing here with "universal inner experience."[18]

An attempt to deny the action axiom involves us in blatant self-contradiction. Denial consists of the use of means (arguments) to achieve ends (conclusions) and, hence, purposeful behavior. In addition, the assumption that men act is a necessary prerequisite for the existence of a scientific community. Arguments, attempts to convince other researchers of a different view, etc., are all fundamentally based on a conception of scientists themselves as engaging in purposeful behavior. To separate out the scientists, and say that while the observers engage in action and the observed do not, would seem to be an artificiality for which no support could be adduced.

While the action axiom is empirical and self-evident, it is, in a sense, also *a priori*.[19] That man acts is logically prior to any concrete manifestation of action. In fact, one must have a *concept* of action before one can even recognize action in the so-called real world. The action axiom is derived from absolutely certain inner experience but is *a priori* to historical phenomena. History, as a complex of human behavior, is analyzed and interpreted by use of praxeological theorems which are, in turn, derived from relatively simple experience.

Praxeology concerns the *form* of action *qua* action. Just because it is not about this specific action or that specific action does not mean that it concerns itself only with words. The category of action is about every action that has and will take place emptied of its specific means-ends content. As such, it is no less about "reality" than any generally recognized empirical statement. All statements about the world involve some degree of abstraction, so it is not the abstraction of praxeological deductions which is at issue. What may be of concern is that they are incapable of falsification. *In principle* the statement "man acts" cannot be falsified since we cannot conceive of the contrary. This is not because we are simply dealing with an arbitrary stipulated definition of "man" as an acting being. Rather, it is because our acquaintance with empirical man as acting is both so intimate and necessary that a purely reacting being would not be human in the only sense we can conceive. The concepts of purposeful behavior and man are linked so tightly not because of arbitrary definition, but because they are necessarily linked in empirical reality. Our language reflects something real, yet necessary.

Praxeology as applied to history (broadly viewed as to include current history) does not depend merely on deductions from the action axiom. It requires subsidiary assumptions derived empirically in order to delimit the scope of a praxeological system.[20] For example, we do not want to develop monetary theory in a world without money. Now, the subsidiary empirical assumptions are not self-evident or necessarily true like the action axiom. These assumptions could conceivably be otherwise, although they may be virtually certain (*e.g.,* the existence of indirect exchange). Insofar as they are uncertain, so too is the applicability of the praxeological statements we can make using them.

To increase the quantitative definiteness of relationships in applied praxeology (economic history), we require increasing specificity of the subsidiary assumptions: These assumptions must become both more numerous and more precise. This, of course, results in conclusions which are no longer apodictically certain. In our terminology, we refer to applied praxeological theory as hypotheses (to indicate their tentative nature). Hence, while economic *theory* is immutable and necessary, economic *hypotheses* are changeable and could be otherwise. The view that economic *theory* is a body of tentative statements about the world (subject to refutation) is implicitly the position that knowledge of social reality is confined solely to historical knowledge.

VII. THE ROLE OF ECONOMETRICS

While it might appear as if econometrics has no role in the advancement of economic theory (defined as deductions from the action axiom), this is not quite accurate (although it may serve as a tolerable first approximation of the truth). Statistical regularities can be the starting point for a purely theoretical investigation, insofar as they raise questions to which the praxeologist addresses himself. But the connection here is more suggestive than logical.

The central role of econometrics is in the application of economic theory to the complex phenomena of history (current or past). There are two questions on which econometric work can shed light:

1. To what extent is a given (historical) instance of human behavior explicable by reference to purposeful activity, *i.e.,* how much does a praxeological hypothesis explain?
2. What is the magnitude of the effect of x on the whole complex phenomenon, y, at some specific point in time?

With regard to the first question, it is important to understand that while man necessarily acts, it does not follow that he *always* acts, *i.e.*, that he *never* engages in automatic response to stimuli or some other kind of nonpurposive behavior. To what extent is a given historical phenomenon the result of some blind emotion aiming at nothing? The answer to this cannot be given *a priori*.[21]

On the second question, it is important to keep in mind that praxeological reasoning *per se* cannot reveal quantitative relations (or even qualitative ones, when many conflicting forces are operative) in economic history. For this, statistical investigations are our only recourse. However, it is important *not* to interpret econometrically derived relations as great constants applicable to all situations at all times. These relations are not theoretical but merely historical. To extrapolate the latter to the former requires an inductive leap that we are not prepared to take.

In answering both of these questions, econometric evidence cannot, of course, give us the same certainty as praxeological reasoning. Answers in economic history must always be uncertain. Nevertheless, this is not the uncertainty of economic theory; rather, it is the uncertainty inherent in the application of a structure (involving the *form* of action) upon historico-temporal actions with specific content. The application of theory to history is not an exercise in deduction; it necessitates the use of judgment or understanding (*verstehen*) in defining the relevant variables and the appropriate means of measuring them.

A *caveat* is, however, in order. Econometrics ought to be only one tool in the apprehension of historical phenomena. Clearly, not all issues of interest are quantifiable. If we try to explain complex phenomena only by reference to quantifiable variables, then we are likely to be throwing away some information that we do, indeed, have. Another danger is that we shall begin to identify reality with statistical data when, in fact, it is just one aspect of reality, a particular transformation of more elementary experience. There is no reason whatever why a specific way of viewing history ought to be identified with history itself or, what is worse, with the whole of social reality.

VIII. CONCLUSIONS AND UNRESOLVED QUESTIONS

The purpose of this paper is primarily to present a critical analysis of "positive economics" and only secondarily to examine the praxeologic alternative. It is in the latter area that a great deal of work needs to be done. At this point, however, a number of concluding observations might be made:

1. A thoroughgoing positivist approach to economics cannot be consistently pursued. The positivist framework creates certain problems that are insoluble from within that framework.

2. Although praxeology is concerned with action *qua* action, *i.e.*, ahistorical and emptied of specific means-ends content, it is still about reality. The *form* of action is no less real than any of the other abstractions necessary in making generally recognized empirical judgments.

3. A crucial problem in praxeology is the epistemological nature of applied praxeology (economic history). How is the transition from theoretical constructs to empirical counterparts to be made? *Verstehen* is too vague an answer.

4. Does a praxeologist do economic history differently from a positive economist? If so, in what way?

In discussing some of the more philosophical issues of economics, it has been our intention to show that the day-to-day issues of explanation, hypothesizing, and testing do not go on in a philosophical vacuum. We do not have a choice as to whether we shall make methodological decisions. Our choice, rather, is whether we shall make them explicitly, examining the various implications and subtleties of meaning, or whether we shall make them implicitly, blind to everything but technique.

REFERENCES

1. Milton Friedman, "The Methodology of Positive Economics," *Essays in Positive Economics* (Chicago, 1953), p. 7.

2. See especially Karl Popper, *Logik der Forschung* (Vienna, 1935). The English translation is Karl Popper, *The Logic of Scientific Discovery* (London, 1962). Other relevant works are Rudolf Carnap, *Philosophy and Logical Syntax* (London, 1935) and A. J. Ayer, *Language, Truth and Logic,* 2nd edition (London, 1946).

3. Stephen Toulmin,*Foresight and Understanding: An Enquiry into the Aims of Science* (Bloomington, 1961), p. 28.

4. *Op. cit.*, p. 28.

5. Some philosophers, such as Popper, make this the criterion of science, and not meaningfulness. However, such a shift does not affect the main argument since we then must return to the question of why we define "science" the way we do. See section I above.

6. Friedman, p. 11.

7. Moritz Schlick, *Gesammelte Aufsätze, 1926-1936* (Vienna, 1938), p. 179 as cited in Brand Blanshard, *Reason and Analysis* (LaSalle, Illinois, 1964), p. 224.

8. Blanshard, p. 229.

9. The word "contradictory" is here used in its technical sense. Hence, the statement "no inflations are caused by increases in the money supply" is *not* the contradictory of the statement in the text. This is because if "no inflations are caused by increases in the money supply" is *false,* then *either* "some inflations are (not) caused. . . ." is true or "all inflations are caused. . . ." is true. "*A* and *O* are mutual contradictories, or negations: *A* is true if and only if *O* is false." On this see W. V. Quine, *Methods of Logic*, 3rd edition (New York, 1972), p. 84.

10. Blanshard, p. 229.

11. The general conception of this and the next section is drawn from Martin Hollis and Edward Nell, *Rational Economic Man* (Cambridge, England, 1975), *passim*. However, in many cases the train of reasoning is different (the reader should beware of assuming that the same point is being made), while in others the argument is expanded.

12. In a somewhat different context, Friedman says, "If there is one hypothesis that is consistent with the available evidence, there are always an infinite number that are." Friedman, p. 9.

13. Imre Lakatos, "Falsification and the Methodology of Scientific Research Programmes," *Criticism and the Growth of Knowledge*, Imre Lakatos and Alan Musgrave, eds. (Cambridge, England, 1970), p. 119.

14. Friedman, pp. 10, 20.

15. Lakatos, p. 118.

16. Friedman, p. 11.

17. Much of what follows in this section is from Hollis and Nell, chapter 4. However, the reader should note that our referential statements are *not* the "criterial statements" of Hollis and Nell.

18. Murray N. Rothbard, "In Defense of 'Extreme Apriorism',"
Southern Economic Journal (January 1957), p. 318.

19. Ludwig von Mises, *Human Action*, 3rd edition (Chicago, 1966),
chapter II.

20. *Op. cit.*, pp. 64-66.

21. For some very preliminary observations on these issues, see
Murray N. Rothbard, "Praxeology: Reply to Mr. Schuller," *American
Economic Review* (December 1951), p. 945.

Economics and Error

Israel M. Kirzner
New York University

The title of this paper, it may correctly be surmised, owes something to the title of the famous 1937 paper of Professor Hayek, "Economics and Knowledge."[1] There lies, Hayek acknowledged, an intentional ambiguity in the title of that paper: we are in fact to learn in his paper that the knowledge which economic analysis conveys depends crucially upon propositions about the knowledge possessed by the different members of society. The not dissimilar ambiguity in the title of the present paper may, one ventures to hope, suggest that a good deal of erroneous thought in economics has its source in confusion concerning the nature and role of *error* in the actions of the different members of society. It is the purpose of this paper to dispel at least some portion of this confusion. If, in the course of this attempt, some incidental light can be thrown, as well, on the problems raised by Hayek in his '37 paper, this will be seen to reflect (once again not accidentally) the symmetrical ambiguities embedded in the titles of the two papers.

EFFICIENCY, WASTE, AND ERROR

Economists have traditionally been concerned with issues related to efficiency. Inefficient action occurs when one places oneself in a position which one views as less desirable than an equally available alternative state of affairs. Inefficiency can therefore not be thought of except as the result of an error, a mistake, an incorrect and wrong move. Much of the work of the modern economist has, in fact, the declared aim of avoiding errors, of achieving efficiency. At the same time, however, as he directs his energies toward the obviation of error, the contemporary economist is frequently to be found pursuing his analysis on the assumption that men do not, and will not, ever fall into error. "Waste," declares Stigler in a recent note, "is error within the framework of modern economic analysis, and it will not become a useful concept until we have a theory of error."[2] Modern economic analysis, we are to understand, lacking a theory of error, can and does proceed only by assuming it away: error and waste simply have no place in the world of economic theory. It is this position that we wish to examine critically. Is it really the case, we must ask, that economic theory requires us to abstract completely from the phenomenon of error? As a preliminary step toward the consideration of this question, it is necessary first to review a number of discussions to be found in the economic literature in which the possibility of error has been seriously canvassed.

MISES, MARKSMEN, AND MISTAKES

In a passage in which he is concerned to explain that human action is *always* rational (in the sense of being designed to attain definite ends), Mises considers the objection that men make mistakes. This does not, Mises points out, constitute irrationality. "To make mistakes in pursuing one's ends is a widespread human weakness.... Error, inefficiency, and failure must not be confused with irrationality. He who shoots wants, as a rule, to hit the mark. If he misses it, he is not 'irrational'; he is a poor marksman. The doctor who chooses the wrong method to treat a patient is not irrational; he may be an incompetent physician. ..."[3] The implication here is that the incompetent physician and the poor marksman may indeed make mistakes and errors. Rational Misesian human actors *are* human enough to err. But it is clear that these errors are not inconsistent with the position (*excluding* errors) cited earlier as taken by Stigler. In fact the reason why these are not errors in the sense relevant to the Stigler position, is entirely similar to the reason why these errors do not, for Mises, constitute irrationality. The mistakes made by the ill-trained medic do not represent a failure by him to attain that which it is within his power to attain. His failure simply reflects lack of the necessary quality of input. An error (in the Stigler sense) occurs only when an input is used in a way that fails to produce what *that* input can produce. When a poor mathematician makes a mistake in arithmetic[4] he is *not*, therefore, making an error; nor is the failure by a poor marksman to hit the mark an error. It is not an error for a physically weak man to be unable to lift a heavy weight. Nor is it an error, in the relevant sense, when one unschooled in medicine fails to prescribe the proper treatment for a patient. (To be sure, it may be that the incompetent physician, indifferent mathematician, and poor marksman ought not to waste their time [and their patients' lives] by engaging in tasks for which they are so definitely ill-suited. But of course Mises is concerned with the mistake the physician makes in the course of the practice of medicine, not with the possible error of his attempting to practice medicine altogether.)

CROCE, TECHNICAL ERROR, AND ECONOMIC ERROR

In the course of his famous correspondence with Pareto at the turn of the century (in the *Giornale degli Economisti*), Benedetto Croce did find a definite place for "economic error." Such an error, Croce explained, must be sharply distinguished from "technical error." Technical error, for Croce, consists in an error of knowledge; it occurs when one is ignorant of the properties of the materials with which one deals (such as when one places a heavy iron girder on a delicate wall too weak to support it). Economic error, on the other hand, occurs for example when, yielding to the temptation of the moment, one pursues a transient fancy which is not one's true goal; it is, Croce explains, an *error of will*, "the failure to aim directly at one's own object: to wish this and that, i.e. not really to wish either this or that."[5] Avoidance of economic error requires that one aim at one's goal; failure to aim at one's goal constitutes, therefore, a special category of error. This error arises out of the incorrectness not of the pattern of acts taken in pursuing one's immediate aim, since these are, from the point of view of *that* aim, entirely appropriate, but of one's immediate aim itself. To pursue this aim is—from the perspective of one's "true" goals—an aberration. One places oneself into contradiction with oneself, one aims at that which one does not, in fact, seek to attain.

Croce's concept of economic error has not found favor among economists. The writer has elsewhere[6] reviewed the careful analysis which Tagliacozzo many years ago made of Croce's position.[7] Briefly the reason why economists have no place for Croce's "economic error" is that it seems impossible, from the point of view of pure science, to distinguish between "true" goals and erroneous, transient ones. Once we have accepted the possibility that man can discard yesterday's goals and adopt new ones towards which he will direct today's purposeful actions—we have surrendered the possibility of labelling the pursuit of any end (no matter how fleeting the "temptation" toward it may be, and no matter how permanent remorse over having "yielded" to it may turn out to become) as, on scientific grounds, an erroneous one. Croce's economic error, it then turns out, emerges only as a result of invoking (unspecified) judgments of value in terms of which to classify, from a man's *own* point of view, those goals of his which it is "correct" to pursue and those the pursuit of which he must consider an error.

It seems worthwhile to digress briefly to note that Mises—in whose writings one finds no room at all for the type of "economic error" identified by Croce—seems to have consistent scientific grounds for his unwillingness to recognize such error. It is well known that Mises denied the independent existence of a scale of values (actuating human choices) *apart from the acts of choice themselves* ("the scale of values . . . manifests itself only in the reality of action").[8] The notion of a given scale of values, Mises is at pains to explain, can therefore not be used to pronounce a real action (at variance with that scale) as "irrational." The logical consistency which human action necessarily displays, by no means entails *constancy* in the ranking of ends.[9] Mises' insistence on the possibility of changes in adopted preference rankings is closely related to his understanding of choice as *undetermined*. Man does not choose as a *reaction* to given circumstances—on the basis of a previously adopted scale of values; he chooses freely at the time he acts, between different ends and different ways of reaching these ends. It follows that the notion of economic error as perceived by Croce has no place in economic *science*.

ERRONEOUS ACTION AND IMPERFECT KNOWLEDGE

That men frequently act on the basis of imperfect knowledge is of course not disputed by writers for whom error in economic theory is excluded. In the passage (cited above) where Mises defends the "rationality" of erroneous actions, he mentions an example which we have not yet cited. "The farmer who in earlier ages tried to increase his crop by resorting to magic rites acted no less rationally than the modern farmer who applies more fertilizer."[10] Men certainly engage in actions which they may regret when they discover the true facts of the situation. Croce, we have seen, termed this kind of mistake a *technical* error. Erroneous action arising from ignorance is not, however, generally seen as a serious threat to an economics which excludes error. With respect to the *perceived* framework of ends and means, error-free decision making can still be postulated. The very notion of an ends-means framework, of preferences and constraints, of indifference curves and budget lines, enables the economist to confine his analysis to choice *within* the given framework. The source of error in such choices, being *outside* that framework, is thus, by the very scope of the analysis, in effect excluded from consideration.

To be sure it is precisely this aspect of modern economics against which Professors Lachmann and Shackle have, among

other matters, so vigorously rebelled. Since all action is future-
oriented, necessarily involving an unknown and unknowable
future, men's actions are inevitably attended by what Knight
called error in the exercise of judgment.[11] Such error may, if one
chooses, be subsumed under Croce's technical error, but the
all-pervasive and inescapable character of such errors in judgment does, in the view of these distinguished critics, seriously
compromise the usefulness of abstractions depending on given,
known, ends-means frameworks. In this paper, we will not pursue further the profound consequences with respect to modern
economics which the Lachmann-Shackle critiques imply. Our
discussion proceeds, instead, in the context of modes of discourse which do perceive continued relevance in theories of
choice dependent on supposedly given, known frameworks of
preferences and constraints.

It should be pointed out that a good deal of modern theorizing
proceeds along a path on which actions based on mistaken
knowledge appear *not* to be errors, in a sense deeper than that so
far discussed in this paper. It is not merely that an action is seen
as "correct" within the framework of the *perceived*—but in fact
the quite wrongly perceived—ends-means framework. The action is frequently seen as correct also in that the ignorance, on
which the mistaken perceptions are to be blamed, may *itself* be
viewed as having been *deliberately* (and quite correctly) cultivated.
Economists have long recognized that men must deliberately
choose what information they wish to acquire at given prices.
One who on a deliberate gamble refrains from acquiring a certain piece of costly knowledge, and who then, in consequence of
his ignorance, makes a "mistake," may indeed regret his lack of
good fortune in having lost as a result of his gamble, but may
nonetheless quite possibly still feel that the chances which he
originally confronted (when deliberating on whether or not to
acquire the costly information) rendered his original decision
the correct one. The relevant ends-means framework, within
which actions have been pronounced consistently errorless, has
now been broadened to embrace the situation within which the
choice was made not to buy improved information. If Mises'

"incompetent" physician had taken a calculated risk in deliberately not studying with sufficient care the treatment of a rare disease, his subsequent errors may indeed be seen as "technical errors"; (they may also, as we have seen earlier, be seen simply as the entirely-to-be-expected shortcoming in output quality consequent on the less-than-perfect quality of medical input). But the ignorance responsible for the technical error in medical treatment (or, if one prefers, for the less-than-perfect quality of medical expertise available for deployment) may itself be the consistent result of a correct, deliberate, choice. This way of seeing imperfect knowledge—as the correctly planned limitation on input quality—permits one to subsume errors arising out of imperfect knowledge under the general class of errors treated above in the section "Mises, Marksmen, and Mistakes," that is, as not constituting errors at all (in the sense of somehow failing to achieve an available preferred state of affairs). This way of looking at things has gained plausibility as a result of the development during the last 15 years by Stigler and others, of the Economics of Information (in which detailed analysis is undertaken of decisions concerning the optimum degree of ignorance to be preserved under different conditions, and of the market consequences of such decisions).

LEIBENSTEIN AND THE LACK OF MOTIVATION

Harvey Leibenstein has written an extensive series of papers developing the concept of X-inefficiency and exploring the extent to which this type of inefficiency has yet to be incorporated into standard economic theory.[12] In this paper we consider only those aspects of his work that bear directly on the possibility of error within the scope of economic analysis. In the present section we briefly take note of some of the objections raised recently by Stigler against certain aspects of Leibenstein's contribution.

For Leibenstein, X-inefficiency (as contrasted with the more conventional allocative inefficiency) is equivalent to what for others is called technical efficiency,[13] the failure of producers to achieve, with the inputs they use, the highest technically possible level of output. Among the sources of this kind of inefficiency, in Leibenstein's view, is inadequacy of motivation and of effort. "The simple fact is that neither individuals nor firms work as hard, nor do they search for information as effectively, as they could."[14] Stigler has severely criticized Leibenstein on his use of language.[15] For the purposes of our discussion of the possibility of error in economics, Stigler's objections can be stated as follows. It is certainly true that greater output could frequently be achieved by greater effort and stronger motivation. But this does not indicate error, in the sense of failing to achieve an available state of affairs more desirable than that actually achieved. If individuals are not sufficiently motivated to work harder, this presumably reflects, deliberately and "correctly," their preference for leisure. If, again, firms have not succeeded in organizing production so as to enhance worker motivation, this constitutes the firm's choice of one "technology" of production, as against the possibility of alternative (more productivity-conscious) technologies. Choice of one technology, yielding lower physical output per week than another available technology, does not, without our knowing all the relevant costs, warrant our asserting the presence of error in the choice of technologies. Stigler's objections are completely convincing. Leibenstein has not, in his exploration of motivational inefficiency, discovered cases of genuine error, in the sense relevant to our discussion. (We will return later in this paper to consider other aspects of Leibenstein's X-inefficiency as more promising in this respect.)

ECONOMICS WITHOUT ERROR?

Let us stand back and observe the position to which we have been led. This position might appear to coincide completely with that in which no place for error exists in economic analysis—if by error one means deliberately placing oneself in a situation which one prefers less than another equally available situation of which one is aware. We have refused to accept Croce's terminology (in which economic error can occur when one has been temporarily seduced to aim deliberately at a goal which one in fact prefers less than another "true" goal). We have, with Stigler, refused to accept Leibenstein's apparent perception of inadequately motivated persons, persons not trying as hard as they really could, as ones who *are* in fact placing themselves in less preferred situations. We have pointed out that errors made by agents whose lack of competence or skill renders such mistakes inevitable, clearly do not involve failure to achieve any attainable preferred position (since the inadequate quality of available inputs places such preferred positions out of reach). And where, as a result of imperfect knowledge, an agent achieves a position less preferred than an equally available alternative position, we have seen that he too cannot, within the framework of the information he believed to be relevant, be convicted of error. Moreover we have seen that insofar as this agent deliberately refrained from acquiring more complete or more accurate knowledge, he cannot even be described as having placed himself in a less preferred situation at all (since in his view the cost of acquiring the more accurate knowledge made ignorance the preferred risk).

It should be observed that our apparent conclusion that error has no place in economics does not depend on any artificial *assumption*, as does, for example, appear to be implied in Stigler. For Stigler, it appears, error is deliberately (and artificially) excluded by the economist from his purview, on the grounds that we lack a theory of error.[16] But for us as Austrians, it should be clear, our conclusions follow strictly from the insight that men are purposeful (or "rational," as Mises uses the word). If men pursue purposes, it follows that of course they do not consciously act to place themselves in situations that are any but the most preferred of those equally available alternatives of which they are aware. If men turn out to have failed to achieve the most preferred situations it must be either that those situations were in fact *not* available, or that (possibly as a result of deliberate, purposeful earlier decisions) these agents were not aware of the full range of alternatives. Not only, that is, have we apparently been led to Stigler's conclusion that there is no place for error in economics, we have been led to this conclusion as implied directly in the very assumption of purposefulness from which we take our point of departure.[17]

Economics, it thus seems to turn out, is peopled by beings whose purposefulness ensures that they can never, in retrospect, reproach themselves for having acted in error. They may, in retrospect, indeed wish that they had been more skillful, or had commanded more inputs, or had been better informed. But they can never upbraid themselves for having acted erroneously in failing to command those superior skills or to acquire more accurate information. They must, at every stage concede that they had, in the past, acted with flawless precision (insofar as they were able). Any reproaches which they may validly wish to direct at themselves—for example for not having tried hard enough or for having succumbed to temptation—arise out of later judgments of value (concerning the significance of leisure or of the goal represented by the fleeting temptation) with which they had, at earlier dates, disagreed. Such self-reproach, we now understand, is not for having acted in error, in the sense relevant to the present discussion.[18]

Indeed the reader might reasonably claim cause for irritation at the *triviality* of our conclusion. Given the paramountcy accorded to purposefulness, and given a definition of error which excludes "wrong" judgments of value as well as failures ascribable to ignorance or inadequacy (whether due to causes beyond the control of the agent or to his past purposeful choices)—surely the conclusion that error is excluded is so obviously implicit in our definitions as to be completely uninteresting.

But, as the remaining pages of this paper will attempt to show, the conclusions to which we have apparently been led by our discussion thus far, are not trivial at all—in fact they are not even true. Not only is there nothing, as we shall see, in the assumptions and definitions on which economic analysis is built, which rules out error—it can be shown that economic analysis can hardly proceed at all without making very important use of the concept of error (as well as of the discovery and correction of error). Let us see how all this can possibly be maintained.

IGNORANCE AND ERROR

Much weight was placed, in earlier pages, on our recognition that mistakes made as a result of ignorance do not qualify as errors (in the sense relevant to our discussion). A man who acted with complete precision, given the knowledge he thought he possessed, could not, we maintained, be reproached with having acted in error. (And where the limits to his stock of knowledge had been deliberately selected, we certainly understood him to have acted, at all times, beyond reproach.) That is, the man at no time refrained from exploiting any known opportunity for achieving the most desirable situation possible. Yet surely we must recognize that, valid though these statements are, within their own framework, they may *not* fully exhaust our interpretation of the situations to which they refer.

A man walks along a street, sees a store with signs offering to sell apples for $1 but, perhaps thinking of other things, enters a second store where he pays $2 for identical apples. He may have "seen" the signs in the first store, but his perception of them was so weak as to mean that, when he paid $2 in the second store he did not, in fact, "know" that he was rejecting a preferred opportunity for one less preferred. Within the framework of his "knowledge," the $2 apples were indeed his best opportunity; he made no error. Yet, surely, in an important sense he will (when he realizes his mistake) reproach himself for having been so absentminded as to pass by the bargain *which he saw*, for the more expensive purchase. In this sense he *did* commit an error, the error of not acting on the information available to him, of not perceiving fully the opportunity before his very nose. He did (without the excuse of not having the necessary information available to him) consciously place himself in a less preferred position than that available to him. It is true that he was not "aware" of the superior alternative. But, because the necessary information *was* available to him, it was surely an error on his part to have failed to act upon it (i.e., to have remained unaware of the superior opportunity). His "unawareness" cannot be "excused" (from conviction of error) on the grounds of inadequacy of inputs (since the information inputs were at hand). It cannot be excused on the grounds of an earlier decision to refrain from acquiring information (since no such decision was made). This unawareness cannot be flatly excluded as impossible (because of inconsistency with purposeful action) because *there is nothing in purposeful action which by itself guarantees that every available opportunity must be instantaneously perceived.*[19]

In the discussion in the first portion of this paper knowledge was treated as something like an input, a "tool." Someone lacking this needed input could not be reproached with error for not succeeding in achieving that for which this input was needed. (And where this input had deliberately and correctly not been acquired because of its cost, this exemption from reproach became even more justified.) But we now see that ignorance may mean something other than lack of command over a needed tool—it may be sheer failure to utilize a resource available and ready at hand. Such failure, moreover, is not inconsistent with purposefulness, since an available resource ready at hand may not be noticed; purposefulness is not necessarily inconsistent with tunnel-vision. (Of course one *might* insist that an agent not blessed with the alertness needed to notice resources available at hand, simply lacks, through no "fault" of his own, *another* "resource" [i.e., "alertness"] necessary to take advantage of the *other* resources with which he *has* been blessed. We cannot set down such a use of terms as *wrong*. We simply point out that while decisions can in principle be made by a person to acquire a resource which he lacks, we can *not* conceive of one lacking "alertness," making a decision to acquire it. This is so because, among other reasons,[20] before a decision to acquire anything can be considered, one must *already* assume the alertness necessary for the perception that such an acquisition is needed and possible at all. Or, to put it somewhat differently, alertness cannot be treated as a resource with respect to which decisions are made on how to use it, since, in order to make such a decision with respect to a resource, one must *already* have been alert to its availability. "Alertness" thus appears to possess a primordial role in decision making which makes it unhelpful for it to be treated, in the analysis of decisions, "as any other resource." We claim, therefore, justification for a terminology which maintains that where ignorance consists, not in lack of available information, but in inexplicably failing to see facts staring one in the face, it represents genuine error, and genuine inefficiency.)[21]

IGNORANCE, ERROR, AND ENTREPRENEURIAL OPPORTUNITIES

We have shown that genuine error is not inconsistent with the fundamental postulates of economics. It remains to show that economic analysis *depends* on the presence of this kind of error for its most elementary and far-reaching theorems. Let us consider the theorem which Jevons correctly called "a general law of the utmost importance in economics," which asserts that "in the same open market, at any one moment, there cannot be two prices for the same kind of article."[22] Now Jevons presented this Law of Indifference as valid only where no imperfection of knowledge exists. Yet surely economists ever since Jevons have understood the law as asserting a *tendency* at all times for divergent prices of identical goods to *converge*, ceteris paribus, toward a single price. That is, the law asserts a tendency for imperfect knowledge to be replaced by more perfect knowledge.[23] Now the existence of such a tendency requires some explanation. If the imperfection of knowledge (responsible for the initial multiplicity of prices) reflected the lack of some "resource" (as where means of communication are absent between different parts of a market), then it is difficult, without additional justification, to see how we can postulate universally a process of spontaneous discovery. If, say, imperfection in knowledge resulted from deliberate unwillingness to incur the costs of search, it is not clear how we can be confident that, in the course of the market process such unwillingness will invariably dissipate, or that the necessary costs of search will invariably fall. (Of course one can construct models in which these costs *may* be supposed to fall. One type of theorizing concerning the nature of the market process has, following on the line of the economics of information, in effect taken this approach.)

Surely our justification for asserting the existence of a tendency for the prices of identical articles to converge rests on our understanding that the imperfection of knowledge (on which one must rely in order to account for the initial multiplicity of prices) reflected, at least in part, sheer error. We understand, that is, that the initial imperfection in knowledge is to be attributed, not to lack of some needed resource, but to failure to notice opportunities ready at hand. The multiplicity of prices represented opportunities for pure entrepreneurial profit; that such multiplicity existed, means that many market participants (those who sold at the lower prices and those who bought at the higher prices) simply overlooked these opportunities. Since these opportunities were left unexploited, *not* because of unavailable needed resources, but because they were simply not noticed, we understand that, as time passes, the lure of available pure profits can be counted upon to alert at least some market participants to the existence of these opportunities. The law of indifference follows from our recognition that error exists, that it consists in available opportunities being overlooked, and that the market process is a process of the systematic discovery and correction of true error. The hypothetical state of equilibrium, it emerges, consists not so much in the perfection of knowledge (since costs of acquiring knowledge may well justify an equilibrium state of ignorance) as in the hypothetical absence of error.

All this permits us to concur (in general terms, if not in matters of detail) with that aspect of Leibenstein's concept of X-inefficiency which he identifies with the scope for entrepreneurship.[24] Scope for entrepreneurship, we have discovered, is present whenever error occurs. Pure profit opportunities exist whenever error occurs. Whenever error occurs in the context of production, inputs are being used to achieve less than the optimum quantity and quality of outputs; the producer is operating inside the "outer-bound production possibility surface consistent with [his] resources."[25] X-inefficiency *is* possible, it reflects error, and is necessarily reflected in the availability of entrepreneurial profit opportunities and scope for entrepreneurial discovery and improvement. That our conclusion with respect to this aspect of Leibenstein's contribution apparently differs from that of Stigler (who rejects the notion of X-inefficiency entirely) is fully consistent with our refusal to accompany Stigler in his insistence on excluding error from economics.

MARSHALL, ROBBINS, AND THE REPRESENTATIVE FIRM

In the course of his critique of Leibenstein, Stigler has valuably recalled our attention to an old issue in the economic literature, the rationale underlying Marshall's concept of the representative firm. It was Lionel (now Lord) Robbins who in 1928[26] explained Marshall's motive in introducing the rather troublesome notion of the representative firm, and who showed, with the most effective logic, that there is in fact no need for this awkward construct at all. Our discussion thus far enables us to make several comments on the issue.

Basing his interpretation on the authoritative opinion of Dennis Robertson, Robbins explains that Marshall devised the representative firm "to meet the difficulties occuring in the analysis of supply when there is a disparity of efficiency as between different producers."[27] This disparity means that part of the total supply of each product (the magnitude of which helps determine price) is produced by producers making zero or negative profits. Consequently it would appear that "the magnitude of net profits is irrelevant to the determination of . . . price." For this reason Marshall explained that price is to be understood in terms of the normal costs (including gross earnings of management) associated with the representative firm.[28]

Robbins went to great pains to show that, insofar as concerns these disparities of efficiency between firms that would not disappear in equilibrium, there is no need at all to invoke the notion of a representative firm. Such disparities in efficiency are to be traced to the presence of entrepreneurs of varying ability. "Just as units of a given supply may be produced on lands of varying efficiency, so their production may be supervised by business men of varying ability. What is normal profit for one will not be normal profit for another, that is all."[29] As Stigler put it, it is inappropriate to use variations in entrepreneurial ability to account for variations in costs among firms: " . . . differences in the quality of an input do not lead to differences in outputs from given inputs. . . . [When] costs of firms differed because of quality of entrepreneurs (or other inputs), the differences in productivity would be reflected in differences in profits (or other input prices)."[30]

In other words, differences in costs of production arising from differences in entrepreneurial ability mean that the equilibrium prices for the various entrepreneurial inputs will be correspondingly different. When account is taken of the costs of these entrepreneurial inputs it will be seen that, in equilibrium, there exist *no* cost variations between entrepreneurs. Stigler appears to conclude that Robbins's discussion justifies the neoclassical practice of viewing each producer as always at a production frontier. If as a result of varying quality of entrepreneurial inputs, there occurs output variation, this is simply because, as a result of the variance in entrepreneurial quality, each producer may have a production frontier above or below that of others.[31] There is no room, in this scheme of things, for Leibenstein's X-inefficiency (which implies the possibility that differences in output are a result of genuine differences in sheer efficiency, *not* attributable to differences in input quality).

For our purposes it is useful to point out that the portion of Robbins's critique of Marshall upon which Stigler draws, is confined explicitly to the state of equilibrium.[32] Under conditions of equilibrium we must indeed reject the possibility of genuine disparities in efficiency among firms that cannot be traced to differences in input qualities. In equilibrium such disparities cannot be traced to sheer error. But under conditions of disequilibrium, when scope exists for entrepreneurial activity, there is no reason why genuine disparities may not exist among different producers, traceable (not to differences in input qualities—since we do not view alertness as an input—but) to differences in the degree to which producers have succumbed to error. Robbins's critique of Marshall does *not*, therefore, imply any need to reject Leibenstein's X-inefficiency (insofar, as we have seen, such inefficiency coincides with the existence of a scope for entrepreneurship).

ERROR IN ECONOMICS: SOME NORMATIVE APPLICATIONS

Our concern in this paper to defend the possibility of genuine error in economics is based on more than our wish to show how positive economic theory cannot proceed without such possibility. Our concern rests, in addition, upon important normative grounds. Allocative inefficiency in a society of errorless individual maximizers must, it appears on reflection, be accounted for only by the existence of prohibitive transaction costs.[33] Improvement in social well-being must, in such a world, appear to be possible only as a result of unexplained technological breakthroughs.

Surely such a picture of the world, a picture in which no genuine opportunities for improvement are permitted to exist, is wholly unsatisfying. Surely we are convinced that enormous scope exists at all times for genuine economic improvement and that the world is chock-full of inefficiencies. It is most embarrassing to have to grapple with the grossly inefficient world we know, with economic tools which assume away the essence of the problem with which we wish to deal.

On the other hand, as soon as we admit genuine error into our purview, our embarrassment fades away. Our world *is* a grossly inefficient world. What is inefficient about the world is surely that, at each instant, enormous scope for improvements exists, is in one way or another ready at hand, and is yet simply not noticed. At each instant, because the market is in a state of disequilibrium, genuine allocative inefficiencies remain yet to be removed simply because entrepreneurs have not yet noticed the profit opportunities represented by these inefficiencies. At each instant available technological improvements (in some sense already ready at hand) remain to be exploited; they remain untapped because entrepreneurs have not yet noticed the profit opportunities embedded in these possibilities. It is genuine error to which we can ascribe much of the world's ills, and we need an economics that can recognize this.

Fortunately, Austrian economics, with its emphasis on disequilibrium and on the entrepreneurial role, is richly suited to fill our need in this respect. Only an economics which recognizes how the profit motive (by which we mean the lure of pure entrepreneurial profits) can harness entrepreneurial activity toward the systematic elimination of error can be of service in pointing the way to those institutional structures necessary for the steady improvement of the lot of mankind.

NOTES

1. F. A. Hayek, "Economics and Knowledge," *Economica*, N.S. Vol. IV, No. 13 (February 1937).
2. G. J. Stigler, "The Xistence of X-Efficiency," *American Economic Review*, March 1976, p. 216.
3. L. Mises, *Theory and History* (New Haven: Yale University Press, 1957), p. 268.
4. See Stigler, *op. cit.* p. 215.
5. B. Croce, "On the Economic Principle," translated in *International Economic Papers*, No. 3, p. 177.
6. I. M. Kirzner, *The Economic Point of View* (Princeton: Van Nostrand, 1960), pp. 169–72.
7. G. Tagliacozzo, "Croce and the Nature of Economic Science," *Quarterly Journal of Economics*, Vol. LIX, No. 3 (May 1945).
8. L. Mises, *Human Action* (New Haven: Yale University Press, 1949), p. 95.

9. *Ibid*. pp. 102f.

10. *Ibid*.

11. F. H. Knight, *Risk, Uncertainty and Profit*, (1921), pp. 225–26.

12. H. Leibenstein, "Allocative Efficiency vs. 'X-Efficiency'," *American Economic Review*, Vol. 56 (June 1966); "Entrepreneurship and Development," *American Economic Review*, Vol. 58 (May 1968); "Competition and X-Efficiency: Reply," *Journal of Political Economy*, Vol. 81, No. 3 (May/June 1973); "Aspects of the X-Efficiency Theory of the Firm," *Bell Journal of Economics*, Vol. 6 (Autumn 1975).

13. H. Leibenstein, "Competition and X-Efficiency: Reply," p. 766.

14. H. Leibenstein, "Allocative Efficiency vs. 'X-Efficiency'," p. 407.

15. G. J. Stigler, *op. cit.*

16. *Ibid*. p. 216.

17. Put differently, our perception of the impossibility of error does not depend on any "arbitrary" assumption of utility- or profit-maximizing behavior. Error is impossible because it is inconsistent with the postulate of purposeful action.

18. The possibility for *social* "inefficiency" of any kind, in such an errorless world, would, it must appear, then rest either on the possibility that high transaction costs make the "correction" in fact uneconomic, or, on the highly dubious notion of an omniscient observer from whose perspective the errorless (but imperfectly omniscient) members of society are overlooking valuable opportunities for improving their positions. On all this see further, I. M. Kirzner, *Competition and Entrepreneurship* (Chicago: University of Chicago Press, 1973), Ch. 6. See also the final section of the present paper.

19. Although, as argued by the writer elsewhere, the extent to which available opportunities *are* perceived is not at all unrelated to the concept of purposeful action.

20. The other reasons include the circumstance that, were one to discover someone whose superior alertness to profitable opportunities one wishes to hire, we would expect that other ("alert one") to have already taken advantage of those opportunities (or at least that he will anyway do so very shortly) on his own account.

21. For further discussion of some of the issues raised in this and the following sections, see the writer's *Competition and Entrepreneurship*, Chapters 2, 3.

22. W. S. Jevons, *The Theory of Political Economy*, 4th Edition, 1911 (Pelican Books, 1970), p. 137.

23. On all this see Hayek's pioneering contribution in his 1937 paper (see footnote 1). See also the writer's unpublished paper, "Hayek, Knowledge, and Market Processes."

24. H. Leibenstein, "Entrepreneurship and Development"; and

Kirzner, *Competition and Entrepreneurship*, p. 46n.

25. H. Leibenstein, "Allocative Efficiency vs. 'X-Efficiency'," p. 413.

26. L. Robbins, "The Representative Firm," *Economic Journal*, Volume 38 (September 1928).

27. Robbins, *op. cit.* p. 391.

28. See A. Marshall, *Principles of Economics* (8th Edition, 1920), pp. 342f.

29. Robbins, p. 393.

30. Stigler, "The Xistence of X-Efficiency", pp. 214f.

31. Stigler, p. 215.

32. Robbins, pp. 392–396.

33. See e.g. G. Calbresi, "Transaction Costs, Resource Allocation and Liability Rules: A Comment," *Journal of Law and Economics*, Vol. 11 (April 1968), p. 68.

The Problem of Social Cost

S. C. Littlechild
The University of Birmingham (United Kingdom)

INTRODUCTION

It is difficult to overestimate the role which social cost plays in modern welfare economics. The ideas of social cost and product lie behind the surplus-maximisation criterion frequently urged upon public utilities, the consequent computation and comparison of social rates of return on road and rail investments, and the philosophy of marginal cost pricing. Following Pigou, the possibility of divergencies between private and social cost or product provides a basis for peak-hour congestion taxes or prices on roads, airports, and telephone systems; for subsidised entrance into the telephone network on the grounds that other subscribers thereby benefit; for regional investment and subsidies or taxes on labour to counter hidden unemployment or social costs of urban growth not reflected in the private calculus; for reduced prices of educational and health services; for subsidies to invention, research and development, and so on.

The criticism of Pigou provided in Coase's article, "The Problem of Social Cost," and the reformulation provided there, have to some extent directed attention away from divergencies between private and social cost towards the possibility of solving social problems through the market by means of an improved definition or reallocation of property rights. Despite this change in approach, the concept of value of social product is retained by both Coase and Pigou, and indeed by the majority of present-day economists, as the basic criterion for comparing alternative social systems. The purpose of the present paper is to examine

77

these notions of social cost and social product from a "subjectivist" or "Austrian" point of view. Apart from its intrinsic importance, the concept of social cost is of particular interest to subjec-
tivists, for Buchanan has suggested that Coase's own work on this
topic is the major success story of the L.S.E. subjectivist school.

Perhaps the most significant L.S.E. impact on modern economics has
come through an indirect application of opportunity-cost theory
rather than through an undermining of basic cost conceptions. "Marginal social cost," enthroned by Pigou as a cornerstone of applied
welfare economics, was successfully challenged by R. H. Coase a
quarter-century after his initial work on cost. His now classic paper on
social cost, which reflects the same cost theory held earlier, succeeded
where the more straightforward earlier attacks on the marginal-cost
pricing norm—attacks by Coase himself, by Thirlby and by
Wiseman—apparently failed (I, pp. 11–12).

However, we shall discover in the present paper that Professor
Coase's work, whatever may be its other substantial merits in
correcting Pigou and in reorienting the economics profession,
does not present an approach to cost which is any more satisfactory, from a subjectivist standpoint, than did Pigou. Indeed,
once it is recognised (a) that social value and social cost are
subjective, rather than objective concepts and (b) that they bear
only a tenuous relationship to the true costs of decision-making,
then it becomes questionable whether the notion of social cost is
the most useful way of approaching the problem.

We shall begin with summaries of the social cost argument and
of the subjectivist approach to economics.

THE NOTIONS OF SOCIAL VALUE AND SOCIAL COST

The concept of social cost is remarkably elusive. Economists
unhesitatingly attribute the concept to Pigou, as expounded in
his *Economics of Welfare*, but in fact in none of the four editions of
that book, nor in his earlier *Wealth and Welfare*, is there any
mention of the term social cost itself. It is perhaps not entirely
coincidental, then, that Coase's own paper, "The Problem of

Social Cost," contains no mention either of the term social cost. The analyses of both authors are, in fact, conducted almost entirely in terms of social product. (I have not yet been able to discover the origin of the term social cost. Knight (VI) used it in his criticism of Pigou without any suggestion that it was original. A. A. Young (XIV), in reviewing *Wealth and Welfare*, referred to a social view of cost. Perhaps this odd situation lends some support to Coase's suggestion that the Pigovian doctrine on these matters was largely the product of an oral tradition.)

Pigou admitted that the elements of welfare were ultimately states of consciousness, but in order to achieve something practicable he felt it necessary to limit his subject matter to "that position of the field in which the methods of science seem likely to work at best advantage," namely, ". . . to that part of social welfare that can be brought directly or indirectly into relation with the measuring-rod of money. This part of welfare may be called economic welfare (VII, p. 11).

The "objective counterpart of economic welfare which economists call the national dividend or national income" was "composed in the last resort of a number of objective services, some of which are embodied in commodities." In order to preserve the measuring rod of money, Pigou decided to include in the national dividend only those goods and services actually sold for money, and for the same reason he rejected consumer surplus as a measure of a change in the national dividend.

Pigou's main instrument of analysis was marginal product, defined as follows:

The marginal social net product is the total net product of physical things or objective services due to the marginal increment of resources in any given use or place, no matter to whom any part of this product may accrue. . . . The marginal private net product is that part of the total net product . . . which accrues in the first instance—*i.e.*, prior to sale—to the person responsible for investing resources there. . . . The value of the marginal social [and private] net product of any quantity of resources employed in any use of place is simply the sum of money which the marginal social net product is worth in the market (VII, pp. 134–35).

If private and social net products coincide, then "the free play of self-interest, so far as it is not hampered by ignorance, will tend to bring about such a distribution of resources . . . as will raise the national dividend and, with it, the sum of economic welfare to a maximum" (VII, p. 143). But if there is a divergence between private and social products (*i.e.*, if there are externalities), then "specific acts of interference with normal economic processes," by means of bounties and taxes, will remove the divergence and increase the dividend (VII, p. 172).

We need not be concerned here with Knight's observation that divergencies between private and social cost depend upon whether or not the road (or other means of production) is privately owned, nor with Coase's suggestion that Pigou was ignorant of the legal position and in any case failed to take into account the response of the party affected by externalities. There are, however, two aspects of Coase's analysis which deserve mention. First, he observed that Pigou's measurement of national dividend in terms of goods and services *actually sold* "means that the value of social product has no social significance whatsoever" (III, p. 40). Coase preferred to value production at its market value regardless of whether payment actually took place. Second, he recommended that

When an economist is comparing alternative social arrangements, the proper procedure is to compare the total social product yielded by these different arrangements. The comparison of private and social products is neither here nor there (III, p. 34).

He later compares this to the opportunity cost approach used in the analysis of the firm. It seems reasonable to infer that the social (opportunity) cost of choosing one social arrangement would be defined as the market value of total product corresponding to the best alternative arrangement not chosen.

THE SUBJECTIVIST APPROACH

For those who are not familiar with the writings of the Austrian school or the L.S.E. subjectivist school, it will be useful to summarise the relevant parts of this approach, beginning with Hayek's work in the 1930s and 1940s, which Buchanan (I, p. 24) has described as laying down the central features of the subjectivist methodology.

In the papers reprinted as Part One of *The Counter Revolution of Science*, Hayek emphasised that the "facts" of the social sciences are human perceptions of the world, beliefs held by people "irrespective of whether they are true or false, and which moreover, we cannot directly observe in the minds of the people but which one can recognise from what they do and say merely because we have ourselves a mind similar to theirs." The objects of human action are not "objective facts" and cannot be defined in purely physical terms. "So far as human actions are concerned, the things are what the acting people think they are." Moreover, "the knowledge and beliefs of different people, while possessing that common structure which makes communication possible, will yet be different and often conflicting in many respects." The term "subjective" thus reflects the idea that actions depend upon perceptions and also the idea that different people will generally have different perceptions.

For present purposes, two implications of this basic insight are of particular relevance. First, as Kirzner (V) has argued, it is no longer appropriate to restrict definition of the "economic problem" to that of allocating scarce resources between competing ends, in the way that Robbins (VIII) had proposed. It is necessary to include the perception of ends and means, rather than to take these as given. Hence we are led to the concept of "entrepreneurship," or alertness to advantageous changes in means or ends, and to Mises' "acting man" rather than to Robbins's "economising man." In turn, the entrepreneurial element in human action can be identified as that which generates a process of change, and indeed the emphasis of the whole Austrian approach is on the market process rather than upon the state of equilibrium.

Kirzner himself has used this notion of perception in commenting upon Coase's analysis of property rights in the social-cost paper already referred to. Coase had argued that, in the absence of transactions costs, market transactions would transfer property rights and allocate resources so as to maximise the value of production, independent of the legal position. Kirzner (V, p. 227) objected that zero transactions costs were neither necessary nor sufficient to ensure that all participants would *notice* the mutually profitable contracts which could be entered into.

The second implication of the subjectivist approach is that cost must be thought of as a subjective, rather than objective, concept, because the elements of individual choice evidently depend upon the alternatives imagined and thought worthy of consideration by the decision-maker, and the choice actually made depends upon his preferences. Buchanan has argued that economists at the L.S.E. (including Coase) have played an important role in developing this subjective theory of cost, and he summarises the theory as follows:

Cost is that which the decision-maker sacrifices or gives up when he selects one alternative rather than another. Cost consists therefore in his own evaluation of the enjoyment or utility that he anticipates having to forgo as a result of choice itself. There are specific implications to be drawn from this choice-bound definition of opportunity cost:

1. Cost must be borne exclusively by the person who makes decisions; it is not possible for this cost to be shifted to or imposed on others.

2. Cost is subjective; it exists only in the mind of the decision-maker or chooser.

3. Cost is based on anticipations; it is necessarily a forward-looking or ex ante concept.

4. Cost can never be realised because of the fact that choice is made; the alternative which is rejected can never itself be enjoyed.

5. Cost cannot be measured by someone other than the chooser since there is no way that subjective mental experience can be directly observed.

6. Cost can be dated at the moment of final decision or choice.

In any general theory of choice cost must be reckoned in a utility rather than in a commodity dimension. From this it follows that the opportunity cost involved in choice cannot be observed and objectified and, more importantly, it cannot be measured in such a way as to allow comparisons over wholly different choice settings (I, pp. 14–15).

Thirlby (1946, 1960) and Wiseman (1953, 1957) have pointed out some of the difficulties of supervision which now arise. Suppose a manager is instructed to maximise net revenue. (We must not say "revenue less cost," since these two concepts are incommensurate: Revenue is measured in terms of money and cost in terms of utility.) Since it is not possible to know with certainty the outcomes of all possible courses of action, it is not possible to make a direct check on the efficiency of the manager. One may make indirect checks by ascertaining which alternatives he considered (*i.e.*, by examining his "plan"), by assessing the actual outcome (*i.e.*, by examining his "account"), and by checking the accuracy of his forecasting (*i.e.*, by comparing his plan with his account). But it is never possible to know whether there were better alternatives which should have been considered or whether the outcomes of alternatives *not* chosen were correctly forecast. Moreover, when indirect checks of this kind are used, the manager is led to modify his actions to take account of them, for the simple reason that the cost, to him, of taking one decision is necessarily his own evaluation of the alternative outcome foregone. It is not net revenue itself, but the *significance to him* of net revenue, which determines his actions.

Let us now apply some of these ideas to the concepts of social value and cost.

SOCIAL COST AND PRODUCT—A RECONSIDERATION

For both Pigou and Coase, social product and social cost are evidently objective concepts. Social product is defined as a stock or flow of specified physical services. The question of what constitutes a good or service, *i.e.*, who perceives it and how, is not raised. There is no uncertainty about the goods and services associated with each possible decision, hence there are no conflicting expectations. Finally, the question of whose valuation is to be used is avoided by reference to the "market value." In these circumstances, the optimal choice is simply a matter of computation and social (opportunity) cost is objective.

It might be conceded that, in practice, the likely outcomes of any particular measure are unsure, as are the likely market prices, but it is necessary to make a "best guess." This element of subjectivity of course raises the difficulties referred to in the last section. Whose guess is appropriate for policy purposes, and how is the efficiency of the guessing procedure to be ascertained? Moreover, there is a crucial difference between this situation and that of the private firm in that no ultimate objective check on efficiency is available: If the decision-making procedure is inefficient, there is no direct feedback comparable to that of financial loss and bankruptcy.

But now suppose that we recognise the full degree of subjectivity of beliefs about situations and no longer assume an objectively specified set of physical products or a market price for these. In this general case, what becomes of the notion of value of social product? Is it possible to reconcile social product and social cost with the subjective theory of cost and choice?

Take first the Pigovian approach. A decision by one person may also affect other people. It is conventional to describe this as a collection of changes in utility levels. The value of (marginal) social product is, then, in some sense, the net change in total utility, but this raises the obvious well-known objections that utilities are ordinal and cannot be aggregated. One therefore attempts to derive a cardinal measure by asking what the change in utility is worth in money terms. This is done by constructing a collection of artificial choice situations, one for each person affected, and asking oneself what this person would be prepared to pay for the decision in question to be taken or not to be taken. The optimal decision depends upon the total sums of money thereby calculated.

Evidently the situation envisaged by Coase does not differ significantly from this. Attention is not focused on a single individual decision-taker, but rather all persons are allowed to respond to each social arrangement (say, legal position) under consideration, with corresponding changes in utility levels which are to be valued in money terms. The optimal choice of social arrangement then depends upon the sum of money values thus obtained.

To what extent is this artificial choice interpretation just described compatible with the subjectivist approach? In effect, we are asking whether it is possible to attach a meaning to the notion of damage or benefit as valued by the person damaged or benefited by the action of another person. If this action had been the result of a contract between the two persons, then we could, in principle, have measured the effect (more precisely, the expected effect) with respect to the alternative choices available, *i.e.*, to the cost of the contract. In the case where no contract is made, we are considering a hypothetical choice and asking how attractive a hypothetical alternative would need to have been in order to be preferred (or how unattractive it could have been and still have been preferred).

The first point to emphasise is that the proposed procedure does not involve choices, albeit hypothetical, by the person in question but rather by an outside observing economist, government official, judge, or politician. As argued earlier, the costs of his choice involve the significance to him of the different answers—for example, whether the answers seem plausible to his peers and supervisors. The valuation put on damage to another person is thus not a cost to that person at all. Moreover, even if the artificial choice were made by the person in question, his costs would involve the benefits of choosing a higher or lower figure in a laboratory situation, and would not measure the costs involved in the intended choice situation (*cf.*, IX).

Second, since this evaluation is not a choice actually made in the market, there is room for considerable uncertainty as to what value would be appropriate. To use the standard terminology, one is simply guessing where the relevant indifference curves lie

(I, p. 72). Different observers could come up with different evaluations, none of which could be proved objectively correct or incorrect.

Third, the intention of the hypothetical choice scheme is to evaluate a person's response to a situation while taking as given his perceived opportunities and objectives. But we have mentioned that, in the subjectivist approach, economics is not simply a matter of known means and ends, but also involves the perception of new possibilities, which in general change one's evaluation of previously perceived opportunities. Suppose that the alternative under consideration by the policymaker had not been conceived by the person whose evaluation it is required to estimate. Then an evaluation can only be obtained by (conceptually) *changing* his existing perceptions. This, of course, raises two problems: how the new alternative should (again conceptually) be presented to the person, and what his reaction would be. The problem applies more generally: Even if he is aware of the possibility of the decision under consideration, he will generally have a different impression of its nature, implications, and likelihood than another person will have. Should the observer/economist take as given his initial, perhaps "incorrect," perceptions or should he (conceptually) modify them? What is a "correct" perception of the consequences of any act?

Even if it were possible to specify the initial reactions of people to a proposed action, what position should be taken concerning subsequent changes in their perceptions and plans? Coase is evidently aware of this difficulty. He refers to the use of bluff in order to induce the other party to make a larger payment, but comments "such manoeuvres are preliminaries to an agreement and do not affect the long run equilibrium position" (III, p. 8). Evidently, he takes the view that it is not the immediate response to a situation which is relevant, but the "equilibrium" response, after appropriate information has been acquired. The difficulty with this position is the precariousness of the notion of equilibrium once economic activity is viewed as a process rather than a state.

CONCLUSION

Let us attempt to summarise the argument of this paper.

It was found that the concept of social cost itself, although widely used, was not used by Pigou and Coase, who preferred to work instead in terms of social product. Despite differences in their usage of this concept, they essentially proposed to use value of social product as a criterion for choosing between alternative situations. This notion depended upon "physical product" composed of specified objective goods and services, to which objectively defined prices were or could be attached.

This approach was shown to lead to certain difficulties. Briefly,

1. The basic assumptions are inconsistent with a subjectivist approach. Goods and prices are defined objectively, so that the optimal choice is simply a matter of computation and cost is objective.

2. If uncertainty of future quantities and prices is admitted, then there is no objectively "right" calculation, there are difficulties in assessing the efficiency of those required to maximise social product, and there is no ultimate test comparable to net revenue in a private firm.

3. The attempt to use artificial choice situations in order to obtain a monetary figure of change in utility means that costs of choice to the observer are not costs which would be experienced in a real choice situation.

4. Some persons may not have perceived the alternative under consideration as relevant, so that an answer to the hypothetical question can only be obtained by (conceptually) changing that person's perceptions. More generally, since different individuals may view alternatives differently, they will not necessarily be appraising the "same"

alternative. How then should the situation be (conceptually) presented?

5. If economic activity is viewed, not as an equilibrium state, but as a process involving changing perceptions and values, then it is not clear at what time, or after what period of reflection, it is appropriate to calculate the value of product.

In this discussion I have tried to show that social cost and product are not objective concepts. This does not mean to say that any particular observer cannot make an estimate of the damage or benefits accruing from any action, but rather that this estimate will necessarily embody elements of his own evaluation and will depend upon his own perceptions and assumptions of what is appropriate. Different individuals will, therefore, make different estimates, and no objective check on efficiency is possible.

This raises the question of whether social product as traditionally conceived is the best concept for use in government decisions. We may, in fact, use Coase's argument against himself. The proper question to ask is not whether this or that social arrangement maximises value of social product, but rather whether using social product as a criterion is preferable to using some other approach. In order to answer this question, it is necessary to know more about how those who have been urged or required to use this criterion have behaved in the past. Here we might examine the decisions of nationalised industries in Britain, and government response to cost-benefit analyses of roads, railways, and airports. Second, it is necessary to know how effective other objective controls have been, such as breakeven requirements or specific constraints on spending or provision of services. Finally, it is necessary to compare government controls of any kind with those imposed by the market. A fruitful start on these problems has been made by Alchian, Stigler, Posner, and others, and one would expect that Coase would sympathise with such an approach.

However, it would seem that social product cannot be used as the final criterion of evaluation, for the reasons given. What other criterion is available? I simply mention here Kirzner's suggestion (V, pp. 216 ff.) that alternative institutions or arrangements can be evaluated in terms of their success in bringing about mutually beneficial contracts. The effectiveness of such a criterion remains to be explored.

POSTSCRIPT

I wish to add a brief comment on the definition of social cost in the literature and a more extensive discussion of social cost as the criterion for action by a public organisation.

Coase implicitly defines the cost of any social arrangement as the market value forgone under an alternative arrangement. This is indeed a cost, in the sense defined by Buchanan, if we think of society as an entity choosing alternative arrangements with the aim of maximising market value (though how these alternatives are generated and evaluated is not specified). However, not all economists adopt this definition. Stigler, for example, discusses a chemical plant which discharges waste into a stream, and says that "the sum of costs to everyone is called the social cost of waste disposal" (*Theory of Price*, 1966). Such a concept is not a cost in Buchanan's sense—indeed, an action by one person cannot impose costs on others. This is not to say that the one definition is superior to the other, of course, but rather that one is (or can more easily be made) consistent with the L.S.E. tradition.

Several of the participants at the Windsor Conference, while broadly sympathetic to the argument of the paper, nevertheless felt uneasy on two counts.

(a) Since the procedure for calculating social costs and benefits appears to be similar to that for private costs and benefits, why is the latter legitimate, but the former illegitimate?

(b) If public organisations are not required to base decisions on social cost, what other instructions should be given them? In this Postscript I shall attempt to answer these questions more directly.

Consider first two ideal types: the businessman interested in maximising net private revenue and the benevolent dictator interested in maximising net social benefit. The problems they have to face are identical, although the criteria they use are different. In neither case is there any distinction to be made between subjective and objective concepts, because in both cases the world is taken to be as the decision-maker perceives it. Those goods are relevant which the decision-maker believes to be relevant; those future prices, future responses, and future values are appropriate which the decision-maker believes to be appropriate. In principle, to calculate net social benefit is no more difficult than to calculate net private revenue.

Putting plans into action generates new information which in turn makes it appropriate, sooner or later, to revise the previous plans. Investments or other commitments may have been made, yet other previous commitments may have expired, and new opportunities may have arisen. The pattern of costs and benefits, and hence the optimal actions, will generally be different from those planned earlier. Revision of plans in this way is necessary regardless of whether the objective is net private revenue or net social benefit, and there is no reason to suppose it is any easier in the one case than in the other.

Finally, suppose that the businessman and the benevolent dictator do not carry out all the actions themselves, but rather instruct subordinates to maximise the respective objectives on their behalf. In each case, it may be assumed that the subordinates have objectives and preferences of their own which they will attempt to satisfy insofar as they are not prevented or discouraged from doing so. The problem of control arises: how to ensure that the subordinates are carrying out their duties efficiently? In neither case is it possible to ascertain directly what is the optimal policy, so it is necessary to develop indirect checks by examining the process of plan preparation, the outcomes of the actions taken, and the accuracy of the forecasting.

Wherein, then, lies the difference between the objectives of net social benefit and net private revenue? It lies, I think, in the degree of difficulty in assessing the outcomes of any series of actions. Both concepts are measured in money terms, but whereas the liquid assets of an organisation at any time can be ascertained reasonably easily and objectively, this is not true of net social benefit. The whole point of a social cost-benefit analysis is to impute to people values which they do not in fact express in the market. There is no "correct" value, there are only different views about values, which may be more or less plausible to others. The problem of control is infinitely more difficult when the outcome of any action is not immediately apparent.

In order to maximise net social benefit it may, paradoxically, be more efficient *not* to set this as a direct objective, simply because of the difficulty of checking performance. As argued elsewhere, the market mechanism, the profit motive, and the possibility of competition provide incentives to discover and meet the wishes of consumers, with monetary success for those who succeed and replacement for those who fail. It is certainly not guaranteed that the market mechanism will ensure that the "correct" decisions are always taken, since these cannot be known, but there are reasons to believe the market is more likely, in the long run, to maximise net social benefit.

It may be objected that competition is not always possible and, indeed, that this is a major reason for replacing the market mechanism with some form of government organisation. As regards the first point, the work of Hayek, Coase, Kirzner, Alchian, Demsetz, and others has gradually provided a better understanding of the nature of competition and market failure. It is now recognised that the efficiency of the market may be enhanced (e.g., by developing property rights) if there is a will to do so. On the second point, whether market failure is the reason for government intervention is debatable. By intervention, the government is, in effect, deliberately isolating an industry from market forces and subjecting it, instead, to political forces. It is expressing the view that the industry should not maximise net social benefit, as expressed in market values, but rather should give greater weight to some particular consumers or producers. It is not surprising to find, then, that those government organisations responsible for monitoring the performance of other government organisations charged with maximising net social benefit show little enthusiasm for their task. Unlike net private revenue, net social benefit is an artificial concept of direct interest only to economists.

This suggests that operating rules for controlling public organisations should satisfy two criteria. First, they should relate to concepts and entities of direct relevance to the people or organisations concerned. Second, the rules should be couched in objective operational terms: It should be possible to check whether or not they have been obeyed.

To illustrate briefly, it is currently British policy to require nationalised industries to assess proposed investments against a "test discount rate." Since in practice it is impossible for an outsider to tell whether the assumptions and forecasts embodied in the appraisal are reasonable (or even what they are!), this rule provides no effective check on efficiency in investment. It would be preferable to replace it by, e.g., a realistic charge for borrowing funds plus a specified rate of return on the borrowing of the industry as a whole. Requiring the industry to invest so as to maximise net social benefit provides not control but only the illusion of control.

BIBLIOGRAPHY

I.   Buchanan, J. M. *Cost and Choice*. Chicago: Markham Publishing Co., 1969.
II. Buchanan, J. M., and Thirlby, G. F., eds. *L.S.E. Essays on Cost*. Weidenfeld & Nicholson, 1973.
III. Coase, R. H. "The Problem of Social Cost." *Journal of Law and Economics* 3 (1960): 1–44.
IV. Hayek, F. A. *The Counter-Revolution of Science*. Glencoe, Ill.: The Free Press, 1952.
V.   Kirzner, I. M. *Competition and Entrepreneurship*. Chicago and London: University of Chicago Press, 1973.

VI. Knight, F. H. "Some Fallacies in the Interpretation of Social Cost." *Quarterly Journal of Economics* 38 (1924): 582–606.

VII. Pigou, A. C. *The Economics of Welfare*. 4th ed. London: Macmillan, 1932.

VIII. Robbins, L. *An Essay on the Nature and Significance of Economic Science*. 2nd ed. London: Macmillan, 1935.

IX. Rothbard, M. N. "Toward a Reconstruction of Utility and Welfare Economics." *On Freedom and Free Enterprise*. Edited by M. Sennholz. Princeton, N.J.: Van Nostrand, 1956.

X. Thirlby, G. F. "The Ruler." *South African Journal of Economics* 14 (1946). Reprinted in Buchanan and Thirlby (1973).

XI. Thirlby, G. F. "Economists' Cost Rules and Equilibrium Theory." *Economica* (1960). Reprinted in Buchanan and Thirlby (1973).

XII. Wiseman, J. "Uncertainty, Costs and Collective Economic Planning." *Economica* (1953). Reprinted in Buchanan and Thirlby (1973).

XIII. Wiseman, J. "The Theory of Public Utility Price—an Empty Box." *Oxford Economic Papers* 9 (1957). Reprinted in Buchanan and Thirlby (1973).

XIV. Young, A. A. "Pigou's Wealth and Welfare." *Quarterly Journal of Economics* 27 (1913): 672–86.

A Critique
of Neoclassical and Austrian
Monopoly Theory

D. T. *Armentano*
University of Hartford

One of the most controversial areas in Austrian economics, and one where even long-established Austrian theorists differ sharply, is monopoly theory. Indeed, as we shall see below, the differences are not merely semantic, nor are they confined to detail or some minor theoretical implication. Rather, there are major and fundamental disagreements between some of the leading Austrians, and these disagreements are created by wholly different theories concerning the *definition* of monopoly, the *origins* of monopoly, and the supposed *effects* of monopoly on consumer sovereignty and efficient resource allocation.

NEOCLASSICAL MONOPOLY THEORY

By way of contrast, and in order to place the Austrian theories of monopoly in perspective, it is perhaps necessary to review and criticize the traditional (neoclassical) theory of monopoly.[1]

A monopolist in neoclassical analysis is a firm that faces the entire demand for the product under consideration. In order to maximize its profits, it produces an output where the marginal revenue associated with the last unit sold is just equal to the marginal costs associated with producing and selling that final unit. But since the demand function facing the monopolist is necessarily sloped downward (perhaps even steeply downward), the price charged for the output is *greater* than both marginal revenue and marginal cost.

This situation, it is argued, compares "unfavorably" with price and output (and cost) under competitive conditions. Under competitive conditions, since price and marginal revenue are equal, price is always identical with marginal cost when profits are maximized. Further, under competitive equilibrium conditions, price is always driven down to the minimum point of the average cost function, so that production tends to take place at its most "efficient" point. Therefore, monopoly prices are higher than competitive prices, outputs are less, and average costs greater than under comparable competitive (cost) conditions.

But, importantly, how is a firm able to *obtain* a monopoly position in the market and, thus, "misallocate" economic resources? In the first place the monopoly could simply be due to governmental prohibition of competitive entry, and there is certainly a recognition of this source of monopoly in the neoclassical literature. However, more recently it has been popular to stress certain *nonlegal* "barriers to entry" that, allegedly, preserve monopoly and resource misallocation.[2] These barriers would include *any* difficulty or impediment that a new firm might have to overcome in order to compete successfully with an existing firm (monopolist). Thus, scale economies enjoyed by an existing firm, or commercially successful product differentiation employed by such a firm, becomes, in the new jargon, a barrier to entry that limits competition and reduces society's "welfare."

CONTEMPORARY MONOPOLY THEORY: A CRITIQUE

There are two avenues of criticism that one might take with respect to neoclassical monopoly theory. In the first place, one might criticize the purely competitive model which is employed as a benchmark and as a basis of comparison with monopolistic situations. And secondly, one might criticize the whole concept of nonlegal barriers to entry, arguing, instead, that it is simply *consumer preference* that "limits competition" and that consequently no misallocation of resources occurs.

Most economists would agree that pure competition is not actually possible. Some would agree, perhaps reluctantly, that it might not even be desirable or optimal if it *could* exist. (If they agree to this, of course, then they must also agree that moving toward pure competition is not necessarily desirable, either.) But few economists have noticed or emphasized the *fundamental* flaw of the purely competitive model, namely, that it is not a description of competition at all.[3] Pure competition is a static, equilibrium condition whose very assumptions are such that competitive process is ruled out by definition. Or to put the matter more charitably, while pure competition may describe the final outcome of a particular competitive situation, the ultimate end result, it does not describe the competitive *process* that produced that particular outcome. The purely competitive theory is *not* a theory of competition as such.

The neoclassical habit of confusing competitive process with a final, static equilibrium condition makes for gross errors in economic analysis. For instance, product differentiation, advertising, price competition (including price discrimination), and innovation are rather routinely condemned as "monopolistic" and, thus, as resource *misallocating* and socially undesirable. This condemnation follows "logically" since not one of these activities is possible under purely competitive conditions. Hence everything that is truly competitive in the real world, truly rivalrous, gets labeled as "monopolistic" and resource misallocating in the Alice-in-Wonderland, purely competitive world. The analytical conclusions one is forced to come to, employing the purely competitive perspective, are not just wrong, not just unrealistic, but the very *opposite* of the truth. Far from being able to "predict," or tell us anything meaningful concerning competitive behavior, pure competition can only describe what things would be like if the world contained zombie-like consumers with homogeneous tastes, atomistically structured firms identical in every important respect, with no locational advantages, no advertising, no entrepreneurship, and no rivalry whatever. Surely this is the major flaw and absurdity inherent in the purely competitive perspective.[4]

BARRIERS TO ENTRY: A CRITIQUE

Discussions about the nonlegal barriers to entry suffer from the same difficulties. The two most popular and important "barriers to entry" are *product differentiation* and *scale economies*. Product differentiation limits competition since it makes competitive entry more costly. To use a favorite neoclassical example, the fact that the major automobile companies change styles every year increases the costs of competing in this industry. Would-be competitors must be willing and able to undergo the same or similar procedures, else they simply cannot compete. Even worse, once competition is "limited," the auto companies routinely pass along the higher costs in the form of higher prices, which contributes, it is alleged, to a real reduction in consumer welfare.

On the other hand—indeed, on the opposite hand—scale economies also limit competition. The fact that certain firms realize lower costs per unit because of large volumes gives these firms the "power" to exclude smaller firms, or smaller potential entrants, from the market. Ergo, we are supposed to regret the reduced competition and consequent resource misallocation since inefficient firms cannot compete with efficient ones.

Actually, of course, the neoclassical theorists have gotten the matter completely and precisely *backward*. It is because, and only because, consumers find resources satisfactorily allocated that would-be competitors find entry difficult or impossible. Product differentiation, especially differentiation that does raise prices, can only act as a barrier to entry if consumers *prefer* that differentiation, and pay the presumably higher prices associated with, say, new annual auto styles. If consumers do not prefer such differentiation and, instead, reward the firms that change styles *less* often, or not at all, then product differentiation could hardly act as a barrier to competitive entry. Indeed, in the case just postulated, product differentiation would be an open invitation to entry and to competition.

To condemn commercially successful product differentiation as a misallocation of scarce resources, therefore, is to condemn the very "resource allocations" that consumers apparently prefer. It is the neoclassical economist's allegedly "optimal" allocation of resources *under purely competitive conditions* that product differentiation upsets, and not any allocation that can be associated with free consumer choice.

The same sort of argument can be made—and even more obviously—with respect to scale economies. Consumers do not regret the economies nor the consequent reduction in competition. Consumers could "increase competition" any time they choose to by indicating their willingness to pay higher prices to cover the higher costs of the smaller firms. That they do not usually do this indicates the resources are correctly allocated so far as they are concerned. Again, it is the economist's vision of the purely competitive wonderland that is upset by the large, efficient firm, and not allocative efficiency from a *consumer* perspective.

The final absurdity in this area is to observe where such incorrect theories of competition are likely to lead. If product differentiation limits competition, i.e., limits the number of competitors, then more competition can be obtained by limiting product differentiation—by law. If efficient techniques of production or scale economies limit competition, i.e., the number of competitors, then more competition can be obtained by raising either costs or prices for the efficient companies—by law. Thus, to take the barriers-to-entry theory seriously is to end up proposing as rational public policy—in the name of consumer welfare—the very procedures that consumers would likely find most harmful. The only thing sadder than all of this is that such ideas have actually been taken seriously in some antitrust circles and by the courts, and we have had some real world legal decisions that reflect such theoretical nonsense.[5]

As should be quite clear from the above review and critique, there is much dissatisfaction with the traditional notions of monopoly and competition, and with the simplistic antitrust policies (antimerger policy, for instance) founded on such assumptions. But if the neoclassical approach to monopoly and competition is defective, what is the correct approach in this area? Indeed, *is* there a logical and rational theory of monopoly and, accordingly, an appropriate public policy to complement that theoretical approach? In the sections below we will turn to a critical examination of Austrian monopoly theory in an attempt to answer these questions. The views of von Mises, Kirzner, and Rothbard will be taken as representative of various Austrian positions concerning monopoly.

MISES' MONOPOLY THEORY

Monopoly exists for Ludwig von Mises when ". . . the whole supply of the commodity is controlled by a single seller or a group of sellers acting in concert."[6] This condition puts the monopolist (or cartel) in the position of being able to restrict supply in order to raise market price without having to "fear that his plans will be frustrated by interference on the part of the other sellers of the *same* commodity."[7] Mises holds, however, that monopoly *prices* do not result unless the restriction in supply produces prices that actually increase the monopolist's "total net proceeds." Only if the demand for the product is inelastic in the price range under discussion could "monopoly prices emerge as differentiated from competitive prices." Hence, it is not "monopoly" as such that is catallactically relevant for Mises, but only the "configuration" of the demand function and the emergence of monopoly prices.[8]

Importantly if such monopoly prices *do* exist, then they are an "infringement of the supremacy of the consumers and the democracy of the market."[9] Mises even goes further:

Monopoly prices are consequential only because they are the outcome of a conduct of business defying the supremacy of the consumers and substituting the private interests of the monopolist for those of the public. They are the only instance in the operation of a market economy in which the distinction between production for profit and production for use could to some extent be made. . . .[10]

And again:

The characteristic feature of monopoly prices is the monopolist's defiance of the wishes of the consumers.[11]

Mises also argues that although most monopolies and monopoly prices are made possible by government intervention in the free market (tariffs, licenses, etc.), there are certain instances in which monopoly (and monopoly prices) arise in the unhampered market. He specifically mentions natural resource monopoly,[12] geographic monopoly,[13] limited-space monopoly,[14] and monopoly that might arise because consumers place a "special confidence . . . on the individual or firm concerned on account of previous experience,"[15] as with certain trademarked drugs.

KIRZNER'S MONOPOLY THEORY

Professor Kirzner's theory of monopoly can be derived logically from his well-articulated theory of the competitive process.[16] Kirzner views the market process as one in which market sellers are continually attempting to inch ahead of rivals by offering more attractive opportunities to potential buyers. And he views this process as *inherently* competitive since the key ingredient that makes the process function—entrepreneurship—can *never* be monopolized. For Kirzner, pure entrepreneurship requires no resources whatsoever; hence the freedom to enter the market is absolute since no obstacles to entry can ever exist in a free market.

However, the exercise of entrepreneurship is quite another matter. Here the exclusive ownership or control of *"all* the current endowment of a certain resource" is defined by Kirzner to *be* monopoly, can indeed block entry into the production of some specific good, and can hamper competition and "impede the course of the market process." A monopoly producer for Kirzner is one whose "exclusive input blocks competitive entry into the production of his products."[17] To employ Kirzner's example, without access to oranges, "production of orange juice is blocked."[18]

Kirzner notes that monopoly should *not* refer to a producer who—in the absence of resource monopoly—is the single supplier of some product in the market. That firm, he reasons, is still fully subject to the market process since entry into competitive production is always possible. On the other hand, when "needed resources" are restricted because of monopoly ownership or control of a certain resource, the very *possibility* of competition—and the benefits to consumers that are the consequences of competition—are eliminated.[19] Here, according to Kirzner, the monopolist is completely "immune from the competition of other entrepreneurs who might, in other circumstances, enter his field of activity."[20]

Kirzner is quick to note, however, that the monopolist is not immune from the competitive process itself. Although entry into some specific activity is by definition blockaded, entry into *similar* activities is not. Monopoly control over a resource simply diverts the competitive, entrepreneurial process into other similar activities, employing other resources which create a "turbulence" that surrounds and impinges upon the monopolist's original activity.

Importantly, Kirzner hints that the equilibrium tendency of a market containing resource monopoly is to produce a *higher* than "competitive-equilibrium price" for the resources and also a higher "surplus" for the product produced with that resource. This surplus can be accomplished by withdrawing some of the stock from the market and "forcing" up the market price.[21] Thus, consumers *might* be harmed by such activity since scarce monopolized resources are not being employed to the "fullest extent compatible with the pattern of consumer tastes in the market."[22]

ROTHBARD'S MONOPOLY THEORY

Professor Rothbard's analysis of monopoly, monopoly price, and the welfare implications of such economic conditions differs radically from that of both Mises and Kirzner. Indeed, in his discussion of monopoly, Rothbard is sharply critical not only of the neoclassical monopoly theories, but also implicitly critical (and occasionally explicitly critical) of views held by his fellow Austrian theorists as well.[23]

As far as Rothbard is concerned, there are three possible definitions of monopoly: one, the single seller of any given good; two, a grant of special privilege by the state, reserving a certain area of production to one particular individual or group; and three, "a person who has achieved a monopoly price."[24]

Although Rothbard admits that the first definition (single seller) is a coherent and even a "legitimate" one, he rejects it as *impractical* because it is too broad and all-inclusive. The impractical nature of this definition can be illustrated, Rothbard argues, by noting that any difference (differentiation) in any two goods or resources and, more importantly, any consumer-*perceived* difference in any two commodities or resources will make them unique (specific) goods and thus, by definition, "monopoly." Hence, "the single seller of any given good" could always reduce to the notion that everyone is a monopolist since each person in a market system is presumed to have exclusive ownership of *his* own (unique) property. But a definition that makes everything monopoly and everyone a monopolist is barren, "confusing," and "absurd" according to Rothbard.[25]

Rothbard clearly prefers the second definition of monopoly—i.e., a grant of privilege from the state restricting competitive production or sale. This is a monopoly since entry into the privileged activity is prohibited by the state; logically, no such monopoly could ever exist in a free market. This definition will be adopted as the "proper" one should the final alternative definition prove nonsensical or illegitimate.[26]

Rothbard's criticism of the theory of "monopoly price" (as well as his criticism of the theory of "competitive price") is certainly a controversial contribution to the literature on monopoly. For here he argues that in a free market there is simply no way of conceptually distinguishing "monopoly price" from a free-market competitive price.

> On the free market there is no way of distinguishing a "monopoly price" or a "subcompetitive price" or of establishing any changes as movements from one to the other. No criteria can be found for making such distinctions. The concept of monopoly price as distinguished from competitive price is therefore untenable. We can speak only of the free market price.[27]

It has been common, of course, to speak of monopoly price as that price accomplished when output is restricted under conditions of inelastic demand, thus increasing the net income of the supplier. Even Mises, it will be recalled, employed the term in this manner and drew some fairly dismal welfare implications from the "restriction."

Rothbard argues, however, that there is no objective way to determine that such a price is a monopoly price or that such a "restriction" is antisocial. All we can know, according to Rothbard, is that *all* firms attempt to produce a stock of goods that maximizes their net income given their *estimation* of demand. They attempt to price (other things being equal) such that the range of demand above the asking price is elastic. If they discover that they can increase their monetary income by producing less—or even destroying existing stock—in the next selling period, then they do so.

Rothbard maintains that to speak of the initial price as the "competitive" price, and the second-period price as the "monopoly" price makes no objective sense. How, he asks, is it to be objectively determined that the first price is really the "competitive" price? Could it, in fact have been a "subcompetitive" price? Indeed, the entire discussion is absurd for Rothbard since there are no *independent* criteria that would allow either determination. All that can be known for sure, he argues, is that the prices both before and after the supply change are free-market prices.

Rothbard also argues that "monopoly" prices cannot be inferred by comparing such prices to prices charged for *similar* factors. So long as the factors are not perfectly identical in the eyes of buyers, the differences in price (or profits) are simply free-market determinations of value for different goods. And any talk of monopoly price or monopoly "gain" when two *different* factors or goods are being compared is analytically incorrect.[28]

Finally, the welfare implications concerning alleged monopoly prices would not follow even if such prices could exist. Since the inelasticity of demand for Rothbard is "purely the result of voluntary demands" of the consumers, and since the exchange (at the higher prices) is completely "voluntary" anyway, there is no way to conclude that consumers or their "welfare" have been injured.[29] Thus, for Rothbard there is no social "problem" associated with monopoly in a free market. Monopoly prices cannot be defined logically, let alone established in a free market.

CRITICAL REVIEW OF AUSTRIAN MONOPOLY THEORY

The views of Kirzner and Mises that monopoly consists of exclusive control over the whole supply of some specific resource creates a number of familiar difficulties. In the first place, there would appear to be no objective way to define *beforehand* some "homogeneous" stock of resources that might be monopolized. All individually owned stocks of a resource could be differentiated at least with respect to location; in addition, the private-property system itself necessarily imparts a "differentiation" to all privately owned stocks. Further, even identical units of some given stock might be regarded differently by potential users, and there would be no way to determine this beforehand. Hence, this view of monopoly could reduce logically to the notion that each and every unit of everyone's property stock is owned "monopolistically."

Rothbard, it will be recalled, was critical of this definition of monopoly because its all-inclusiveness made it "impractical," confusing, and, ultimately, "absurd." But we can be critical of it on different grounds, employing Professor Kirzner's own (correct) view of the competitive market process. It will be recalled that Kirzner had argued that the key to competition was freedom of entry and that entry was impossible if potential entrepreneurs could not gain access to monopolized resources.[30] Yet, as has been noted above, if *all* individual stocks of resources are, in fact, *monopolized*, it would seem to follow that Kirzner's definition of monopoly would completely negate his own views on competition and market process. Indeed, it is difficult to understand how any competition or market process would even be possible with this definitional approach. How could *any* competition occur if *all* resources are monopolized?

Even if it were to be assumed for the moment that resources are *not* uniquely specific and are, instead, completely homogeneous, additional difficulties remain. Why, for instance, ought monopoly ownership to preclude the *possibility* of competition from potentially rivalrous entrepreneurs that *purchase* needed resources? Indeed, Kirzner himself has already stated that the market process is *"always"* competitive so long as there is freedom to buy and sell in the market.[31] Even monopoly ownership does not erase the freedom to buy and sell since it is possible that access to resources could be obtained, say, through purchase. Yet Kirzner argues that the *"very possibilities themselves"* of competition may be eliminated by monopoly ownership of a resource.[32]

Another difficulty with Professor Kirzner's approach is his use of the qualifying term, *"current* endowment of a certain resource."[33] Obviously, nothing prevents potentially rivalrous entrepreneurs from exploring for and exploiting *new* supplies of a specific resource. Indeed, "current endowment" of a resource is an ambiguous phrase since supplies of resources are normally classified as "proved," "probable," and "possible."

If Kirzner means to imply that a monopoly over the current *proved* endowment of a particular resource precludes the *possibility* of competition and allows the resource owner to be "immune from entrepreneurial competition,"[34] he would be arguing a tenuous point at best. Clearly such a "monopoly" allows no such thing. In this example, future[35] entry is clearly possible and cannot be precluded *a priori*. And since the entire Austrian tradition in this area is to treat the competitive process as one that unfolds through *time* anyway, how are the potential entrepreneurs effectively blocked from "discovering unexploited opportunities for profit"?

As a final point, monopoly over a resource would appear to make rational economic calculation difficult (if not impossible) since no "market" would then exist for the resource.[36] Without markets economic calculation is impossible since objective prices cannot be determined. A firm that monopolized "oranges" for instance, would have no objective way of knowing, subsequently, whether it was employing its resources efficiently in the production of "orange juice," or even whether it ought to be producing orange juice at all. This "definition" of monopoly, therefore, would appear to be operationally self-destructive. The monopoly position would tend to generate inevitable irrationalities in production since entrepreneurs would have no objective way to calculate "costs."

Mises, it will be recalled, realized the inherent difficulties of defining monopoly, and so he moved on to the catallactic significance of monopoly: obtaining the monopoly price and, thus, frustrating "the wishes of the consumers." Professor Kirzner, although he denies that the elasticity of the demand function has any bearing whatever on whether a monopoly exists or not, nonetheless does argue that resource monopoly is likely to result in a restricted employment of such resources, higher prices, and larger surpluses for the producer employing the resource.[37] Importantly, such ownership (at least in the short run) has "harmful effects" since it creates an incentive "for not using a scarce resource to the fullest extent compatible with the pattern of consumer's tastes in the market."[38]

It is really difficult to see, however, why any of this argument necessarily follows. The "pattern of consumer tastes in the market" would appear to be, simply, consumer demand. Consumer demand is the variable amount of some homogeneous stock that consumers would be willing and able to purchase at various prices. The important point to be made here is that in a free market such "demand" determinations by consumers are completely *voluntary* on their part, and all price-output combinations on that hypothetical function faithfully reflect that choice and relate those "wishes" to the producers. Consequently, consumers are at all times in complete control of (fully *sovereign* over) their own property at any given price-output combination.

It appears completely arbitrary to argue that only "low" prices, or "lower" prices induced by "supply increases," or only the "elastic" portions of a consumer's demand function are compatible with consumer sovereignty. Why are not consumers fully "sovereign" throughout the entire price-output range of their *own* demand function? After all it is *they* who determine, in certain instances, that they will trade greater volumes of dollars for fewer units of some good. Indeed, to prevent them from engaging in such exchanges would more accurately infringe upon their "sovereignty." If and when consumers become dissatisfied with such combinations, they are perfectly free to change the "elasticity" of their own demand to combinations that they *do* prefer.

If the above analysis is correct, it follows that resource owners or producers that voluntarily "restrict" their supplies to obtain higher prices (not "force" them up as Professor Kirzner asserts)[39] have committed no socially harmful act. Restricted supplies and higher prices *relative* to what? *All suppliers in free markets restrict their supplies in the sense that they only supply as much of a good or resource as they determine will maximize their monetary or physic income. But, importantly, this is precisely what the "monopolist" does.* If his action is "harmful," then so is the economic activity of all other suppliers in the market.

Alternatively, it cannot be argued that what distinguishes "monopoly" supply from "competitive" supply is the consequently higher prices. In the first place we have already argued that the new price-output combination is perfectly compatible with expressed consumer demand and, therefore, with consumer sovereignty. Secondly, prices are always "high" relative to lower prices that *could* exist, but do not. Indeed, any price at all is "high," "frustrates" consumers, and reduces their ultimate utility from consumption. But surely the ability to charge a lower price than the prevailing market price, or no price at all, can hardly be a correct criterion for judging whether a supply is competitive or monopolistic. Indeed, since producers are *also* sovereign under free-market conditions, we must conclude that *any* supply is competitive and *any* price is "compatible" with consumer sovereignty and consumer satisfaction.

ROTHBARD'S MONOPOLY THEORY RECONSIDERED

Rothbard it will be recalled had defined monopoly as "a grant of special privilege from the State reserving a certain area of production to one particular individual or group." This definition of monopoly would appear to be immune from the sort of criticism employed above against both the neoclassical and Mises-Kirzner theories of monopoly. In the first place, we can be confident that competition is "lessened" by this sort of monopoly, and that resources are nonoptimally allocated so far as consumers are concerned, since governmental monopoly restricts *by law* both competitive entry and, consequently, free consumer *choice*. Legal barriers to entry restrict entry by definition. Areas of production that are truly "naturally" monopolistic would hardly require *governmental* entry restrictions. Consequently, consumer choice *must* be distorted, and the subsequent resource allocations *must* be "inefficient," since consumers are prevented by law from making choices that differ from those already made for them by the political authority. Hence, we conclude that governmental monopoly *always* restricts competition, *always* violates consumer (and producer) sovereignty, and *always* "injures" consumer welfare.

It would be tempting to argue that these "restrictions" and "injuries" are, perhaps, minor in the case of "minor" legal impediments to either production or exchange. Yet, there is no satisfactory way to cardinally measure either "competition" or consumer "utility." Since utility is a completely subjective notion, and since interpersonal comparisons of utility are not possible, there is no objective way to determine how severe even "minor" state impediments to entry and competition actually are. It is completely possible, for instance, that what may *appear* to be an extremely inoffensive governmental regulation, i.e., setting minimum safety standards for sellers, may in fact be harmful in the extreme with respect to certain potential businessmen and specific classes of consumers.

We conclude, therefore, that any and *all* state restrictions are "monopolistic," competition reducing, and destructive of consumer satisfaction vis-à-vis alternative free-market situations. We also conclude, in summary, that this particular theory of monopoly is the *only* theory that meets all the standard critical objections and remains entirely consistent with the general Austrian methodology.

NOTES

1. For a review of this position see, for instance, Edwin Mansfield, *Microeconomics*, Second Edition (Norton, 1975), Chapters 9 & 10.

2. Willard F. Mueller, *A Primer on Monopoly and Competition* (Random House, 1970), Chapter 2.

3. Israel M. Kirzner, *Competition and Entrepreneurship* (University of Chicago Press, 1973).

4. D. T. Armentano, *The Myths of Antitrust: Economic Theory and Legal Cases* (Arlington house, 1972), Chapter 2.

5. *Ibid.*, pp. 212–15, 246, 267–68.

6. Ludwig von Mises, *Human Action* (Yale University Press, 1963), p. 358.

7. *Ibid.*

8. *Ibid.*, pp. 358–60.

9. *Ibid.*, p. 358.

10. *Ibid.*, p. 371.

11. *Ibid.*, p. 373.

12. *Ibid.*, p. 371.

13. *Ibid.*, p. 373.

14. *Ibid.*, p. 375.

15. *Ibid.*, p. 364.
16. Kirzner, *op. cit.*, Chapter I.
17. *Ibid.*, p. 21.
18. *Ibid.*, p. 103.
19. *Ibid.*
20. *Ibid.*, p. 105.
21. *Ibid.*, p. 110.
22. *Ibid.*, p. 111.
23. Murray N. Rothbard, *Man, Economy, and State*, Volume II (D. Van Nostrand Company, Inc., 1962), pp. 561–66. See also *Journal of Economic Literature*, September-October, 1974, pp. 902–3.
24. Rothbard, *op. cit.*, pp. 590–93.
25. *Ibid.*, p. 591.
26. *Ibid.*, p. 593.
27. *Ibid.*, p. 614.
28. *Ibid.*, pp. 608–9.
29. *Ibid.*, p. 564.
30. Kirzner, *op. cit.*, p. 103.
31. *Ibid.*, p. 20. This statement would seem to refute Kirzner's entire position on monopoly. If markets are *always* competitive so long as there is *freedom* to buy and sell, then in a free market there is always competition and *never* any monopoly.
32. *Ibid.*, p. 103.
33. *Ibid.*, p. 21.
34. *Ibid.*, p. 110.
35. And "future" in an entrepreneurial sense can mean the *next* moment competitive supply appears or threatens to appear.
36. See Rothbard's discussion of similar problems for cartels in *Man, Economy, and State*.
37. Kirzner, *op. cit.*, p. 110.
38. *Ibid.*, p. 111.
39. *Ibid.*, p. 110.

Spontaneous Order and the Coordination of Economic Activities*

Gerald P. O'Driscoll, Jr.
Iowa State University

This paper is an essay on the coordination of economic activities. It is exploratory and speculative, connecting arguments that I have made in several other places. The essay is an attempt to give a coherent picture of some of the theoretical and practical problems facing economists, as well as society in general. Written for a conference on Austrian economics, this paper deals with questions specifically from that distinctive viewpoint. It is not that I propose to defend the proposition that economists of this school possess a uniquely correct perspective of the issues, but merely that they have much to say on the particular questions with which I will deal. I trust that my references to economists not normally considered to be members of the Austrian School will demonstrate the universality of the problems discussed here.

Those economists who view a system of free exchange—Adam Smith's "obvious and simple system of natural liberty"[1]—as the solution of the coordination problem in economics face intellectual challenges from at least four sources: first, the continuing challenge of the Keynesian legacy; second, the challenge from what James Buchanan has termed the "modern Ricardians";

*This essay appeared in *The Journal of Libertarian Studies* 1 (Spring 1977): 137–51. Copyright © 1977 Pergamon Press Ltd.

third, the challenge from the new movement for national planning; and finally, the challenge from certain economists in the Austrian School.

In previous papers, I have dealt with the Austrian analysis of monetary theory (or macroeconomics) as it is concerned with the coordination of economic activities. Accordingly, I will begin with this general problem.

THE KEYNESIAN LEGACY

It has become clear in recent years that Keynes's *General Theory* is a very confused work, so much that it is virtually an ink-blot test for economists: an economist's perception of its contents tells more about the beliefs of the reader than the contents of that book.[2] Indeed, Keynes's sympathetic critics are compelled to point out these confusions in their attempts to argue that he made a significant contribution to our understanding of the economic system. The best example of this is Axel Leijonhuf- vud's *On Keynesian Economics and the Economics of Keynes*.[3] Leijonhufvud argues there that Keynes had important insights into coordination failures in market systems. Specifically, Leijonhufvud's Keynes argued that banking and financial systems can operate so as to impede rather than to facilitate the adjustment to a change in the equilibrium rate of interest. Securities markets are incapable of moving from a higher to a lower equilibrium rate of interest, without attendant fluctuations in income and employment. This is true whether the assumed disturbance consists of a downward shift in the marginal efficiency of investment (Keynes's marginal efficiency of capital), or an increase in the savings schedule (a decreased marginal propensity to consume out of current income). The existence of bearish speculators in securities markets impedes smooth adjustment of those markets. Keynes's bears do this by speculating against any rise in the prices of long-lived assets, real or financial.[4] Keynesian bears speculate on the basis of the historical perception that they possess of a "normal" long run rate of interest. If this normal long-rate could be taken as summarizing the real forces determining the equilibrium rate of interest, then it is quite reasonable, from a profit-maximizing viewpoint, for speculators to treat deviations from the rate as temporary fluctuations.[5] Indeed, Keynes's speculators behave precisely the way textbook examples suggest, in that they act so as to hasten the return to the *perceived* equilibrium position (though this effect is not part of their intention, of course). But in this instance, speculative activity, following a guide that normally proves reliable, proves to be disequilibrating in its effects. Speculators are misled into identifying as but a transitory fluctuation what in fact is the consequence of a shift in parameters.

In microtheory it is customary to point out that speculators who misidentify an equilibrium position will suffer capital losses, and that, in any case, market forces will restore equilibrium. But Keynes raised an important issue: bearish speculators, in exhibiting liquidity preference, can initiate deflationary pressures.[6] Unless we assume that wage and price changes occur *infinitely* fast, then price deflation will be accompanied by quantity-adjustments.[7] In effect, the resulting speculative losses become socialized. To put a Keynesian proposition in Hayekian terms, the unintended consequences of a speculative search for liquidity generate falling income and general illiquidity. If one adopts the position—as do most Austrians—that the market *process* is a continuing search for opportunities, one cannot dismiss out of hand the possibility that speculation of the ·Keynesian variety could inhibit the equilibrating market forces. And unless one adopts the view that prices are always correct, which no Austrian would do, then one must confront this Keynesian information problem.

Several points need to be made here. I have been talking of "Leijonhufvud's Keynes," because of the problematical nature of *The General Theory.* Yet my paraphrase of Leijonhufvud's interpretation is a fairly straightforward argument about discoordinating market processes. The obvious question that comes to mind in this context is why Keynes didn't say all this explicitly and simply if this is what he meant? The thesis, as I have presented it, can obviously be put very succinctly. What makes Leijonhufvud's presentation of it so difficult is the web of confusion woven by Keynes.

In order to show that his interpretation has captured the authentic Keynes, Leijonhufvud not only must criticize conflicting interpretations, but he must deal with Keynes's own imprecision and confusion. The clearest example of these problems occurs in Leijonhufvud's discussion of Keynes's views on capital Before examining this discussion, however, one must consider the intellectual background to the treatment of capital questions in *The General Theory*.

Hayek was quite critical of Keynes's earlier book, the *Treatise on Money*, when he reviewed that work. The general tenor of his criticism is that Keynes, at the time he wrote that book, was largely ignorant of capital theory. Hayek recognized that Keynes had developed a neo-Wicksellian theory, but without the necessary theoretical foundations.[8] And he observed that:

It is *a priori* unlikely that an attempt to utilise the conclusions drawn from a certain theory without accepting that theory itself should be successful. But, in the case of an author of Mr. Keynes' intellectual calibre, the attempt produces results which are truly remarkable.[9]

In an amazing piece of candor, Keynes all but admitted the legitimacy of Hayek's criticism; after defending himself by observing that there was no "satisfactory theory" of capital in "completed form," Keynes stated:

Nevertheless, substantially I concede Dr. Hayek's point. I agree with him that a clear account of the factors determining the natural rate of interest ought to have a place in a completed *Treatise on Money*, and that it is lacking in mine: and I can only plead that I had much to say for which such a theory is not required and that my own ideas about it were still too much in embryo to deserve publication. Later on, I will endeavor to make good this deficiency.[10]

Did Keynes ever "make good this deficiency"? I do not believe so, and I offer the following observations in support of this judgment. Much of the confusion surrounding the nature of

Keynes's message can be accounted for if one accepts the thesis that Keynes remained largely ignorant of capital theory. He had difficulty, then, in presenting his message because he did not possess the requisite technical knowledge. Of course, one could also infer that Keynes was not sure of the message that he wished to present. There is evidence for this interpretation in the recent observation of one of his close associates at Cambridge, Joan Robinson, who noted that certain of Keynes's putative followers " . . . had some trouble in getting Maynard to see what the point of his revolution really was. . . ."[11]

But I would offer as a final judgment of Keynes the observation of his recent interpreter, Axel Leijonhufvud. By far the most difficult chapter of the latter's book is the fourth, "The General Theory of Liquidity Preference," in which both the state of capital theory in the thirties and Keynes's own views on the subject are presented. Of this complexity, Leijonhufvud remarks: "This chapter will be a lengthy affair, partly because of the intrinsic difficulty of capital theory, partly because Keynes did not work out his ideas on the subject in much detail so that we are left with only what amounts to an unfinished sketch."[12] In short, Keynes never made up the self-admitted deficiency of the *Treatise*. Moreover, it is only by having thus demonstrated Keynes's lack of knowledge and clarity that Leijonhufvud can make it at all plausible that Keynes had a comparatively simple point to make (i.e., stickiness of interest rates), though this point is not the one commonly attributed to him (i.e., stickiness of money wage rates).

There are several approaches that one can take to Keynes's challenge. Conceptual errors abound in *The General Theory*; and I have suggested that in the area of capital theory, Keynes is quite confused. One can fairly easily engage in piecemeal criticism of Keynes's ideas. I do not believe that the Keynesian system can stand up to such a criticism. But I am not sure that this is a fruitful approach, though I myself have adopted it on previous occasions.[13] The reasons are several-fold. First, no one, I believe, can get beyond the exegetical problem—I refer the reader again to my ink-blot analogy. No matter which Keynes one criticizes, a new Keynes is proffered in its stead. More to the point, one m st consider the possibility that the most interesting recent interpretation bears scant resemblance to Keynes's ideas. Yeager has argued, for instance, that Leijonhufvud and Clower both seem prepared to credit Keynes with their own, original contributions.[14] Perhaps, then Keynes is the wrong target of any criticism.

Nonetheless, the Keynesian *debate* does raise important theoretical issues that Austrians must confront, regardless of who is adjudged the author of particular views. And I believe that there is one unifying theme running through most, if not all, versions of Keynesian economics: the self-correcting forces of the market economy cannot be relied upon to maintain full-employment and reasonable price stability. In its most extreme version, this criticism would even deny the existence of self-correcting market forces. It is to the issue of the strength of these market forces that Austrians should address themselves, for it is now becoming increasingly accepted that macroeconomics is in fact concerned with the coordination of economic activities. Leijonhufvud has stated the problem as follows:

. . . The central issue in macroeconomic theory is—once again—the extent to which the economy, or at least its market sectors, may properly be regarded as a self-regulating system. . . . How well or badly, do its "automatic" mechanisms perform?[15]

Before continuing, it would be well to consider this latter issue in detail.

THE PRINCIPLE OF SPONTANEOUS ORDER

The principle of spontaneous order—or of "undesigned order," as it might more properly be called—can be viewed as the first principle of economics. Indeed, James Buchanan has recently gone so far as to suggest that it is the *only* principle of economics. The principle is, in any case, a cornerstone of modern economics, whether we trace modern (i.e., post-mercantilist) economics back to Adam Smith and the other Scottish moral philosophers, or to the Physiocrats. With this principle, scholars for the first time could see economic phenomena as interdependent events. Indeed, this principle made it possible to reason systematically and coherently about economic phenomena. Much of nineteenth century economics can be seen as consisting of developments of this principle (along with minority criticisms of the principle and the systems of thought deduced therefrom).

On the other hand, most of twentieth century economics has consisted of reactions against systems in which this principle plays a central role. In this, Keynesian economics is but one among a family of theories that deny the existence of a spontaneous or undesigned market order in which plans are coordinated. The reaction has been so complete that what was taken by earlier economists to be an empirical law—the existence of a spontaneous market order—is now frequently viewed as the product of ideological bias or prejudice. If anything, modern economic discussions presuppose the absence of the very order whose existence was the cornerstone of much of nineteenth century economics. In this sense, modern economics is fundamentally inconsistent.[16]

It is apparent now that the principle was not firmly enough established in economics to withstand the criticisms that were levied against it. Yet the question of the existence of a spontaneously generated order remains the central question of economics—and of social theory generally—even though it is seldom recognized as such. Theories of the instability of investment, of saving, and of aggregate demand are all variants of the general proposition that the economy lacks strong forces leading to an undesigned order. These are not simply disputes of technical economics, narrowly defined, though they too long have been treated as such. The question of the necessary amount of governmental stabilization policy will not be decided by running yet another money-demand equation through a computer. Nonetheless, it is imperative that the question be addressed directly once again.[17]

As intellectual descendants of Carl Menger, most Austrian

economists have defended the proposition that spontaneous market forces are capable of producing an overall order in society. Hayek, for one, is well-known for his emphasis on the role of nonpurposive social organizations in this process.[18] Indeed, the persistence of members of this school in their views in the face of the contrary opinion of much of the profession has contributed to their intellectual isolation. In this sense, and alone among the neoclassical schools, the Austrians can today lay claim to being the inheritors of the Smithian system. In this, the bicentenary of the publication of *The Wealth of Nations*, it would be well for Austrian economists to seize the opportunity to reestablish the importance of the principle of spontaneous order—an order that, though designed by no one, emerges from the individual and independent planning of market transactors.

THE NEW RICARDIANS[19]

There is yet another tradition in the history of economics, distinct from both the Austrian and Smithian traditions, and from those that are overtly hostile to these traditions. It is a tradition epitomized by David Ricardo's general approach to economic questions. In the Ricardian tradition, attention is focused on the long run, in which full adjustment to all disturbances has occurred. Periods of transition are abstracted from.[20] It would be anachronistic to credit Ricardo with a theory of perfect information, but he wrote as though the laborers, capitalists, and rentiers of his system had full access to future events. The difference between the Smithian and Ricardian traditions is a subtle, though important one; and it separates theorists even today.

In Smith's world, changes are constantly occurring, and adaptations to these changes are never complete. These changes may be of comparatively simple variety, such as variations in the corn harvest from year to year (with attendant effects on real wage rates).[21] More importantly, Smith was concerned with the continuous process of market adaptation to invention and further extensions of the division of labor. Changes in institutions and the legal structure are of prime concern.[22] It is not, of course, that Smith had nothing to say about the long run. His value theory is a long-run theory, though I find it one of the least developed parts of his system.[23] Nonetheless, the emphasis in *The Wealth of Nations* is on change. Moreover, Smith's actors suffer various illusions and misunderstandings about future events, and, indeed, about their own self-interest. None of this would make sense in a Ricardian world.

Whether it is a question of monetary economics or of fiscal policy, Ricardo generally treats all disturbances as though they were fully and completely anticipated.[24] In the Ricardian world, then, the problem of coordination disappears. It is not that Ricardo denied the principle of spontaneous order. Rather he did not treat the emergence of coordinated behavior on the market as a problem. He in effect *assumed* that economic behavior will be coordinated. Most importantly, and unlike Smith, Ricardo generally ignored the question of what institutional arrangements are necessary for the emergence of that order upon which the soundness of his arguments depends.

The institutional setting and the allocation mechanism matter in economics precisely because behavior in a changing world is not automatically coordinated. Laws and institutions have a significant impact on human behavior precisely because some facilitate and some inhibit the flow of information that is necessary for adaptation in a changing world. This realization is certainly contained in *The Wealth of Nations*—Smith's emphasis on the importance of these matters suffuses that work. Not so with Ricardo's *Principles*.

Professor Lachmann has recently reminded us that the problem of economic coordination is intimately involved with the twin problems of acquisition and diffusion of knowledge among transactors. In dealing with the characteristic assumption that the state of knowledge is among the data of the system, he queries:

Do we assume that all market actors know all the tastes and resources in all markets in which they, actually or potentially, do or might operate? But if so, equilibrium should at once be attained in all markets. If we were to make this assumption, there could be no disequilibrium, no dealings at "false prices." Walras's "auctioneer" would become super-fluous. If, on the other hand, we do not make it, how do we delimit the extent of each actor's knowledge at each point of time, and how do we deal with the flow of knowledge between actors over time?[25]

Discussion about the importance of information may seem prosaic to economists at this point. But the radical implications of imperfect knowledge have simply not been generally absorbed in economic theory. For, *inter alia*, imperfection of knowledge means that prices do not necessarily coordinate economic be-havior, as those prices are influenced by the inconsistent expec-tations on the basis of "false" price signals. To justify one's faith in the coordinating function of markets, one cannot simply assume that prices are coordinating, or at their equilibrium level. Rather, one must be concerned with the institutional environ-ment of economic systems and with the appropriateness of these institutions for the emergence of a spontaneous market order. One must be concerned, then, with specifying the situations in which prices will coordinate, and those situations in which prices will not coordinate, economic activity. By his attention to the long run, in which, *ex hypothesi*, all such problems disappear because full adjustment to all changes has occurred, Ricardo (and his followers) ignored these difficulties.

The problem of economic coordination is a theoretical and practical issue not merely because decision-making is decen-tralized, though this is an important aspect of the problem. Of even more importance is the fact that we live in a world of constant change. Were there decentralized decision-making, but an unchanging environment, it might be reasonable to suppose that economic activity could be coordinated under a wide variety of institutional and allocational arrangements. Learning would occur due to the repetition of events, with adjustments made as past errors were revealed.[26] A price system and appropriate market institutions are of practical significance precisely because of the need to register the effects of continuous changes in the data, changes which are given to no one in their entirety. On the other hand, it is doubtful whether money, prices, or the market system would exist in the stationary state. Those who ignore this aspect of imperfect information are caught in the dilemma of dealing with phenomena, most of which would not exist in the world as they assume that world to exist—a world of perfectly coordinated plans.[27]

Ricardo and his epigones thus obscured the basic questions of social order that Smith had raised. They shifted the emphasis away from these questions to the theorems and lemmas of value theory. Their legacy is still with us today. Walras and the Lausanne School introduced the concept of *general* equilibrium into economics. But in other respects the Walrasian system is quite similar to the Ricardian: both are perfectly coordinated systems. By the sheer logic of these systems, neither is obviously concerned with the coordination of economic activities—this coordination is implicitly assumed to take place. In such systems laws and institutions do not matter. Monetary disturbances can have no significant effects—for the transition periods in which money clearly matters are de-emphasized or ignored in the Ricardian system.[28] In such systems, the market would not be viewed as a process in which continual adjustment to continual change occurs, but a state of affairs in which this process was at an end.

The Chicago School can be fairly described as the modern Ricardians. In Kirzner's terminology, the transactors in the Chicago world are nothing but Robbinsian maximizers.[29] Chicago economists are Ricardian in their approach to questions of tax and expenditure policy and monetary policy, to cite two examples previously mentioned for Ricardo. The Ricardian bent of the Chicago School is important to the Austrian School for at least two reasons.

First, the time has passed when members of the Chicago School were articulate, but minority members of the profession. Increasingly, economic discussions and debates are influenced by their approach. Second, on issues involving coordination questions, their Ricardian leanings *re-enforce* the Walrasian approach of the dominant mathematical, general equilibrium theorists. This is an important point because economists are beginning to recognize the distinctiveness of the Marshallian approach (*vis à vis* the Walrasian approach) of Chicago School economists. And the differences between Chicago School economists and the rest of the profession are important for a wide variety of issues, such as the role of empirical research, partial vs. general equilibrium analysis, etc. But as regards the coordination of economic activities, the new Ricardians and the neo-Walrasians are more of one mind. They tend to take for granted that markets coordinate economic activities. By doing so, they ignore the complex questions of economic coordination, upon the solution of which depends the degree of economic coordination. This approach is objectionable because of the conclusions it engenders when markets demonstrably are not coordinating economic activity. The "market failure" mentality is an effect of this approach.[30] "The market system" is adjudged a failure in such cases, with scant recognition that "the market" is a metaphor for a complex of interrelationships and institutions, any one of which may be the source of the problem. That members of the Chicago School are generally more sanguine about the efficacy of this system hardly mitigates the methodological point being made here.

Austrian economists and other adherents to the principle of spontaneous order will receive little support and should generally expect overt hostility from the Chicago School on a wide range of economic questions.[31] Austrian economists tend to view most economic questions as issues involving the principle of spontaneous order. Accordingly, they take characteristic positions on these questions. Two of the areas where disagreement between the two schools is particularly intense are monetary and capital theory. Quite apart from their differences over the determination of the *equilibrium* values of interest rates, the two schools are sharply divided over the approach to questions of capital and interest theory, as well as those of monetary theory. Being Ricardians, members of the Chicago School naturally keep questions of monetary theory and capital theory quite distinct, since these are distinct problems in long-run equilibrium analysis. As did Ricardo, they treat deviations from the equilibrium rate of interest as temporary fluctuations. The transitional periods in which monetary disturbances influence the accumulation of capital and the level of rate of interest are typically ignored or at least de-emphasized.

On the other hand, many of the twentieth century members of the Austrian School have dealt with the interface between monetary and capital theory. Mises and Hayek were most persistent in their analysis of the interrelation between monetary and capital questions, precisely because of their interest in adjustment problems. Hayek, for instance, has been consistent in treating economic fluctuations as manifestations of economic discoordination, brought on by monetary disturbances.[32] For Hayek, monetary disturbances change entrepreneurial expectations and lead to capital accumulation that, *ex post*, is revealed to have been malinvestment. These malinvestments cause real scarcities, whose existence becomes manifest in subsequent price changes. The price changes compel entrepreneurs—because of the capital losses that they eventually incur—to revise their investment plans. It is in this sense that modern Austrians view cyclical expansions brought about by monetary and credit inflation as self-reversing and inherently unstable.[33]

Hayek and Mises thus dealt with phenomena virtually ignored by monetary theorists of the Chicago School—the transition period between a monetary disturbance and complete adjustment to its effects.[34] To the extent that Professor Friedman, for instance, deals with the transition period, it is only in terms of one, comparatively narrow problem—anticipation of future price levels.[35] As a practical matter, monetarists generally view inflation as synchronized inflation, with all prices rising *pari passu*. For Hayek and Mises, synchronized inflation is a fantasy, so long as monetary disturbances impinge at specific points.[36] And full adjustment to inflation would be all but inconceivable, as it would involve each actor's anticipating correctly the precise changes in each relative price that will occur in each future period, due to the assumed monetary disturbances.[37]

Once again, the Ricardian approach to monetary questions
blinds its users to the issues considered paramount by the Austrians. In so doing, this approach inhibits an understanding of
important issues confronting market economists. For the Ricardian, quantity theory approach is one in which prices continue
their coordinating function even in an inflation. Yet, the point at
issue is whether spontaneous market forces operate as usual in
an inflation. If monetary disturbances not only generate pure
price inflation, but also interfere with the coordinating
mechanisms in an economy, then the quantity theory approach
ignores an important research programme in economics—the
study of the monetary framework necessary for prices to fulfill
their coordinating function.[38] In the words of one expositor of
Hayek's ideas:

[Hayek] regarded prices . . . as empirical reflectors of specific circumstances and price changes as an *inter-related* series of changes in
these "signals," which produced a gradual adaptation in the entire
price structure (and hence in the outputs of different commodities and
services) to the constant, unpredictable changes in the real world.
Pricing, in short, is seen as a continuous information-collecting and
disseminating process, but it is the institutional framework that determines both the extent to which and the degree of success with which,
prices are enabled to perform this potential signalling or allocative
function.[39]

PLANNING[40]

That nonpurposive social organizations will naturally evolve
and that an undesigned order can be the product of self-
regarding acts are radical ideas in Western thought. These ideas
run counter to the dominant approach to social questions and
were in ascendency for only a brief period in Western intellectual history. It is not, then, entirely surprising that in economics
these ideas have not gained complete acceptance; and that
among the general public, even the so-called educated public,
they are scarcely understood at all. But there is danger that
because of essentially reactionary developments in social

thought, the insights that were the product of the Enlightenment will be all but lost in practice. Adam Smith has aptly
characterized the far older conception of social order:

The man of system. . . . seems to imagine that he can arrange the
different members of a great society with as much ease as the hand
arranges the different pieces upon a chess-board; he does not consider
that the pieces upon the chess-board have no other principle of motion
besides that which the hand impresses upon them; but that, in the great
chess-board of human society, every single piece has a principle of
motion of its own, altogether different from that which the legislature
might choose to impress upon it. If those two principles coincide and
act in the same direction, the game of human society will go on easily
and harmoniously, and is very likely to be happy and successful. If they
are opposite or different, the game will go on miserably, and the society
must be at all times in the highest degree of disorder.[41]

The liberal conception of society of Adam Smith and the
classical economists stands in sharp contrast with this older view.
Yet once again in the United States, we see evidence of this older
conception's becoming prominent, under the guise of national
economic planning. Proposals for planning are embodiments of
the chess-game conception of social affairs, adapted to the problem of economic allocation. These proposals implicitly or
explicitly deny that market forces guide decision making, so as to
produce an overall, yet undesigned order; and they virtually
ignore the function and role of nonpurposive economic organizations.

It is not that the arguments for national (i.e., central) economic
planning constitute a direct *intellectual* challenge to opponents of
such planning. As Professor Hayek has recently demonstrated in
a devastating rebuttal of these proposals, modern exponents of
"planning" possess as naive and ill-thought-out an approach to
the problem as did the Bolsheviks and European socialists in the
immediate post–World War I period. As he notes:

The conception [collectivist economic planning], originally developed
by some of the organizers of the German war economy during World
War I, was thoroughly discussed by economists in the 1920's and

1930's; and all those familiar with that discussion will agree that it greatly contributed to the clarification of concepts and that one ought today to be entitled to assume that no competent economist who lived through that discussion would ever again talk about the issues in terms of the vague and confused concepts initially bandied about.[42]

Indeed, if this debate were being carried out in the scholarly arena, I doubt that the proposals put forth by those in favor of central planning would survive Hayek's recent criticisms. Unfortunately, the debate is not being carried forth in learned journals, or, generally, by learned men; rather, the proposals are being developed in the pages of the *New York Times*, and are being presented by politicians, businessmen, and labor union leaders. This is an instance in which those who accept the Smithian insights have won the intellectual battle, but are in danger of seeing their arguments lose out in practice. This situation surely represents a dilemma for economists. Economists generally disdain polemics, but they now face a situation in which influencing important political questions depends on their ability to present economic ideas in a polemical fashion. Certainly those economists who have chosen, for whatever reasons,[43] to ally themselves with the misleading arguments of the "planners" have not eschewed polemics.[44]

Hayek has done an admirable job of marshalling the chief arguments against central planning in his recent article. I do not intend to repeat these arguments here. But it is worth reminding ourselves of the central confusion of the early advocates of central planning, as it is the central confusion of the current advocates. The confusion concerns the very concept of "planning." If nothing else developed from the earlier debates over the question, it was the realization that a market economy is characterized by *continual* planning and plan-revision, albeit on a decentralized level.[45] As Hayek put it over thirty years ago, and recently repeated:

The dispute between the modern planners and their opponents, is, therefore, *not* a dispute on whether we ought to choose intelligently between the various possible organizations of society; it is not a dispute on whether we ought to employ foresight and systematic thinking in planning our common affairs. It is a dispute about what is the best way of so doing. The question is whether for this purpose it is better that the holder of coercive power should confine himself in general to creating conditions under which the knowledge and initiative of individuals are given the best scope so that *they* can plan most successfully; or whether a rational utilization of our resources requires *central* direction and organization of all our activities according to some consciously constructed "blueprint." The socialists of all parties have appropriated the term "planning" for planning of the latter type, and it is now generally accepted in this sense. But though this is meant to suggest that this is the only rational way of handling our affairs, it does not, of course, prove this. It remains the point on which the planners and the liberals disagree.[46]

The challenge of "planning" confronts liberal economists with both the necessity and the opportunity of once again entering the popular debate over the trend of society that we will shape for the future. For it must be remembered that in constructing economics upon the principle of spontaneous order, earlier economists were ultimately interested in the problem of social and political organization. In part, then, I am proposing a return to an earlier conception of our task as engaging in political economy, though we now recognize a specifically scientific part of this field, *viz.*, economics. If economists do not conceive of their task thusly, it is doubtful whether there will be any practical opportunity in the future for the *scientific* pursuit of the implications of the principle of spontaneous order.

In order to pursue this goal, however, Austrian economists in particular must settle among themselves certain theoretical and seemingly purely scientific issues. I have argued above that among the neoclassical economists, the Austrians have most consistently adhered to Adam Smith's conception of the economic problem. Ironically, recent debates indicate anything but agreement among living members of this school. The positions of some could be construed as an implicit attack on the idea that there is a spontaneous market order in the economy. It is thus that I am led into a final section, involving a discussion of the Austrian approach to the question of the operation of spontaneously generated forces in a market economy.

THE AUSTRIAN SCHOOL AND SPONTANEOUS ORDERING FORCES

In a recent paper, Professor Kirzner speculates about the exact status of the proposition that profitable opportunities have a tendency to be exploited.[47] He concludes that the propensity to discover opportunities is "inseparable from our insight that human beings act purposefully."[48] In fact, he even suggests a sympathetic reinterpretation of the perfect knowledge assumption of neoclassical price theory. Though orthodox use of the assumption is "carefree,"[49] it does reflect a real insight: our "instinct" is seen as assuring us that profitable opportunities will be discovered. He then concludes that: "The perfect knowledge assumption of neo-classical economics carried this instinctive assurance to altogether unjustified lengths. In rejecting this dangerous assumption, we must take care not to expunge the entirely healthy instinct on which it rested."[50]

Kirzner's approach to the issue of profit exploitation in a market economy differs markedly from Lachmann's. Nonetheless, this proposition is not easily demonstrated, for two, interrelated reasons. First, Lachmann to my knowledge nowhere *explicitly* asserts the contrary proposition, *viz.*, that we have no grounds for believing that market participants will discover and exploit profitable opportunities. Second, though the figure of Professor Lachmann lurks in the background throughout the second half of Kirzner's paper, the latter never brings this figure into the foreground.

The best way of elucidating this issue is to turn to Lachmann's own recent paper. Toward the end of his paper, Lachmann notes that:

...Skepticism about equilibrium need not deter us from appraising the relative strength and weakness of the equilibrating forces in various situations. In fact, it must encourage us to do so. To make confident use of the notion of equilibrium means to imply that the equilibrating forces will always be of sufficient strength to triumph over all obstacles. A skeptic might readily admit that such situations may exist, but he will probably doubt whether they occur with sufficient frequency to warrant our treating them as the norm. The more skeptical we are about general equilibrium as the central notion of economic analysis, the more incumbent on us it becomes to examine each situation individually with respect to the balance of strength of equilibrating and disequilibrating forces.[51]

It must be noted here that Kirzner's position is *not* that we should admire neoclassical price theory for its treatment of general equilibrium as "the central notion of economic analysis" or as "the norm." Rather, he suggests that we accept the proposition that equilibrating tendencies are strong. If the propensity to discover opportunities is "inseparable from our insight that human beings act purposefully," then we must likewise acknowledge a *tendency* toward equilibrium in all markets. *A fortiori*, there exist strong tendencies toward an overall or general equilibrium *at each moment*. Individuals are, then, constantly revising their plans in a way that brings them into greater uniformity. This latter proposition, when thus phrased in dynamic terms, does embody the principle of an undesigned order. It remains questionable, however, whether Lachmann wishes to embrace this principle. Thus he argues that:

Experience shows that in the real world of disequilibrium different persons will typically hold different expectations about the same future event. If so, at best one person's expectation can be confirmed and all other expectations will be disappointed. Hence the "assumption that all other expectations are confirmed" cannot possibly hold. Nobody can take his equilibrium bearings if he does not know how others will act. In such a situation, which we have every reason to regard as normal, his equilibrium, as Hayek admits, cannot serve as a source of a "feedback mechanism." *The beacon that had been designed to keep entrepreneurs from straying from the narrow path of convergent expectations turns out, on most nights, to be rather dim.*[52]

Lachmann makes much of "the autonomy of the human mind" (as must all Austrians):

This source of . . . new knowledge may well be past experience, but the latter requires interpretation by a discerning mind, and optimists will interpret it differently from pessimists. The human mind is a filter of experience, but each individual's filter is different from every other filter. Divergent expectations are thus as "natural," a feature of the social landscape as are divergent tastes. Changes in the constellation of knowledge are an inevitable concomitant of the passing of time, and changes in the constellation of expectations are bound to follow them.[53]

There is no denying the autonomy of the human mind, but one is reluctant to follow Lachmann in his apparent conclusion that we can say nothing about the likelihood that individuals will make consistent and coordinated decisions in the face of new knowledge. If anything, he seems to be saying that they will not coordinate plans. Yet, one always supposed it was an Hayekian insight that prices facilitate the diffusion of information and the coordination of plans.[54]

We are faced here with an important question: Do different and disparate individuals have a common reaction to shared experience? We certainly would not want to say they always do, or there would be little sense in referring to "individuals." Yet, there are obvious cases in which people do react to shared experiences in the same or similar ways: the perception of a fire in an enclosed room will lead to virtually everyone's making for an exit. Each person could form a reasonable expectation about what the others will do.

Moreover, many events are implicit demonstrations of the degree to which expectations do coincide. Changes in clothing fashion might be cited as an example. The "agreement" among separate manufacturers of apparel can be amazing, though clearly retail customers do not register their preferences for new fashion in a clothing futures market. Apparently individual entrepreneurs, experiencing the same signals and trends, will often form similar expectations.

None of these considerations is decisive, of course, but they are suggestive. Lachmann has clearly done a great service in pointing out forcefully the absurdity of an approach in which expectations *always* prove consistent. It is an essential feature of markets that not everyone reacts equally quickly to the continual changes in the data.[55] But it is true of at least some changes that they occur only because actors share a unanimous opinion about the future course of events.

Having eschewed the approach of assuming consistency among expectations at all times, one is not justified, without further argument, in arguing that economists can make no assumptions about a tendency toward such uniformity, where this tendency is based on a universally recognized "propensity to discover opportunities." To do so would involve a non sequitur. Again, to assume that all opportunities are at any moment fully exploited (and thus do not really exist as opportunities) would be, to paraphrase Kirzner, a "carefree" use of concepts. But we must surely accept the existence of the propensity, or forsake the principle of spontaneous order. This point can be elaborated by recounting an event that happened at a December, 1975, conference on Austrian economics.

Professor Lerner argued that without the concept of general equilibrium, defenders of the market system have no basis from which to carry on their defense. His criticism was in response to Lachmann's approach to the question of general equilibrium. I confess that I rose to the latter's defense at the time, by pointing out that we need only assume that there is market-day equilibrium. If prices clear existing supplies, then markets can operate successfully. "That is all we need." I am now not sure that I did not err. Lerner may have been raising an important issue for Austrians.

We must distinguish two functions of markets. The first consists simply in a method of allocating existing supplies peacefully. Without prices and free markets, society requires guns and dictatorship. Examples of the latter type of social allocation of resources are numerous. But I am not sure that defenders of the market system can be satisfied with demonstrating that free trade is an alternative to the "war of all against all," however important this insight may be. For if supplies of goods are autonomous, if not gratuitous, it is dubious in what sense it can be said that prices coordinate activity. Indeed, I suspect that there is no coordination in the conventional sense in Lachmann's system. For him apparently, *ex ante* plans bear no relation to *ex post* reality. There is not even reason to believe that actors will move in the right direction in correcting past errors.

Lachmann does feel that the market "cannot make bulls and bears change their expectations, but it nevertheless can coordinate these." He continues:

> To coordinate bullish and bearish expectations is, as Keynes showed, the economic function of the Stock Exchange and of asset markets in general. This is achieved because in such markets the price will move until the whole market is divided into equal halves of bulls and bears. In this way divergent expectations are cast into a coherent pattern and a measure of coordination is accomplished.[56]

"Coordination" is being used here in a highly ambiguous sense. As Lachmann notes subsequently, he is talking not about *ex ante* consistency, but about a Marshallian *ex post*, market-day equilibrium.[57] This usage of coordination is in sharp contrast to the more conventional one, and the usage that Austrians have traditionally employed.[58] "Coordination of plans" in traditional usage means there is *ex ante* consistency among transactors' plans. It is certainly scant comfort for one interested in this problem to be informed that there will be "coordination" *ex post*. Though related, *ex ante* and *ex post* "coordination" are conceptually distinct issues. To conflate the two issues is scarcely to contribute to the solution of either problem.[59]

It is certainly not the case that Austrian economists maintain that there ever exists *ex ante* consistency among all transactors' plans. But they have traditionally maintained, as Lachmann himself notes, that there is a *strong* tendency toward diffusion of knowledge and increased consistency of plans. In other words, Austrian economists have always viewed the problem of economic coordination in dynamic terms. Do plans become more consistent over time? Lachmann apparently sloughs over the distinction between two very different propositions:

1. Economic activities are coordinated in the sense that all

plans are successfully executed ("general equilibrium").
2. Economic activities are coordinated in the sense that a mechanism exists (i.e., the price system) that facilitates rational plan revision *and* leads to greater consistency of plans over time.

Lachmann switches back and forth between discussions of "the relative strength and weakness of the equilibrating forces," and "general equilibrium as the central notion of economic analysis" as though he were talking about the same problem (see p. 129). Surely, the statement that "the market produces strong equilibrating forces" is fundamentally different than the assertion that "the market is always in (general) equilibrium." Does Professor Lachmann acknowledge the difference? It is certainly not clear that his arguments against the first class of statements are telling against the second. It is true that elsewhere Lachmann apparently acknowledges the existence of a tendency toward equilibrium in some areas: "A tendency toward the integration of the [capital] structure does exist."[60] But even there, he seemingly takes back what he has just granted.[61] I am afraid his occasional concessions to the existence of a tendency to greater consistency of plans in markets only confuses matters.

What I find most disturbing about Lachmann's position is that he criticizes a *static* general equilibrium model, but concludes that the modern Austrian approach to coordination, in a *dynamic* sense, is thereby called into question. I am not at all clear what he thinks "the general equilibrium perspective" is. The reader is told that Hayek's "early work was clearly under the influence of the general equilibrium model."[62] Elsewhere the reader is reminded that as early as 1933 (in "Price Expectations, Monetary Disturbances and Malinvestments") Hayek dealt with expectations. It was in 1936 ("Economics and Knowledge") that Hayek launched his attack on the static, general equilibrium models of mathematical economics. From this, one must conclude that Lachmann is critical even of theories espousing a tendency toward overall equilibrium (i.e., he denies the principle of spontaneous order). I can draw no other conclusion.

It also seems that what Kirzner treats as the "equilibrating market process," Lachmann treats as a "disequilibrating" process. At first, I thought there was a mere semantic confusion. I now believe the apparent semantic confusion is masking real conceptual differences. Kirzner sees any disturbance as developing equilibrating market forces. Lachmann sees change as disequilibrating.[63] The only reason that I can adduce is that Lachmann does not see market forces as being equilibrating in nature. If this is his position for markets as a whole, then he is generalizing the position taken by Keynes about securities markets to markets as a whole, *viz.*, that we cannot rely on spontaneous market forces to bring us to an equilibrium position after a disturbance. And if this be the case, then Lachmann's views represent a radical challenge not only to his fellow Austrians, but to all those who accept the existence of an undesigned market order. For it certainly seems that the only effective answer to the challenges with which I have been concerned lies in Kirzner's characterization of the entrepreneurial role.

As a final note, if I have misread Lachmann, I hope this section will at least serve to clarify issues and develop implications of the principle of spontaneous order. If the paper succeeded in nothing else, it would have served its purpose.

CONCLUSIONS

I would like to remind the reader that my original task was to demonstrate that seemingly diverse and particular problems are really instances of a more general theoretical disagreement. For it is only by directly addressing this general theoretical disagreement—disagreement that I have identified as devolving around the existence of an undesigned market order—that a fruitful search toward solutions of these individual problems can be begun. It is in the nature of an endeavor to demonstrate the interconnections between such seemingly disparate (but really connected) issues that no one of them is adequately treated. If the reader feels that each section calls for a separate paper on its topic, the author can only agree and express the hope that more papers on these subjects will be forthcoming, albeit papers informed by the realization of the overall problem being studied.

NOTES

1. Adam Smith, *The Wealth of Nations*, ed. by Edwin Cannan (New York: The Modern Library, 1937), p. 651.
It is frequently forgotten that Smith's defense of a relatively unhampered market is partly based on considerations of justice. See Smith, pp. 141, 308 and 497. The ethical basis of Smith's system is emphasized in a paper by Joseph Cropsey, "The Invisible Hand: Moral and Political Consideration," delivered as part of the Harry Girvetz Memorial Lecture Series at the University of California, Santa Barbara. Also see James M. Buchanan, "The Justice of Natural Liberty," *The Journal of Legal Studies*, V (January, 1976): 1–16.
2. My colleague, Roy Adams, first suggested this very apt analogy to me. Also: " . . . You can find in Keynes, as in Marx, almost anything . . ." F. A. Hayek, "No Escape: Unemployment Must Follow Inflation," in *Full Employment at Any Price?* (London: Institute of Economic Affairs, 1975), p. 43.
3. New York: Oxford University Press, 1968; hereafter, *Keynesian Economics*. Leijonhufvud's "Keynes and the Classics" (London: Institute of Economic Affairs, 1969) is also of importance here.
4. Leijonhufvud has argued that, contrary to contemporary practice, Keynes aggregated assets according to their term to maturity, and not according to whether they are real or financial. Cf. Leijonhufvud, *Keynesian Economics*, pp. 130–57.
5. Sir John Hicks has demonstrated the remarkable stability of the return on British consols in the nineteenth century. If the yield of consols can be taken as proxy for the long-rate, then his findings give some empirical basis to Keynes's hypothesis. See John R. Hicks, "The Yield on Consols," in *Critical Essays on Monetary Theory* (Oxford: The Clarendon Press, 1967), pp. 83–102.
6. It would be well to recall why speculators seek liquidity in this hypothetical situation; or, more precisely, why they attempt to shift their holdings from long-lived to short-lived assets. If long-rates are falling, but are expected to rise once again, then wealth-holders have a double incentive to sell long assets and purchase short assets. By selling at the long end of the yield spectrum, they can capture capital gains. By "going short" in the interim, they can purchase these assets back at lower prices and higher yields, once interest rates have risen again.

All this assumes, of course, that in the aggregate, transactors seek to avoid capital uncertainty. On this point, cf. Leijonhufvud, *Keynesian Economics*, pp. 45–46; 282–314.

7. Cf. ibid., pp. 49–109.

8. See F. A. von Hayek, "Reflections on the Pure Theory of Money of Mr. J. M. Keynes, Part I," *Economica*, XI (August, 1931): 279.

9. Ibid.

10. J. M. Keynes, "The Pure Theory of Money. A Reply to Dr. Hayek," *Economica*, XI (November, 1931): 394–95. Of course, the question of whether the issues with which Keynes dealt could be treated without reference to capital theory was one of the chief points of dispute.

11. Joan Robinson, "What has become of the Keynesian Revolution?" in Milo Keynes (ed.), *Essays on John Maynard Keynes* (Cambridge: Cambridge University Press, 1975), p. 125; quoted in F. A. Hayek, "No Escape: Unemployment Must Follow Inflation," p. 43.

12. Leijonhufvud, *Keynesian Economics*, p. 43.

13. Cf. "Hayek and Keynes: A Retrospective Assessment," Iowa State University Department of Economics Staff Paper No. 20 (Ames, Iowa: Photocopy, 1975).

14. See Leland Yeager, "The Keynesian Diversion," *Western Economic Journal*, XI (June, 1973): 150–63.

It should be noted that what Clower and Leijonhufvud have done is to present an interpretation of Keynes that rationalizes his doubts concerning the strength of the spontaneous forces operating to maintain or restore full employment. This in no way indicates that these two authors share these doubts. Nonetheless, it is frequently assumed, without any firm basis, that because Leijonhufvud and Clower have attempted to explicate Keynes's views, they agree with them in their entirety!

15. Axel Leijonhufvud, "Effective Demand Failures," *Swedish Journal of Economics*, 75 (1973): 28. Leijonhufvud continues, noting that this issue "lies at the heart of two of the most prominent controversies in the field over the last decade: the Fiscalist vs. Monetarist controversy . . . and the controversy over the long-run stability of the Phillips-curve. The volume of writings on each of these continues to mount steadily with no clear-cut resolution in sight—in large measure because this central issue is not being effectively addressed."

16. Discussions about the energy problem are a prime example of this. They almost never even consider what spontaneous market forces might exist that would lead to the discovery of a new, coordinated solution to the allocation of energy resources. One very probable solution—perhaps the most probable if market forces were permitted

to operate unfettered—would involve the destruction of the international oil cartel, whose existence makes a reallocation of energy resources appear necessary. And it is not merely noneconomists who are guilty of ignoring these market forces.

On a more sophisticated level, modern welfare economics is virtually predicated on the absence of a spontaneous order in society, though part of the problem here is the static quality of welfare analysis.

On the general, 20th century reaction against the principle of spontaneous order, cf. Leijonhufvud, "Effective Demand Failures," 31–32. Though the principle of spontaneous order continues as a cornerstone of economics—particularly of microeconomics—this only shows the inconsistency of current micro and macro economics—a point Leijonhufvud develops at length. Ibid., 28–33.

17. The reader is referred to footnote 15 and the relevant portion of the text footnoted therein.

18. As but one example, see F. A. Hayek, *The Counter-Revolution of Science* (New York: The Free Press of Glencoe, 1955), pp. 25–35.

19. I adopt here James Buchanan's terminology to describe the Chicago School. Professor Lachmann has proposed the term "Neo-Ricardian" to refer to the distinct foibles of yet another school of theorists, the Cambridge (U.K.) School.

20. As one example of this Ricardian tendency, see the discussion of the general glut controversy in Thomas Sowell, *Classical Economics Reconsidered* (Princeton: Princeton University Press, 1974), pp. 46ff.

21. See Smith, pp. 35–36.

22. On this point, cf. James M. Buchanan, "Public Goods and Natural Liberty" (Blacksburg, Virginia: Photocopy, 1976), especially 3–10.

23. Thus, theorists disagree over whether Smith held a labor cost theory of value, an entrepreneurial cost theory, or merely a labor measure theory. Smith may also have been unwittingly articulating a factor-exhaustion theorem for the long run. Nor could he seemingly distinguish between quasi-historical observations about the role of labor in production and theoretical statements of labor's contribution. This latter difficulty reflects Smith's "speculative" or "theoretical" approach to history. On this, cf. A. Skinner, "Economics and History—The Scottish Enlightenment," *Scottish Journal of Political Economy* (February, 1965): 1–22.

24. An example of Ricardo's approach is his treatment of the effects of an increase in the money supply. On this, see Gerald P. O'Driscoll, Jr., *Economics as a Coordination Problem: The Contributions of Friedrich A. Hayek* (Kansas City: Sheed Andrews and McMeel, Inc., 1977), pp. 37–43.

Ricardo is also famous for his so-called "Equivalence Theorem" for taxation and public debt. But though this may be the most famous case of the Ricardian vice, it is the one case where Ricardo was *not* a Ricardian! See *The Works and Correspondence of David Ricardo*, Vol. I: *On the Principles of Political Economy and Taxation*, ed. by Piero Sraffa (Cambridge: Cambridge University Press, 1951), pp. 247–48; Ibid., Vol. VI: *Pamphlets and Papers, 1815–1823*, pp. 185–87; Sowell, pp. 67–68; and Gerald P. O'Driscoll, Jr., *The Ricardian Nonequivalence Theorem*, *Journal of Political Economy*, 85 (February, 1977): 207–10.

25. Ludwig M. Lachmann, "From Mises to Shackle: An Essay on Austrian Economics and the Kaleidic Society," *Journal of Economic Literature*, XIV (March, 1976): 55. Cf. Hayek, *The Counter-Revolution of Science*, pp. 29–30.

26. Cf. Hayek, "The Meaning of Competition," in *Individualism and Economic Order* (Chicago: University of Chicago Press, 1948), pp. 97–98.

27. An example of this dilemma is the role of money in a general equilibrium model. On this, see Hayek, *The Pure Theory of Capital* (Chicago: University of Chicago Press, 1941), p. 31. Also see Ludwig von Mises, *Human Action*, 3rd ed. (Chicago: Henry Regnery Co., 1966), pp. 416–19.

28. Cf. Sowell, pp. 58–59.

29. Cf. Israel M. Kirzner, *Competition and Entrepreneurship* (Chicago: University of Chicago Press, 1973), pp. 32–37.

30. Ignoring the factors that govern the emergence of a spontaneous order is in some sense more objectionable (from the viewpoint of one who accepts the principle) than denying its relevance. Failure to discuss the conditions under which a spontaneous order would emerge in an economic system prejudices the case against unhampered, decentralized decision-making. Thus, when obvious misallocations and "market failures" develop in an economy, suggestions that policy be directed toward *freer* markets will be met with incredulity.

In a letter to me (dated February 2, 1977), Professor Richard Wagner argued persuasively that in the *Principles* Marshall was more aware of these problems than those claiming to be influenced by him, especially if we look to the Marshall of the text rather than of the footnotes. I am inclined to agree with Professor Wagner.

On Walras's assumption that markets will clear so as to produce an overall order, cf. O'Driscoll, *Economics as a Coordination Problem*, pp. 18–19 and Note 16 on pp. 30–31.

31. The hostility of the Chicago School to the approach of the Austrian School is a fact. What calls for explanation is the reason, which involves far more than a "family" squabble. The divisions between the two schools antedate each in the history of economic thought.

For a recent example of the Chicago attitude toward the Austrian conception of economics, see the *Review of Competition and Entrepreneurship* by Benjamin Klein, *Journal of Political Economy*, 83 (December, 1975): 1305–09. For an earlier example of similar treatment, see the Review of *Capital and Its Structure* by Martin J. Bailey, *Journal of Political Economy*, LXV (June, 1957): 265–66.

32. For instance, see the discussion in Hayek, *Monetary Theory and the Trade Cycle*, translated by N. Kaldor and H. M. Croome (New York: Augustus M. Kelley, 1966), pp. 43–45.

In what follows, I will draw on my paper, "Friedrich Hayek and the Science of Choice," Iowa State University Staff Paper in Economics No. 24 (Ames, Iowa: Photocopy, 1975).

33. Cf. Friedrich A. Hayek, *The Pure Theory of Capital*, pp. 33–34.

34. "Of course, it is one thing to assert that monetary changes are the key to major movements in money income; it is quite a different thing to know in any detail what is the mechanism that links monetary change to economic change; how the influence of the one is transmitted to the other; what sectors of the economy will be affected first; what the time pattern of the impacts will be, and so on. We have great confidence in the first assertion. We have little confidence in our knowledge of the transmission mechanism, except in such broad and vague terms as to constitute little more than an impressionistic representation rather than an engineering blueprint." Milton Friedman and Anna J. Schwartz, "Money and Business Cycles," in Friedman, *The Optimum Quantity of Money* (Chicago: Aldine Publishing Co., 1969), p. 222.

Commenting on Ricardo's inattention to transitional periods, Schumpeter has remarked: ". . . In matters of monetary as of general theory, Ricardian teaching is a detour and . . . it slowed up the advance of analysis, which would have been much quicker and smoother had [Henry] Thornton's lead been followed—had Ricardo's force not prevailed over Thornton's insight." Joseph A. Schumpeter, *History of Economic Analysis* (New York: Oxford University Press, 1954), p. 704n.

35. Cf. Gerald P. O'Driscoll, Jr. and Sudha R. Shenoy, "Inflation, Recession and Stagflation," in Edwin G. Dolan, ed., *The Foundations of Modern Austrian Economics* (Kansas City: Sheed & Ward, 1976), pp. 190–93.

For recent statements of Friedman's position, see "A Theoretical Framework for Monetary Analysis," *Journal of Political Economy*, 78 (March/April, 1970): 193–238; and "A Monetary Theory of National Income," *Journal of Political Economy*, 79 (March/April, 1971): 323–37.

36. I am referring here to the problem of distributional, or Cantillon-effects, which have been so long ignored in monetary theory. This gap in monetary theory is not accidental, for most theories of money incorporate neutrality assumptions. If money is neutral, then

indeed there are no distribution effects. It is not remarkable, then, that monetary economists generally ignore the problem of distribution effects. What is remarkable is that the almost fantastic assumption of neutrality of money generally does not give economists pause. While it would be beyond the scope of this paper to demonstrate this proposition, it does seem that an economy in which money could be neutral is one in which there would be no demand for money. For, where else but in a world of correct expectations and perfect coordination would changes in the supply-demand relation of money be neutral in their effects?

The issue of the neutrality of money and distribution effects is considered in Friedrich A. Lutz, "On Neutral Money," in Erich Streissler, Gottfried Haberler, Friedrich A. Lutz and Fritz Machlup, *Roads to Freedom* (New York: Augustus M. Kelley, 1969), pp. 105–16.

37. Cf. O'Driscoll, *Economics as a Coordination Problem*, pp. 106–08.

38. I am quite aware that to some extent Friedman has dealt with the general institutional framework necessary for economic stability. And, indeed, I find his earlier work of more interest in this regard. I would point out that even in that he focused on price *levels*, and did not develop the problem of *coordination* at length. Cf. Milton Friedman, *A Program for Monetary Stability* (New York: Fordham University Press, 1960).

39. From the editorial introduction by Sudha R. Shenoy, ed., *A Tiger by the Tail* (London: Institute of Economic Affairs, 1972), p. 8.

40. The argument appearing in the beginning of this section was strongly influenced by a talk, "Adam Smith in Theory and Practice," delivered by Thomas Sowell in the Harry Girvetz Memorial Lecture Series at the University of California, Santa Barbara.

41. Adam Smith, *Theory of Moral Sentiments* (London: Henry G. Bohn, 1853), pp. 342–43.

42. Hayek, *The Morgan Guaranty Survey* (January, 1976): 4.

43. For one reason that might attract economists to this movement, see Hayek, *The Morgan Guaranty Survey*: 11.

44. See Wassily Leontief, "For a National Economic Planning Board," *The New York Times* (March 14, 1974): 37.

45. The modern Austrians have specifically emphasized this point. The work of Mises, Hayek, Lachmann and Kirzner are notable in this respect. For a recent example of a work written in the Austrian tradition that emphasizes the role of decentralized planning in a market economy, see Kirzner's *Competition and Entrepreneurship*.

46. This quotation appears in Chapter III of Hayek, *The Road to Serfdom* (Chicago: University of Chicago Press, 1944), pp. 35–36; it is cited in Hayek, *The Morgan Guaranty Survey* (January, 1976): 5–6.

The word "liberal" refers here, of course, to classical English liberalism, and not to twentieth century American liberalism.

47. Israel M. Kirzner, "Hayek, Knowledge and Market Processes," Paper Delivered at the Allied Social Science Association Meetings in Dallas, Texas (New York: Photocopy, 1975); especially 28–29.

48. Kirzner, "Hayek, Knowledge and Market Processes," p. 29.

49. Kirzner, "Hayek, Knowledge and Market Processes," p. 32.

50. Kirzner, "Hayek, Knowledge and Market Processes," p. 33.

51. L. M. Lachmann, "Reflections on Hayekian Capital Theory," Paper Delivered at the Allied Social Science Association Meetings in Dallas, Texas (New York: Photocopy, 1975): 13.

52. Lachmann, "Reflections. . . ," 8–9. Emphasis added. Also, cf. Lachmann, "From Mises to Shackle," 59–61.

53. Lachmann, "Reflections. . . ," 9. "The Future is unknowable, though not unimaginable. Future knowledge cannot be had now, but it can cast its shadow ahead. In each mind, however, the shadow assumes a different shape, hence the divergence of expectations. The formation of expectations is an act of our minds by means of which we try to catch a glimpse of the unknown. Each one of us catches a different glimpse." Lachmann, "From Mises to Shackle. . . ," 59.

54. In his most recent work, Lachmann notes that Mises, Hayek and Kirzner have emphasized the diffusion of knowledge in the market process. But he denies that the market can diffuse expectations in the same way. Cf. Lachmann, "From Mises to Shackle," 59. I believe the distinction between knowledge and expectations is a spurious one.

55. Cf. Kirzner, "Hayek, Knowledge and Market Processes," 30–31.

56. Lachmann, "From Mises to Shackle," 59.

57. Ibid., p. 61.

58. Cf. Hayek, "Economics and Knowledge," in *Individualism and Economic Order*, pp. 39–45.

59. It is true that one can find recent instances in which prominent economists imply "coordination" in the *ex post* sense. For instance, cf. Leijonhufvud, "Effective Demand Failures," 29. But there Leijonhufvud is dealing, *inter alia*, with the question of whether markets clear at all. But the general issue with which Lachmann is dealing is surely the problem of *ex ante* coordination. If not, one must ask "why all the fuss?" Generally it is not denied by non-Marxists that at least output markets clear.

60. Ludwig M. Lachmann, "On Austrian Capital Theory," in Dolan, ed., *The Foundations of Modern Austrian Economics*, p. 149.

61. " . . . Expectations of early change in the present situation may impede the process of adjustment, and even when this does not happen, the forces of adjustment themselves may be overtaken by other

forces." Lachmann, "On Austrian Capital Theory," pp. 149–50.

62. Lachmann, "From Mises to Shackle," 60; also see 58n of that article.

63. In any event, this is what I make of his public statements on the issue, made at various times. Also, note the last sentence of the first quotation appearing on p. 20. Lachmann juxtaposes "the forces of equilibrium" and "the forces of change." Lachmann, "From Mises to Shackle," 61.

Austrian Definitions of the Supply of Money

Murray N. Rothbard
Polytechnic Institute of New York

I. THE DEFINITION OF THE SUPPLY OF MONEY

The concept of the supply of money plays a vitally important role, in differing ways, in both the Austrian and the Chicago schools of economics. Yet, neither school has defined the concept in a full or satisfactory manner; as a result, we are never sure to which of the numerous alternative definitions of the money supply either school is referring.

The Chicago School definition is hopeless from the start. For, in a question-begging attempt to reach the conclusion that the money supply is the major determinant of national income, and to reach it by statistical rather than theoretical means, the Chicago School *defines* the money supply as that entity which correlates most closely with national income. This is one of the most flagrant examples of the Chicagoite desire to avoid essentialist concepts, and to "test" theory by statistical correlation; with the result that the supply of money is not really defined at all. Furthermore, the approach overlooks the fact that statistical correlation cannot establish causal connections; this can only be done by a genuine theory that works with definable and defined concepts.[1]

In Austrian economics, Ludwig von Mises set forth the essentials of the concept of the money supply in his *Theory of Money and*

143

Credit, but no Austrian has developed the concept since then, and unsettled questions remain (e.g., are savings deposits properly to be included in the money supply?).[2] And since the concept of the supply of money is vital both for the theory and for applied historical analysis of such consequences as inflation and business cycles, it becomes vitally important to try to settle these questions, and to demarcate the supply of money in the modern world. In *The Theory of Money and Credit*, Mises set down the correct guidelines: money is the general medium of exchange, the thing that all other goods and services are traded for, the final payment for such goods on the market.

In contemporary economics, definitions of the money supply range widely from cash + demand deposits (M_1) up to the inclusion of virtually all liquid assets (a stratospherically high M). No contemporary economist excludes demand deposits from his definition of money. But it is useful to consider exactly why this should be so. When Mises wrote *The Theory of Money and Credit* in 1912, the inclusion of demand deposits in the money supply was not yet a settled question in economic thought. Indeed, a controversy over the precise role of demand deposits had raged throughout the nineteenth century. And when Irving Fisher wrote his *Purchasing Power of Money* in 1913, he still felt it necessary to distinguish between M (the supply of standard cash) and M', the total of demand deposits.[3] Why then did Mises, the developer of the Austrian theory of money, argue for including demand deposits as part of the money supply "in the broader sense"? Because, as he pointed out, bank demand deposits were not *other* goods and services, other assets exchangeable for cash; they were, instead, redeemable for cash at par on demand. Since they were so redeemable, they functioned, not as a good or service exchanging for cash, but rather as a warehouse receipt for cash, redeemable on demand at par as in the case of any other warehouse. Demand deposits were therefore "money-substitutes" and functioned as equivalent to money in the market. Instead of exchanging cash for a good, the owner of a demand deposit and the seller of the good would both treat the deposit *as if* it were cash, a surrogate for money. Hence, receipt of the demand deposit was accepted by the seller as final payment for his product. And *so long as* demand deposits *are* accepted as equivalent to standard money, they will function as part of the money supply.

It is important to recognize that demand deposits are not automatically part of the money supply by virtue of their very existence; they continue as equivalent to money only so long as the subjective estimates of the sellers of goods on the market *think* that they are so equivalent and accept them as such in exchange. Let us hark back, for example, to the good old days before federal deposit insurance, when banks were liable to bank runs at any time. Suppose that the Jonesville Bank has outstanding demand deposits of $1 million; that million dollars is then its contribution to the aggregate money supply of the country. But suppose that suddenly the soundness of the Jonesville Bank is severely called into question; and Jonesville demand deposits are accepted only at a discount, or even not at all. In that case, as a run on the bank develops, its demand deposits no longer function as part of the money supply, certainly not at par. So that a bank's demand deposit only functions as part of the money supply so long as it is treated as an equivalent substitute for cash.[4]

It might well be objected that since, in the era of fractional reserve banking, demand deposits are not *really* redeemable at par on demand, that then only standard cash (whether gold or fiat paper, depending upon the standard) can be considered part of the money supply. This contrasts with 100 percent reserve banking, when demand deposits are *genuinely* redeemable in cash, and function as genuine, rather than pseudo, warehouse receipts to money. Such an objection would be plausible, but would overlook the Austrian emphasis on the central importance in the market of *subjective* estimates of importance and value. Deposits are not *in fact* all redeemable in cash in a system of fractional reserve banking; but so long as individuals on the market *think* that they are so redeemable, they continue to function as part of the money supply. Indeed, it is precisely the expansion of bank demand deposits beyond their reserves that accounts for the phenomena of inflation and business cycles. As

noted above, demand deposits must be included in the concept
of the money supply so long as the market *treats* them as equivalent; that is, so long as individuals *think* that they are redeemable
in cash. In the current era of federal deposit insurance, added to
the existence of a central bank that prints standard money and
functions as a lender of last resort, it is doubtful that this confidence in redeemability can ever be shaken.

All economists, of course, include standard money in their
concept of the money supply. The justification for including
demand deposits, as we have seen, is that people believe that
these deposits are redeemable in standard money on demand,
and therefore treat them as equivalent, accepting the payment of
demand deposits as a surrogate for the payment of cash. But if
demand deposits are to be included in the money supply for this
reason, then it follows that any other entities that follow the same
rules must also be included in the supply of money.

Let us consider the case of savings deposits. There are several
common arguments for *not* including savings deposits in the
money supply: (1) they are not redeemable on demand, the bank
being legally able to force the depositors to wait a certain amount
of time (usually 30 days) before paying cash; (2) they cannot be
used directly for payment. Checks can be drawn on demand
deposits, but savings deposits must first be redeemed in cash
upon presentation of a passbook; (3) demand deposits are
pyramided upon a base of total reserves as a multiple of reserves,
whereas savings deposits (at least in savings banks and savings
and loan associations) can only pyramid on a one-to-one basis on
top of demand deposits (since such deposits will rapidly "leak
out" of savings and into demand deposits).

Objection (1), however, fails from focusing on the legalities
rather than on the economic realities of the situation; in particular, the objection fails to focus on the *subjective* estimates of the
situation on the part of the depositors. In reality, the power to
enforce a thirty-day notice on savings depositors is never en-
forced; hence, the depositor invariably thinks of his savings
account as redeemable in cash on demand. Indeed, when, in the
1929 depression, banks tried to enforce this forgotten provision

in their savings deposits, bank runs promptly ensued.[5]

Objection (2) fails as well, when we consider that, even within the stock of standard money, some part of one's cash will be traded more actively or directly than others. Thus, suppose someone holds part of his supply of cash in his wallet, and another part buried under the floorboards. The cash in the wallet will be exchanged and turned over rapidly; the floorboard money might not be used for decades. But surely no one would deny that the person's floorboard hoard is just as much part of his money stock as the cash in his wallet. So that mere lack of activity of part of the money stock in no way negates its inclusion as part of his supply of money. Similarly, the fact that passbooks must be presented before a savings deposit can be used in exchange should not negate its inclusion in the money supply. As I have written elsewhere, suppose that for some cultural quirk—say widespread revulsion against the number "5"—no seller will accept a five-dollar bill in exchange, but only ones or tens. In order to use five-dollar bills, then, their owner would first have to go to a bank to exchange them for ones or tens, and *then* use those ones or tens in exchange. But surely, such a necessity would not mean that someone's stock of five-dollar bills was not part of his money supply.[6]

Neither is Objection (3) persuasive. For while it is true that demand deposits are a multiple pyramid on reserves, whereas savings bank deposits are only a one-to-one pyramid on demand deposits, this distinguishes the sources or volatility of different forms of money, but should not exclude savings deposits from the supply of money. For demand deposits, in turn, pyramid on top of cash, and yet, while each of these forms of money is generated quite differently, so long as they exist each forms part of the total supply of money in the country. The same should then be true of savings deposits, whether they be deposits in commercial or in savings banks.

A fourth objection, based on the third, holds that savings deposits should not be considered as part of the money supply because they are efficiently if indirectly controllable by the Federal Reserve through its control of commercial bank total re-

serves and reserve requirements for demand deposits. Such
control is indeed a fact, but the argument proves far too much;
for, after all, demand deposits are themselves and in turn indirectly but efficiently controllable by the Fed through its control
of total reserves and reserve requirements. In fact, control of
savings deposits is not nearly as efficient as of demand deposits;
if, for example, savings depositors would keep their money and
active payments in the savings banks, instead of invariably "leak-
ing" back to checking accounts, savings banks *would* be able to
pyramid new savings deposits on top of commercial bank demand deposits by a large multiple.[7]

Not only, then, should savings deposits be included as part of
the money supply, but our argument leads to the conclusion that
no valid distinction can be made between savings deposits in
commercial banks (included in M_2) and in savings banks or
savings and loan associations (also included in M_3).[8] Once savings
deposits are conceded to be part of the money supply, there is no
sound reason for balking at the inclusion of deposits of the latter
banks.

On the other hand, a *genuine* time deposit—a bank deposit that
would indeed only be redeemable at a certain point of time in the
future, would merit very different treatment. Such a time deposit, not being redeemable on demand, would instead be a
credit instrument rather than a form of warehouse receipt. It
would be the result of a credit transaction rather than a
warehouse claim on cash; it would therefore not function in the
market as a surrogate for cash.

Ludwig von Mises distinguished carefully between a *credit* and
a *claim* transaction: a credit transaction is an exchange of a
present good (e.g., money which can be used in exchange at any
present moment) for a future good (e.g., an IOU for money that
will only be available in the future). In this sense, a demand
deposit, while legally designated as credit, is actually a present
good—a warehouse claim to a present good that is similar to a
bailment transaction, in which the warehouse pledges to redeem
the ticket at any time on demand.

Thus, Mises wrote:

It is usual to reckon the acceptance of a deposit which can be drawn upon at any time by means of notes or cheques as a type of credit transaction and juristically this view is, of course, justified; but economically, the case is not one of a credit transaction. If *credit* in the economic sense means the exchange of a present good or a present service against a future good or a future service, then it is hardly possible to include the transactions in question under the conception of credit. A depositor of a sum of money who acquires in exchange for it a claim convertible into money at any time which will perform exactly the same service for him as the sum it refers to has exchanged no present good for a future good. The claim that he has acquired by his deposit is also a present good for him. The depositing of the money in no way means that he has renounced immediate disposal over the utility it commands.[9]

It might be, and has been, objected that credit instruments, such as bills of exchange or Treasury bills, can often be sold easily on credit markets—either by the rediscounting of bills or in selling old bonds on the bond market; and that therefore they should be considered as money. But many assets are "liquid," i.e., can easily be sold for money. Blue-chip stocks, for example, can be easily sold for money, yet no one would include such stocks as part of the money supply. The operative difference, then, is not whether an asset is liquid or not (since stocks are no more part of the money supply than, say, real estate) but whether the asset is redeemable at a fixed rate, at par, in money. Credit instruments, similarly to the case of shares of stock, are sold *for* money on the market at fluctuating rates. The current tendency of some economists to include assets as money purely because of their liquidity must be rejected; after all, in some cases, inventories of retail goods might be as liquid as stocks or bonds, and yet surely no one would list these inventories as part of the money supply. They are *other* goods sold for money on the market.[10]

One of the most noninflationary developments in recent American banking has been the emergence of *certificates of deposit* (CDs), which are genuine time and credit transactions. The purchaser of the CD, or at least the large-demonination CD, knows that he has loaned money to the bank which the bank is only bound to repay at a specific date in the future; hence, large-scale CDs are properly not included in the M_2 and M_3 definitions of the supply of money. The same might be said to be true of various programs of time deposits which savings banks and commercial banks have been developing in recent years: in which the depositor agrees to retain his money in the bank for a specified period of years in exchange for a higher interest return.

There are worrisome problems, however, that are attached to the latter programs, as well as to *small-denomination* CDs; for in these cases, the deposits *are* redeemable before the date of redemption at fixed rates, but at penalty discounts rather than at par. Let us assume a hypothetical time deposit, due in five years' time at $10,000, but redeemable at present at a penalty discount of $9,000. We have seen that such a time deposit should certainly not be included in the money supply in the amount of $10,000. But should it be included at the fixed though penalty rate of $9,000, or *not* be included at all? Unfortunately, there is no guidance on this problem in the Austrian literature. Our inclination is to include these instruments in the money supply at the penalty level (e.g., $9,000), since the operative distinction, in our view, is not so much the par redemption as the ever-ready possibility of redemption at some fixed rate. If this is true, then we must also include in the concept of the money supply federal savings bonds, which are redeemable at fixed, though penalty rates, until the date of official maturation.

Another entity which should be included in the total money supply on our definition is *cash surrender values* of life insurance policies; these values represent the investment rather than the insurance part of life insurance and are redeemable in cash (or rather in bank demand deposits) at any time on demand. (There are, of course, no possibilities of cash surrender in other forms of insurance, such as term life, fire, accident, or medical.) Statistically, cash surrender values may be gauged by the total of policy reserves less policy loans outstanding, since policies on which money has been borrowed from the insurance company by the policyholder are not subject to immediate withdrawal. Again, the objection that policyholders are reluctant to cash in their surrender values does not negate their inclusion in the supply of money; such reluctance simply means that this part of an individual's money stock is relatively inactive.[11]

One caveat on the inclusion of noncommercial bank deposits and other fixed liabilities into the money supply: just as the cash and other reserves of the commercial banks are not included in the money supply, since that would be double counting once demand deposits are included; in the same way, the demand deposits owned by these noncommercial bank creators of the money supply (savings banks, savings and loan companies, life insurance companies, etc.) should be deducted from the total demand deposits that are included in the supply of money. In short, if a commercial bank has demand deposit liabilities of $1 million, of which $100,000 are owned by a savings bank as a reserve for its outstanding savings deposits of $2 million, then the total money supply to be attributed to these two banks would be $2.9 million, deducting the savings bank reserve that is the base for its own liabilities.

One anomaly in American monetary statistics should also be cleared up: for a reason that remains obscure, demand deposits in commercial banks or in the Federal Reserve Banks owned by the Treasury are excluded from the total money supply. If, for example, the Treasury taxes citizens by $1 billion, and their demand deposits are shifted from public accounts to the Treasury account, the total supply of money is considered to have fallen by $1 billion, when what has really happened is that $1 billion worth of money has (temporarily) shifted from private to governmental hands. Clearly, Treasury deposits should be included in the national total of the money supply.

Thus, we propose that the money supply should be defined as all entities which are redeemable on demand in standard cash at a fixed rate, and that, in the United States at the present time, this criterion translates into:

M_a (a = Austrian) = total supply of cash-cash held in the banks + total demand deposits + total savings deposits in commercial and savings banks + total shares in savings and loan associations + time deposits and small CDs at current redemption rates +

total policy reserves of life insurance companies—policy loans outstanding—demand deposits owned by savings banks, saving and loan associations, and life insurance companies + savings bonds, at current rates of redemption.

M_a hews to the Austrian theory of money, and, in so doing, broadens the definition of the money supply far beyond the narrow M_1, and yet avoids the path of those who would broaden the definition to the virtual inclusion of all liquid assets, and who thus would obliterate the uniqueness of the money phenonemon as the final means of payment for all other goods and services.

II. *THE MONEY SUPPLY AND CREDIT EXPANSION TO BUSINESS*

In contrast to the Chicago School, the Austrian economist cannot rest content with arriving at the proper concept of the supply of money. For while the supply of money (M_a) is the vitally important supply side of the "money relation" (the supply of and demand for money) that determines the array of prices, and is therefore the relevant concept for analyzing price inflation, different parts of the money supply play very different roles in affecting the business cycle. For the Austrian theory of the trade cycle reveals that *only* the inflationary bank credit expansion that enters the market through new business loans (or through purchase of business bonds) generates the over-investment in higher-order capital goods that leads to the boom-bust cycle. Inflationary bank credit that enters the market through financing government deficits does *not* generate the business cycle; for, instead of causing overinvestment in higher-order capital goods, it simply reallocates resources from the private to the public sector, and also tends to drive up prices. Thus, Mises distinguished between "simple inflation," in which the banks create more deposits through purchase of government bonds, and genuine "credit expansion," which enters the business loan market and generates the business cycle. As Mises writes:

In dealing with the [business cycle] we assumed that the total amount of additional fiduciary media enters the market system via the loan market as advances to business. . . .

There are, however, instances in which the legal and technical methods of credit expansion are used for a procedure catallactically utterly different from genuine credit expansion. Political and institutional convenience sometimes makes it expedient for a government to take advantage of the facilities of banking as a substitute for issuing government fiat money. The treasury borrows from the bank, and the bank provides the funds needed by issuing additional banknotes or crediting the government on a deposit account. Legally the bank becomes the treasury's creditor. In fact the whole transaction amounts to fiat money inflation. The additional fiduciary media enter the market by way of the treasury as payment for various items of government expenditure. . . . They affect the loan market and the gross market rate of interest, apart from the emergence of a positive price premium, only if a part of them reaches the loan market at a time at which their effects upon commodity prices and wage rates have not yet been consummated.[12]

Mises did not deal with the relatively new post–World War II phenomenon of large-scale bank loans to consumers, but these too cannot be said to generate a business cycle. Inflationary bank loans to consumers will artificially deflect social resources to consumption rather than investment, as compared to the unhampered desires and preferences of the consumers. But they will *not* generate a boom-bust cycle, because they will not result in "over" investment, which must be liquidated in a recession. Not enough investments will be made, but at least there will be no flood of investments which will later have to be liquidated. Hence, the effects of diverting consumption investment proportions away from consumer time preferences will be asymmetrical, with the overinvestment–business cycle effects only resulting from inflationary bank loans to business. Indeed, the reason why bank financing of government deficits may be called simple rather than cyclical inflation is because government demands are "consumption" uses as decided by the preferences of the ruling government officials.

In addition to M_a, then, Austrian economists should be interested in *how much* of a new supply of bank money enters the market through new loans to business. We might call the portion of new M_a that is created in the course of business lending, M_b (standing for either business loans or business cycle). If, for example, a bank creates $1 million of deposits in a given time period, and $400,000 goes into consumer loans and government bonds, while $600,000 goes into business loans and investments, then M_b will have increased by $600,000 in that period.

In examining M_b on the American financial scene, we can ignore savings banks and savings and loan associations, whose assets are almost exclusively invested in residential mortgages. Savings bonds, of course, simply help finance government activity. We are left, then, with commercial banks (as well as life insurance investments). Commercial bank assets are comprised of reserves, government bonds, consumer loans, and business loans and investments (corporate bonds). Their liabilities consist of demand deposits, time deposits (omitting large CDs), large CDs, and capital. In trying to discover movements of M_b with any precision, we founder on the difficulty that it is impossible in practice to decide to what extent any increases of business loans and investments have been financed by an increase of deposits, thus increasing M_b, and how much they have been financed by increases of capital and large CDs. Looking at the problem another way, it is impossible to determine how much of an increase in deposits (increase in M_a) went to finance business loans and investments, and how much went into reserves or consumer loans. In trying to determine increases in M_b for any given period, then, it is impossible to be scientifically precise, and the economic historian must act as an "artist" rather than as an apodictic scientist. In practice, since bank capital is relatively small, as are bank investments in corporate bonds, the figure for commercial bank loans to business can provide a rough estimate of movements in M_b.

With the development of the concepts of M_a (total supply of money) and M_b (total new money supply going into business credit), we have attempted to give more precision to the Austrian theory of money, and to the theoretical as well as historical Austrian analysis of monetary and business cycle phenomena.

NOTES

1. In a critique of the Chicago approach, Leland Yeager writes: "But it would be awkward if the definition of money accordingly had to change from time to time and country to country. Furthermore, even if money defined to include certain near-moneys does correlate somewhat more closely with income than money narrowly defined, that fact does not necessarily impose the broad definition. Perhaps the amount of these near-moneys depends on the level of money-income and in turn on the amount of medium of exchange. . . . More generally, it is not obvious why the magnitude with which some other magnitude correlates most closely deserves overriding attention. . . . The number of bathers at a beach may correlate more closely with the number of cars parked there than with either the temperature or the price of admission, yet the former correlation may be less interesting or useful than either of the latter" (Leland B. Yeager, "Essential Properties of the Medium of Exchange," *Kyklos* [1968], reprinted in *Monetary Theory*, ed. R. W. Clower [London: Penguin Books, 1969], p. 38). Also see, Murray N. Rothbard, "The Austrian Theory of Money," in E. Dolan, ed., *The Foundations of Modern Austrian Economics* (Kansas City, Kansas: Sheed & Ward, 1976), pp. 179–82.

2. Ludwig von Mises, *The Theory of Money and Credit*, 3rd ed. (New Haven: Yale University Press, 1953).

3. Irving Fisher, *The Purchasing Power of Money* (New York: Macmillan, 1913).

4. Even now, in the golden days of federal deposit insurance, a demand deposit is not always equivalent to cash, as anyone who is told that it will take 15 banking days to clear a check from California to New York can attest.

5. On the equivalence of demand and savings deposits during the Great Depression, and on the bank runs resulting from attempts to enforce the 30-day wait for redemption, see Murray N. Rothbard, *America's Great Depression*, 3rd ed. (Kansas City, Kansas: Sheed & Ward, 1975), pp. 84, 316. Also see Lin Lin, "Are Time Deposits Money?" *American Economic Review* (March 1937), pp. 76–86.

6. Rothbard, "The Austrian Theory of Money," p. 181.

7. In the United States, the latter is beginning to be the case, as

savings banks are increasingly being allowed to issue checks on their savings deposits. If that became the rule, moreover, Objection (2) would then fall on this ground alone.

8. Regardless of the legal form, the "shares" of formal ownership in savings and loan associations are economically precisely equivalent to the new deposits in savings banks, an equivalence that is universally acknowledged by economists.

9. Mises, *Theory of Money and Credit*, p. 268.

10. For Mises' critique of the view that endorsed bills of exchange in early nineteenth-century Europe were really part of the money supply, see *ibid.*, pp. 284–86.

11. For hints on the possible inclusion of life insurance cash surrender values in the supply of money, see Gordon W. McKinley, "Effects of Federal Reserve Policy on Nonmonetary Financial Institutions," in Herbert V. Prochnow, ed., *The Federal Reserve System* (New York: Harper & Bros., 1960), p. 217n; and Arthur F. Burns, *Prosperity without Inflation* (Buffalo: Economica Books, 1958), p. 50.

12. Ludwig von Mises, *Human Action*, 3rd rev. ed. (Chicago: Henry Regnery, 1966), p. 570.

The Emergence of Interest in a Pure Exchange Economy: Notes on a Theorem Attributed to Ludwig von Mises

Laurence S. Moss
Babson College

1. Individuals faced with alternatives equally attractive in all respects except their position in time prefer proximate enjoyments to those more remote. According to Ludwig von Mises, this preference for earlier rather than later enjoyments is inherent in all acts of individual choice and is termed "time preference."[1] It has been claimed that Misesian time preference guarantees the emergence of a positive rate of interest in a pure exchange economy, that is, where there is no production and the economic future is known with certainty.[2] Furthermore, the interest rate that "invariably" emerges results entirely from the interaction of valuing minds and is therefore a subjective phenomenon, not being dependent on the technology of production or the productivity of capital. Interest is not a payment for a monopolized agent of production, nor does it reflect a particular distribution of the means of production that can be done away with by reorganizing the social order in a manner prescribed by Socialist visionaries.[3]

The claim that a positive rate of interest will emerge in a pure exchange economy seems fundamental to, and consistent with,

Mises' entire theoretical system. While in his early economic writings Mises embraced Eugen von Böhm-Bawerk's theory that the height of the interest rate is determined by the technological superiority of roundabout methods of production, his later writings repudiated the productivity theory of interest rate determination in favor of the pure time-preference theory advanced in the United States by Frank A. Fetter at the turn of this century.[4] As has been claimed by recent Austrian economists, Mises' adoption of the so-called pure time-preference concept indicates an abandonment of Böhm-Bawerkian theory and a return to the more thoroughgoing subjectivism characteristic of Carl Menger's thought.[5] In fact, a fundamental theoretical difference between Mises and Friedrich A. Hayek may well turn on the issue of the influence the material structure of the world exerts on the individual's personal valuation of goods now as opposed to goods later.[6] To the extent that the payment of interest is necessitated by the material conditions surrounding the production and distribution of commodities rather than by man's subjective estimate of future enjoyments, then to that extent the capitalist system (i.e., the market economy) seems less permanent and more dependent on a historical stage in the evolution of these material conditions. Thus, modern Austrian economists who view capitalism as the only social system compatible with the nature of man attach great importance to their interest theory and to the theorem I shall discuss in this paper.[7]

What I offer here is a model of a pure exchange economy with an analysis of the circumstances under which a positive market rate of interest will emerge. I shall show that much of the misunderstanding regarding Mises' interest theory has to do with the special meaning Mises attached to the term *time preference*. Still, when Mises' theorem is correctly stated and understood, it will be seen that the emergence of interest is not inevitable but depends in part on the existence of certain objective conditions that prevent the individual from "internally financing" an increase in present consumption even when he can afford to do so. And these objective conditions that make possible the emergence of interest are hardly the sort that can be eliminated by a reorganization of the social order along the lines advocated by antimarket reformers.

2. Consider an economy consisting of a number of individuals each facing a time horizon made up of n consumption periods. Also, assume that each individual is guaranteed an endowment of a single consumption good (apples) and knows how many units of this single consumption good will be made available to him at the beginning of each of the n consumption periods. We assume the individual is able to rank this particular time allocation among all other conceivable time allocations, and we write the individual's utility function as follows:

$$U_I^a = f\,(C_1^a, C_2^a, C_3^a, \ldots C_n^a) \qquad (1)$$

where U represents, for individual I, the utility level associated with the time pattern of consumption offered by his original endowment, and C represents the number of units of a consumption good available to the individual at the beginning of the ith period of consumption (where i ranges over the n periods).

It may be useful to think of a prisoner of war camp where each of the prisoners is told in advance how many apples he will be given at each of n successive dates in the future. Each individual is absolutely certain that he will obtain that number of apples on schedule as promised.[8] Now suppose that after this information is disclosed, each prisoner is given the option of transferring some of the apples promised in remoter consumption periods to periods more proximate. For example, an individual may request that an apple promised in period number 10 be supplied in period number 3. Also, if we assume that storage costs are zero, individuals can always move apples from earlier periods to later periods simply by holding them in the form of inventory.[9] In such a world each individual will redistribute his consumption stream over time so that he can achieve a preferred level of satisfaction over the whole planning period. Let us represent this preferred allocation as follows:

$$U_{I}^d = f\,(C_1^d, C_2^d, C_3^d, \ldots C_n^d), \qquad (2)$$

where U_I^d represents the *desired* level of satisfaction of individual I and C represents the *desired* number of apples to be consumed in the ith period. As should be clear from the description of the problem, the arithmetic sum of apples consumed over the entire planning horizon must be equal to the sum of apples promised in the original situation, that is,

$$\sum_{i=1}^{n} C_I^d = \sum_{i=1}^{n} C_I^a. \tag{3}$$

Stated another way, if we define net borrowing between any two periods as

$$C_I^d - C_I^a, \tag{4}$$

then the sum of net borrowing over the entire planning horizon must be zero, or

$$\sum_{i=1}^{n} [C_I^d - C_I^a] = 0. \tag{5}$$

3. It is clear that, if the individual chooses to increase his apple consumption in some periods, he must decrease it in other periods by an exact amount.[10] The utility maximizing allocation has the property that the marginal utility of apple consumption is roughly equal in each period, or the marginal rate of substitution between apples in any two periods is equal to unity and is the same for all individuals.[11] It may at first seem that the marginal utility of an apple scheduled to be received x periods in the future must be perceived as being of smaller intensity than it will actually turn out to be when that period of consumption is reached.[12] It may be realistic to assume this in actual life situations where individuals often fail to provide adequately for their old age, but in our model the assumption of perfect knowledge assures us that no such shortsighted valuation takes place. The individual is equipped with the power to project his feelings (or

value orderings) forward in time and anticipate quite accurately what his future requirements will be.

It is apparent that individuals starting out with identical apple endowments will not necessarily arrive at identical consumption plans. Economists such as Irving Fisher and more recently Gary Becker tried to say something more definite about the relationship between individual tastes and final consumption patterns. For this purpose they distinguished among positive, negative, and zero (or neutral) time preference.[13] An individual who possesses positive time preference will, when given an equal endowment of apples in two adjacent periods, trade more than one future apple for one present apple. On the other hand the individual who is willing to give up more than one present apple for a future apple when his endowment of apples is the same in the two adjacent periods is said to possess negative time preference (though we would not observe such a trade, as I shall argue below). Finally, an individual satisfied with an equal number of apples in each time period is said to display neutral or zero time preference. Since any one of these three situations is evidence for what Mises called "time preference," he must have meant by the term something different from what has become standard terminology among neoclassical economists.

In Mises' view an individual demonstrates time preference in any period simply by consuming some apples in that period rather than none at all. If (in terms of our n-period model) an individual reallocated his apple endowment so that he consumed nothing in the first $n-1$ periods and everything in the last period, we would have a situation close to what Mises described as the *absence* of time preference.[14] According to Mises, the very act of consuming during the planning period demonstrates (positive) time preference. In Mises' writings this concept might better be termed *time allocation* than *time preference*.

I do not wish to enter into a discussion of which definition of time preference is best for modern economics. I do wish to point out, however, that (1) the Misesian notion of time preference (that is, time allocation) does not make use of the notion of "choice at the margin," or at least it is obscure as to what and

where the notion of the margin might enter into such a definition;[15] and (2) when semantic considerations are put aside, there
is no fundamental issue separating Mises from the remainder of
the economics profession. A great deal of confusion has resulted
from Mises' frequent use of the expression *time preference* to
mean time allocation without indicating that his special use of the
term was different from that of those whom he credited with
originating the concept.[16]

4. We may now ask whether Mises was correct when he insisted
that time allocation gives rise to a market for claims to future
consumption (that is, a bond market) with a positive rate of
interest. Obviously, we would not observe a negative interest rate
in our model of a pure exchange economy where storage costs
are assumed to be zero. No one would trade a present apple for a
claim to *less than one* future apple when he could obtain a whole
future apple simply by storing the present apple until that later
date. If consumption goods could be transferred not only from
the present to the future but also from the future to the present,
no one would find it economical to trade a claim for more than
one unit of future consumption goods for a unit of present
goods when that same present good could be obtained more
cheaply by transferring goods back through time. In a world
with this type of symmetrical time transfer, an individual time
allocator would trade only with himself, and there would be no
economic incentive to create a market in which claims on future
goods are exchanged.

It is only when we drop the assumption that apples can be
transferred from the future to the present (though present
apples can still be held for future consumption) that a (bond)
market will merge in which claims to future apples are exchanged. Here individuals who want more than one future
apple for a present apple and are unable to acquire that apple
from their future endowment induce others by means of an
interest payment to give up some of their current stock of apples.
The actual market rate of interest will move to equate the supply
of, and demand for, goods. Furthermore, the equilibrium in-

terest rate can never fall below zero, because individuals can always hold present goods until a later period at zero cost.

The existence of an organized market in which claims to future consumption are traded now makes it possible for a single individual's total n-period consumption to be greater or less than his total aggregate apple endowment. Whether it will be greater or less depends, of course, on whether over the n periods he was a net interest payer or receiver. It remains true, however, that total apple consumption for the entire society must equal total apple endowment when both totals are summed over all individuals and all periods. That is,

$$\sum_{i=1}^{n} \sum_{j=1}^{k} (C_{ij}^{d} - C_{ij}^{a}) = 0, \qquad (6)$$

where all symbols are defined as before and j ranges over all k members of society. It is interesting to point out the major difference between a pure exchange economy and an economy with production and exchange: Production removes the constraint on societal consumption represented by equation (6). With production it is possible for all members of society simultaneously to reduce present consumption and have future consumption rise by an even greater amount. It was this phenomenon Böhm-Bawerk had in mind when he wrote of the productivity of roundabout methods of production.[17] It is not my purpose here to explore any further the interesting dynamics of the production economy.

5. In conclusion, we say that in a pure exchange economy a market will emerge in which claims to future consumer goods are sold at positive prices. If it were technologically possible to order up future goods ahead of time (and storage costs were zero), then no economizing individual would pay more than one unit of a present good for a claim to a future good. In such a world, there would be no economic incentive to create a bond market, and a zero rate of interest would prevail. It is only

because of the asymmetry in the time market, namely, that present goods can be costlessly transferred to the future but future goods cannot be conjured to the present, that we have every reason to expect the emergence of a market for claims to future goods along with a positive interest rate.

Thus, interest will emerge in a Socialist economy as it does in a market economy because time allocation proceeds in a world where the present gradually unfolds into the future rather than the other way around. Mises' attempt to present a purely subjective time preference (read "time allocation") theory of interest must at the very least admit the empirical or broadly technological assumption that the transfer of goods through time is indeed a one-way street.

NOTES

1. Ludwig von Mises, *Human Action: A Treatise on Economics* (Chicago: Henry Regnery Co., 1966), pp. 479–90; idem, "A Critique of Böhm-Bawerk's Reasoning in Support of His Time Preference Theory," in Percy L. Greaves, Jr., *Mises Made Easier: A Glossary for Ludwig von Mises' Human Action* (New York: Free Market Books, 1974), pp. 150–57.

2. See Israel M. Kirzner, "Ludwig von Mises and the Theory of Capital and Interest," in *The Economics of Ludwig von Mises: Toward a Critical Reappraisal*, ed. Laurence S. Moss (Kansas City: Sheed & Ward, 1976), pp. 61–65. Kirzner wrote, "Mises' views on capital and on interest may be conveniently summarized as follows . . . interest expresses the universal . . . phenomenon of time preference and will therefore inevitably emerge also in a pure exchange economy without production" (p. 53).

We are trying to explain what Mises called "originary interest," which is the market rate of interest less a premium for uncertainty (or risk) and less the anticipated rate of price inflation.

3. Mises, *Human Action*, pp. 458, 528, 532.

4. On Fetter's contribution, see the introduction to Frank A. Fetter, *Capital, Interest, and Rent: Essays in the Theory of Distribution*, ed. Murray N. Rothbard (Kansas City: Sheed Andrews and McMeel, 1977), pp. 1–24. On Mises' adoption and subsequent dissatis-

faction with Böhm-Bawerk's theory, see Ludwig von Mises, *The Theory of Money and Credit* (New Haven: Yale University Press, 1959), p. 24; Kirzner, "Mises and the Theory of Capital," p. 52; and Mises, "A Critique of Böhm-Bawerk's Reasoning in Support of His Time Preference Theory," in Percy L. Greaves, Jr., *Mises Made Easier* (New York: Free Market Book, 1974), pp. 150–57.

5. See Ludwig M. Lachmann, "On Austrian Capital Theory," in *The Foundations of Modern Austrian Economics*, ed. Edwin G. Dolan (Kansas City: Sheed & Ward, 1976), pp. 145–51.

6. Cf. Friedrich A. Hayek, "Time Preference and Productivity: A Reconsideration," *Economica* 12 (February 1945): 22–25.

7. Murray N. Rothbard, *Man, Economy, and State*, 2 vols. (New York: D. Van Nostrand, 1962), 1:350–56.

8. Cf. R. A. Radford, "The Economic Organization of a P.O.W. Camp," *Economica* 12 (November 1945): 189–201.

9. I am also assuming that the apples do not spoil and that there is no possibility of theft or accidental destruction.

10. There are no fraudulent traders in our model economy; accordingly, without production one cannot promise to pay more than one's assets will allow.

11. If the marginal utility of an apple in period m is significantly greater than the marginal utility in period n, then the individual would do better to reallocate his apples out of period-n consumption and into period-m consumption. By the familiar law of diminishing returns the marginal utility of apples in period m falls and rises in period n. This will continue so long as the marginal utilities in any two periods are larger than some value say ϕ, i.e.,

> When $(MU_m - MU_n) > \phi$ then apples are transferred from period n to period m.

The size of ϕ depends on the perceived opportunity costs of making such a transfer. This last value will differ among individuals. When ϕ is small and the same for all consumers, then reallocation will continue until

$$MU_m = MU_n.$$

Multiplying both sides of this equality by ΔA and dividing by MU_n yields,

$$MU_m/MU_n = \Delta A/\Delta A$$

Now the left-hand side is the marginal rate of substitution for any individual and the right-hand side the "terms of trade" between period *m* and *n* which is 1 by the assumptions of this model.

12. This is an important point. Böhm-Bawerk and other writers tried to explain interest by postulating a psychological tendency for individuals to systematically *undervalue* their future needs. Besides being bad psychology, in that it disregards at the very least the paranoid miser who does quite the opposite, such misvaluation is ruled out by my assumption of certainty about future conditions and needs. Cf. Mises, "A Critique of Böhm-Bawerk's Reasoning," pp. 150–55.

13. Irving Fisher, *The Theory of Interest as Determined by Impatience to Spend Income and Opportunity to Invest It* (New York: Macmillan Co., 1930), pp. 61–68; see also, for example, Gilbert R. Ghez and Gary S. Becker, *The Allocation of Time and Goods over the Life Cycle* (New York: National Bureau of Economic Research, 1975), pp. 8–14.

14. This is how I interpret the following passage by Mises in the context of an *n*-period model: "Whoever eats and consumes anything is making a choice between a satisfaction in the immediate future and one in the more distant future. If he were to decide differently, that is, if he were not to prefer the earlier to the later satisfaction, he would never be able to consume at all. He could not even eat and consume tomorrow, because when tomorrow became today, and the day after tomorrow became tomorrow, the decision to consume would still call for valuing an earlier satisfaction more than a later satisfaction. Otherwise, consumption would have to be delayed still further" (Mises, "A Critique of Böhm-Bawerk's Reasoning," p. 157).

15. See Roger W. Garrison, "Reflections on Misesian Time Preference" (paper presented at Seminar in Austrian Economics, University of Virginia, April 1975), pp. 4–5.

16. Mises, *Human Action,* p. 489; see also Garrison, "Reflections," pp. 9–13.

17. Eugen von Böhm-Bawerk, "Positive Theory of Capital," in *Capital and Interest*, trans. George D. Hunche and Hans F. Sennholz (South Holland, Ill.: Libertarian Press; 1959), pp. 10–12.

Austrian Macroeconomics: A Diagrammatical Exposition

Roger W. Garrison
University of Virginia

INTRODUCTION

The object of this paper is the development of a diagrammatic model representing the Austrian view of macroeconomic relationships. More explicitly, the model will be designed to faithfully reflect the macroeconomic relationships found in the writings of Mises,[1] Hayek,[2] and Rothbard.[3] At this stage in its development the model is little more than a skeletal outline. It is a framework that can facilitate a fuller discussion of the actual adjustment mechanisms—the processes by which the economy is moved toward an equilibrium position. Because of the brevity of such discussions in this paper, the model may appear to be unfaithful to the Austrian view in one respect: It focuses on aggregates rather than on processes. Hopefully, this unfaithfulness is only apparent. Although the model is constructed with aggregate quantities and deals with the relationships between these quantities, no attempt is made to "explain" one aggregate in terms of another. It is fully recognized that, ultimately, each aggregate must be explained or accounted for in terms of the

---

Graphics by Cheryl L. Mallory

individual choices and actions of market participants. It is in this sense that the model is consistent with the methodological individualism so characteristic of Austrian theory.

Before we begin the actual construction of the model, a preview of some of its primary characteristics may be in order. The purpose of the preview is twofold. Firstly, it will suggest that the model is in fact worth developing. Many of the following characteristics are desirable ones and give the Austrian model an edge over the more orthodox models. Secondly, it should help those readers uninitiated in Austrian macroeconomics to follow the development of the model more easily.

1. The capital stock in Austrian theory is made up of heterogeneous capital. The relationship between the various pieces of capital can be one of substitutability or complementarity. The individual pieces of capital (both fixed and circulating) are integrated into a "structure of production." (Although the nature of capital is obscured by simplifying assumptions in the first section of this paper, it is taken into account more fully in subsequent sections.)

2. The size of the capital stock is treated as a variable in the model. The usual assumption is that even though investment of some positive amount is realized each period, the stock of capital remains constant.[4] With the Austrian model this assumption is unnecessary. This has the important consequence of integrating macroeconomic theory, growth theory, and business cycle theory. Explanations of both growth and cyclical activity are based on the same macroeconomic model.

3. The Austrian model is not a full-employment model in the sense that it assumes full employment. The analysis does begin, however, with an economy that is fully employed: "[W]e have to start where general economic theory stops; that is to say at a condition of equilibrium when no unused resources exist. The existence of unused resources is itself a fact which needs explanation."[5] The model does in fact explain the abnormally high

levels of unemployment that accompany the contraction phase of the business cycle.

4. The Austrian model takes explicit account of the time element in the production process. It does not simply add "lags" as an afterthought to an otherwise timeless model. It accounts for the fact that production takes time and that more production takes more time.

5. Austrian macroeconomic theory is not a theory of real income determination. Ultimately, it is a theory of co-ordination[6]—of how the production process is co-ordinated with the tastes of individuals (their time and liquidity preferences), and how monetary disturbances affect this co-ordination. Because of its focus on the co-ordination problem, there is no *sharp* distinction between Austrian macroeconomics and Austrian microeconomics.

THE STRUCTURE OF PRODUCTION

One of the most distinctive features of Austrian macroeconomic theory is its use of the concept of a "structure of production."[7] This concept was formulated to give explicit recognition to the notion that capital (and the capital structure) has two dimensions. It has a value dimension which can be expressed in monetary terms, and it has a time dimension which is an expression of the time that elapses between the application of the "original means of production"[8] (labor and land) and the eventual emergence of the consumption goods associated with them. The development of the notion of two-dimensional capital has its roots, of course, in the writings of Jevons.[9] It can be traced from Jevons to Cassel[10] and Böhm-Bawerk[11] and then to Mises,[12] and from Mises to Hayek,[13] Rothbard,[14] and other contemporary Austrian theorists. This view of capital, then, is neither new nor is it strictly Austrian, yet the notion of two-dimensional capital is by no means readily accepted by capital theorists in general.

A third though not independent dimension of capital can be envisaged which represents a composite of the two dimensions described above. Again, Jevons was the first to synthesize this third dimension. He made the distinction between the "quantity of capital" and the "length of time during which it remains invested." He then devised the third dimension of capital by " . . . multiplying each portion of capital invested at any moment by the length of time for which it remains invested."[15] The compounding of interest was ignored for the sake of simplicity. The resulting composite dimension was shown to have the units of "dollar-years." (The units are Americanized here. Jevons, of course, used "pound-years.")[16]

Cassel followed thirty years later with a similar formulation: " . . . interest is paid in proportion to the capital lent and in proportion to the duration of the loan, i.e., in proportion to the *product* of value and time" (emphasis added).[17] Cassel's product and Jevons's composite dimension measure the same thing. They are indications of the extent to which capital is "tied-up" in the production process. No claim is made here that this product can be calculated directly, but if we can conceive of interest income and of the rate of interest, then we can conceive of this composite dimension of capital—the amount of "waiting" or postponement of consumption brought about by the payment of interest.

This composite dimension will be referred to as "aggregate production time"[18] or simply as "production time." For sure, there are problems in aggregating (even conceptually) the production time associated with different pieces of capital just as there are problems with all macroeconomic aggregates. Much ambiguity will be avoided, however, by using the concept of *aggregate* production time rather than *average* production time or *average* period of production. These latter concepts were used by both Jevons[19] and Böhm-Bawerk,[20] but were rejected by Mises,[21] Hayek,[22] and Rothbard.[23] Many of the problems of Böhm-Bawerk's capital theory had their roots in his use of the average period of production: Because the denominator of his average was the value dimension of the structure of production (value reckoned in labor units), and because changes in the numerator of his average are typically accompanied by changes in the denominator in the same direction, the direction of change in the average period of production is generally ambiguous. Further problems derive from Böhm-Bawerk's incautious generalizations about changes in the average period of production that were based on the analysis of an oversimplified model.

With a full awareness of the difficulties of working with aggregates in general and of working with aggregate production time in particular, the structure of production will be defined in terms of the value of the capital at each stage in the production process and the aggregate production time associated with the process. The difficulties encountered by Böhm-Bawerk will be avoided by relying on a somewhat less rigorous interpretation of "changes in aggregate production time," but discussion of this interpretation will be deferred to a later section of the paper. The actual modeling can begin with an examination of earlier treatments of the structure of production.

The first graphical representation of the structure of production in the Austrian literature is found in *Prices and Production* in the form of the famous Hayekian triangles.[24] Such a triangle has been reproduced in Figure 1. (The axes have been reversed for convenience of exposition.) Hayek envisaged a vertically integrated production process in which the " . . . original means of production are expended continuously during the whole process of production."[25] Again, "original means" refers to the non-produced (or non-reproducible) means of production, i.e., to labor and land. (In our discussion we will associate the original means with "laborers" and the produced means with "capitalists." The terms laborers and capitalists, of course, are used in a functional sense and do not refer to particular individuals.) The production process begins at point *T* in Figure 1 and proceeds leftward. At the conclusion of the process consumption goods with a dollar value of *OY* emerge. At point *T* no capital exists. At point *D*, one of the intermediate stages of production, there exists capital with a dollar value of *DD'*. This capital can be viewed as simply the unfinished consumption goods that will be valued at *OY* when the production process is completed.

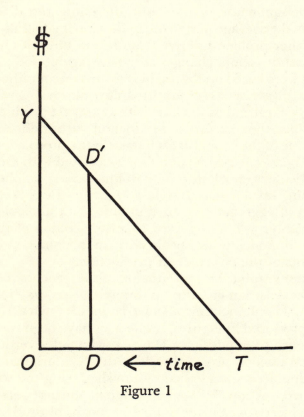

Figure 1

The Hayekian triangle has two mutually re-enforcing interpretations.[26] On the one hand, it can depict the flow of capital in real time from its inception at point *T* through the numerous stages of production until it emerges as consumption goods valued at *OY*. This is the interpretation adopted in the preceding paragraph. On the other hand, if the production process is in equilibrium, or to be more vivid, if it is in the state referred to by

Mises as the "evenly rotating economy,"[27] then the triangle represents all of the various stages of production that co-exist at each and every point in time. At any given point in time, for instance, consumption goods *OY* will be emerging from the production process, and at the same time the unfinished goods *DD'* will be in existence destined to emerge at a later date as consumption goods.

The dollar amount represented by *DD'* is less than that represented by *OY* for two reasons. Firstly, additional quantities of the original means (i.e., labor) are yet to be applied to the unfinished product that exists at point *D*. Secondly, *OY* and *DD'* represent consumption goods available at different points in time. If *OY* is available now, *DD'* will be available for consumption only at some future date. *DD'*, then, is discounted with respect to *OY*. To separate these two influences on the value of *DD'* with respect to *OY*, the model will be modified. Instead of conceiving, as Hayek did, of a process in which the original means of production are applied continuously, we will conceive of a production process in which the original means are applied only at the beginning of the process. The Hayekian triangle is abandoned in favor of a trapezoid. In Figure 2, the production process begins at point *T* with the application of labor services having a dollar value of *TF*. These original means grow in value as they pass through the numerous stages of production, finally emerging as consumption goods valued at *OY* dollars.

A second modification has been made in Figure 2. The horizontal axis now represents the aggregate production time (*APT*) associated with the structure of production. This allows the relaxation of the assumption that the structure is characterized by complete vertical integration. The slope of line *FY*, then, represents the rate of increase in value per unit of time per dollar invested at point *T*. That is, the slope of line *FY* is the (simple) rate of interest (profit) when the economy is in equilibrium.

Of course, this is a highly stylized representation of the actual structure of production. The development of the Austrian model, however, will be accompanied by discussions of the actual processes that take place in the real-world structure of produc-

tion. These discussions will recognize that capital and labor
services are applied in each of the stages of production. Changes
in the structure, for instance, will be couched in terms of labor

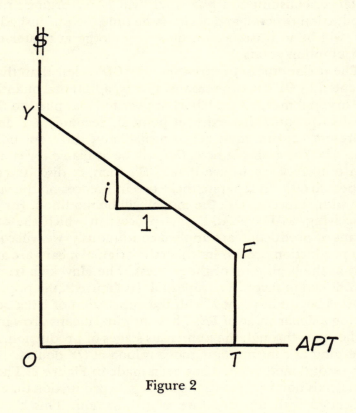

Figure 2

and capital being moved out of the stages relatively close to the
final (consumption) stage and into stages relatively remote from
the consumption stage (or *vice versa*) in response to (intertemporal) price changes and profit opportunities. This corresponds
to a lengthening (or shortening) of the structure. Changes in the
shape of the stylized representation of the structure of production will be an indication of the nature of the changes in the
real-world structure.

INTERTEMPORAL EXCHANGE

Intertemporal exchange is the exchange of present consumption goods for future consumption goods and *vice versa*. This type of market transaction is generally introduced by first allowing for pure consumption loans only. Investment loans are brought into view only after consumption loans have established some initial terms of trade in the intertemporal market. The Austrian model, though, will account for intertemporal exchange by initially abstracting from the pure consumption loan. This will allow us to focus on the type of intertemporal exchange that is inherent in the production process. The intertemporal market, then, can be thought of as dealing with direct purchases of investment goods as well as with loans made for the purpose of purchasing investment goods.

In the context of the present model intertemporal exchange can be accounted for in terms of the original means of production, i.e., in terms of the market for labor services. The labor services represent future consumption goods, which is to say that they can be converted into consumption goods only by allowing them to pass through the time-consuming production process. Laborers sell their services (future consumption goods) receiving in exchange dollars that can be used to purchase presently existing consumption goods. The sale of labor services, then, constitutes the demand for present goods (and the supply of future goods). Looking at the other side of the market for intertemporal exchange, the labor services are purchased by the capitalists. The capitalists exchange dollars for labor services and, *ipso facto*, register a demand for future goods. At the same time they constitute the supply of present goods. (Of course, this is an "excess" supply: At the end of the production process the capitalists own OY of consumption goods. They consume OY-TF and supply the remaining TF to the laborers.)

The supply and demand for present goods are represented diagrammatically in Figure 3. This market for intertemporal exchange is equilibrated by adjustments in the intertemporal price ratio—the rate of interest. The particular shape and positioning of these curves is determined by the individuals' (laborers' and capitalists') relative evaluations of present as opposed to future goods, i.e., by their time preferences. The *technical* aspects of transforming the labor services into consumption goods, as might be represented by a technical transformation function, are kept in the background here. The Austrian model focuses not on the technical considerations *per se* but rather on the alternative combinations of present and future goods that indi-

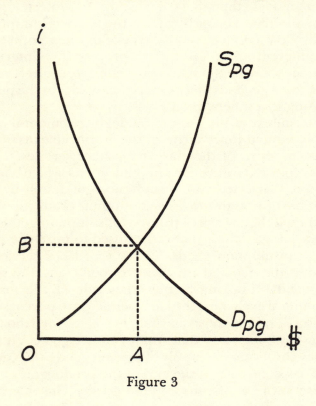

Figure 3

viduals perceive to be possible. Of course, when the economy is in equilibrium (the Misesian evenly rotating economy), individuals *know* what alternatives are possible so that the transformations that are perceived to be possible and the actual transformations are one and the same. When the economy is out of equilibrium, however, individuals will act on the basis of what they perceive the possibilities to be and not on the basis of what the possibilities actually are in some technological sense. This (fundamentally Austrian) distinction is an important one and will come into play in understanding the workings of the Austrian model under disequilibrium conditions.

Rothbard makes use of a diagram essentially identical to the one in Figure 3.[28] He points out that the intersection of the two curves determines the equilibrium rate of interest and the equilibrium amount of (gross) savings. (Net savings are zero.) Given the stylized structure of production of the present model, these (gross) savings manifest themselves as payments for labor services. When the economy is in equilibrium, the rate of interest is given by *OB*; the total payment for labor services by *OA*.

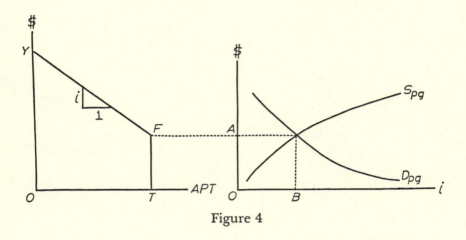

Figure 4

It should be noted at this point that *OA* in Figure 3 measures the same payment that is measured by *TF* in Figure 2. In recognition of this connection between the market for intertemporal exchange and the structure of production, Figure 3 can be inverted, rotated, and juxtaposed with Figure 2 to yield the summary diagram shown in Figure 4. There is a second connection between the two panels of Figure 4. The rate of interest is represented by *OB* in the right-hand panel and by the slope of the line *FY* in the left-hand panel. In equilibrium, of course, these two representations must reflect the same rate of interest.

It may be helpful at this point to show the relationship between this simple Austrian model and the corresponding Keynesian model. The point of commonality is the magnitude *OY* which represents the equilibrium dollar value of consumption goods. In the simple Keynesian model point *Y* is the intersection of the consumption function and the 45° reference line. *OY* is the distance from that intersection to the horizontal (or vertical) axis. Figure 5 shows the two models drawn on vertical planes perpendicular to one another and intersecting along *OY*. (This comparison may do some violence to the Keynesian model in that all magnitudes are expressed in dollar terms rather than real terms.)

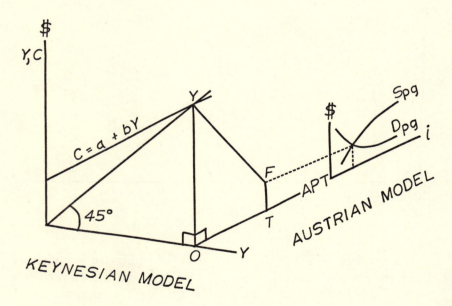

Figure 5

INVESTMENT

In order to deal with (net) investment an additional relationship must be introduced into the model, namely the relationship between the quantity of capital (dollar value) in the structure of production and the production time associated with it. ("Quantity of capital" here refers to *all* the capital in the structure of production. In Figure 2 it referred to the quantity that exists *at each stage* of the structure of production.) Although these two dimensions of the structure of production (quantity of capital and production time) are defined independently of one another, there is, according to Austrian theory, a relationship between them. Again, this relationship has its genesis in the writings of Jevons: "Capital simply allows us to expend labor in advance."[29] *More* capital, Jevons went on to show, allows us to expend labor *further* in advance.[30]

The positive relationship between capital and production time has suffered several set-backs during its development. Böhm-Bawerk, for instance, couched it in terms of the "average period of production," inadvertently causing the formulation to be ambiguous. But Mises and the contemporary Austrian theorists (e.g., Hayek and Rothbard) fully recognize the errors in Böhm-Bawerk's formulation.[31] They still accept, however, the basic notion that there is a positive relationship between the quantity of capital and the production time associated with it. Mises, for instance, argues that " . . . every increase in the supply of capital goods available results in a lengthening of the period of production, and of waiting time, . . ."[32] and conversely that " . . . [a]n increase in the quantity of capital goods available is a necessary condition for the adoption of processes in which the period of production and therefore waiting time are longer."[33] Similar statements can be found in Rothbard's formulation: "Any increase in capital goods can serve only to lengthen the structure, i.e., to enable the adoption of longer . . . processes."[34]

Hayek points out the difficulties of talking about "changes in the period of production" when the term refers to the actual aggregation of investment periods. He goes on, though, to say that

> ... since the use of the expression "changes in the length of the process" is a convenient way of describing the type of changes in the whole process where the changes in the investment periods are predominantly in one direction, there is probably something to be said for retaining it, provided that it is used cautiously. . . .[35]

With this somewhat less rigorous view "changes in production time" is more of a "shorthand" for the type of changes being made to the structure of production than a change in a genuine aggregate.

The relationship between the quantity of capital and production time has been called into question in recent years by the so-called "double-switching and capital-reversing debates."[36] The possibility of capital reversing (which involves an apparent violation of the Austrian relationship) has been the source of much controversy in Cambridge capital theory. Although there is good reason to believe that the problems created by double switching and capital reversing are confined to the Cambridge paradigm itself, the Austrian model will eventually have to be defended against the Cambridge charges. But this task will not be undertaken here. Rather, our concern with the problem will end with the observation that even those who think that capital reversing is possible consider it extremely unlikely: "[Capital reversing] could happen, but it looks like being on the edge of things that could happen."[37] (!)

The positive relationship between the quantity of capital (dollar value) and production time is introduced diagrammatically in the upper panel of Figure 6. The "wavy" shape of the curve is simply a way of indicating that no claims are made about the rate of change in the slope of the curve. The only significant feature of the curve is that its slope is positive. That the curve should begin at the origin seems obvious enough: There can be no production time if there is no capital. The origin, then, may represent the hand-to-mouth existence of a Robinson Crusoe,

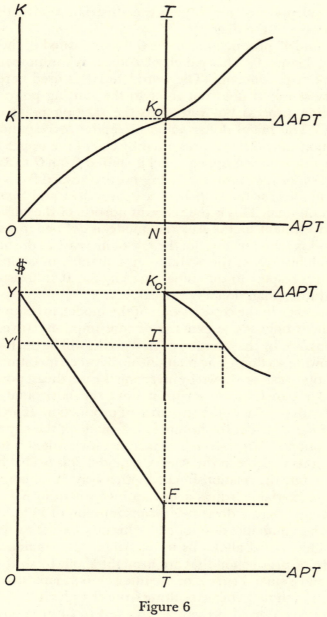

Figure 6

but for purposes of developing the Austrian model, this is a trivial aspect of the diagram.

The "initial" production time is OT as indicated in the lower panel of Figure 6. This panel, of course, is the now-familiar structure of production. (The word "initial" is used here in an arbitrary sense: It does not refer to the starting point of the production process but rather to the starting point of our analysis.) The initial dollar value of capital corresponding to production time OT is represented by OK in the upper panel.

If the origin in the upper panel is shifted from O to K_o, then the portion of the curve extending northeastward from K_o will represent the relationship between *investment* and *changes* in production time. This is the relevant portion of the curve. The term "investment" in the Austrian model is defined in a slightly unorthodox manner. It is not the *rate* of increase in the quantity of capital, but rather the addition of a quantity of capital measured with respect to the initial quantity K_o. It is measured in dollars rather than dollars per year.

At this stage in the construction of the model, investment can come about only at the expense of consumption. (Investment made possible by the creation of new credit will be dealt with in the following section.) The relationship between investment and consumption can be shown by inverting the northeast portion of the upper panel and lowering it until the horizontal axis is aligned with point Y of the structure of production. If an investment of K_oI is made, for instance, it is made at the expense of consumption YY'. In view of the fact that investment is to be an endogenous variable in the Austrian model, it is probably preferable to state the relationship in another way. If a change in an exogenous variable brings about an investment of K_oI, it, *ipso facto*, brings about a decrease in consumption of YY'.

The diagrammatics developed to this point are shown in Figure 7. This model allows us to determine the changes in the structure of production that are brought about by shifts in the supply and demand curves of the intertemporal market. These shifts can be thought of as resulting from changes in individuals' relative evaluation of present as opposed to future goods, i.e.,

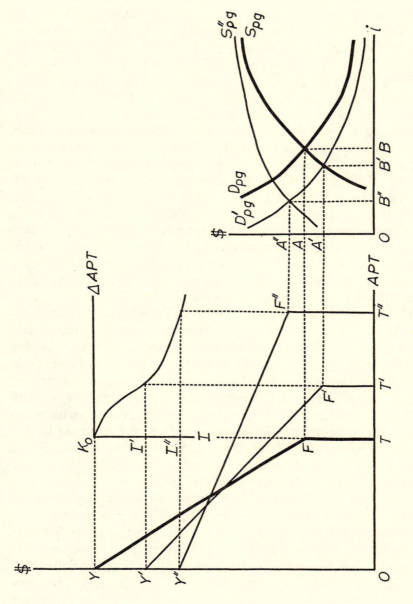

Figure 7

changes in their time preferences. A decrease in the time preferences of laborers, for example, can be represented by a shift in
the demand for present goods from D_{pg} to D'_{pg}, which intersects
the original supply-of-present-goods curve at coordinates OA'
and OB'. (To this point the magnitude OA has been taken to
represent both the amount paid for labor services and the dollar
value of present goods consumed by laborers. For this equality to
hold requires the tacit assumption that laborers are neither
increasing nor decreasing their cash holdings. However, if the
demand for present goods shifts without causing a corresponding shift in the supply of present goods (demand for future
goods), then there must be a change in the cash holdings of
laborers (from Walras's Law). That is, a shift in just one of the
two curves, D_{pg} and S_{pg}, must correspond to a change in both
time and liquidity preferences. OA, then, represents the dollar
value of present goods consumed by laborers—which equals the
amount paid to laborers minus the change in their cash holdings.
(For our immediate purposes, though, this change in cash holdings will be kept in the background.)

The diagrammatic representation of the structure of production is uniquely determined by the shift in the demand for
present goods. The amount of present goods advanced to laborers is now $T'F'$ ($=OA'$), and the new equilibrium rate of interest is
OB' ($<OB$), which is reflected as a less steep slope in the structure
of production diagram. (The slope of $F'Y'$ is less than the slope of
FY.) An investment of K_oI' is realized, which involves an increase
in production time of TT'. In other words, the decrease in the
time preferences (of laborers) has allowed resources that would
otherwise have been used for current consumption to be used
instead for investment purposes. The accompanying decrease in
the rate of interest has made it profitable to employ these resources in more time-consuming methods of production.

In the real-world structure of production the actual process
might be described as follows: Capitalists in their entrepreneurial roles sense that individuals are now willing to forgo consumption in the near future in order to achieve even greater consumption in the more distant future. This change in time preferences

creates profit opportunities that cause the capitalists to bid capital and labor services away from the stages of production relatively close to the final (consumption) stage and into stages relatively remote from the consumption stage. They are also induced by the lowering of the interest rate to create additional stages that had previously been unprofitable.[38]

Although the dollar expenditure on consumption goods decreases from OY to OY', consumption in real terms decreases only temporarily and then rises to a new high once the additional investment comes to fruition. It is this additional quantity of consumption goods coming into the market, of course, that allows the prices of consumption goods to be bid down to a level consistent with OY'.

The above description of changes in the structure of production brought about by a decrease in time preferences is very similar to the discussion found in *Prices and Production* of the change in the shape of a Hayekian triangle brought about by voluntary savings:

If we compare the two diagrams [representing the structure of production before and after the change in voluntary savings] we see at once that the nature of the change consists in a stretching [of the structure]. . . . Its [height at the final stage], which measures the amount of money spent during the period of time on consumers' goods, . . . has permanently decreased. . . . This means that the price of a unit of consumers' goods, the output of which has increased as a consequence of the more capitalistic methods of production, will fall. . . . The amount of money spent in each of the later stages of production has also decreased, while the amount used in the earlier stages has increased, and the total spent on intermediate products has increased also because of the addition of . . . new stage[s] of production.[39]

Although the price level and the real level of consumption are accounted for in the discussion of the workings of the Austrian model, they do not appear in the diagrammatical representation in any explicit form. Austrian macroeconomics has never been concerned directly with the general price *level*, but has been concerned instead with the *relative* price of consumption goods as opposed to investment goods—or, in terms of the present model, the *relative* amounts paid for consumption goods as opposed to labor services. This is a fundamental aspect of Austrian theory that sets it apart from the more orthodox macroeconomic theory. Patinkin, for instance, lumps "consumer commodities" and "investment commodities" into a single aggregate and then tells us that " . . . [t]he prices of these two categories are assumed to change in the same proportion."[40] By disallowing relative price changes between these two categories of commodities, Patinkin puts the structure of production in a straitjacket. This throws the entire burden of moving the economy from one equilibrium position to another on the real cash balance effect.[41]

A shift in the supply of present goods from S_{pg} to S_{pg}'' could be the result of a decrease in the time preferences of capitalists. The effects of this shift on the structure of production can be analyzed in the same manner and with similar results. The new equilibrium (associated with D_{pg}' and S_{pg}'') is shown with double-prime notation. The only significant difference is that the amount of present goods consumed by laborers has increased when before it decreased. But this difference was to be expected: A decrease in the time preferences of *laborers* means that they are willing to consume *fewer* present goods now in order to enjoy greater (real) consumption later; a decrease in the time preferences of *capitalists* means that they are willing to advance *more* present goods to laborers now in order to enjoy more (real) consumption later.

A change in time preferences is not the only change in tastes that can cause a shift in the supply and demand for present goods, although it seems to be the one that the Austrian theorists are most concerned with. But shifts of the curves can also result from changes in the demand for money, e.g., from increases or decreases in liquidity preferences. (Hayek was aware in his early writings of the need to incorporate the analysis of liquidity preferences into Austrian macroeconomic theory.)[42] To accommodate the analysis of liquidity preferences the structure-of-production diagram must be interpreted so as to include cash balances. In other words, OY must include the quantity of cash balances "consumed." Where a change in time preferences (laborers' and capitalists') will cause both curves of the intertemporal market to shift either east or west, a change in liquidity preferences (laborers' and capitalists') will cause both curves to shift either north or south. A neutral change in liquidity preference would be one in which both curves shifted in such a way as to leave the rate of interest unchanged. The effects of a change in liquidity preferences can be analyzed in terms of the Austrian model of Figure 7, but the details will not be described here. It can be said, however, that the results of such an analysis, whether the change in liquidity preferences is neutral or non-neutral, confront us with no surprises.

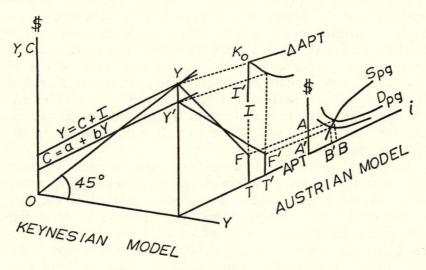

Figure 8

In concluding this section it may be helpful to follow up on the comparison of the Austrian model and the corresponding Keynesian model. The two models are shown in Figure 8 in the same format as was used in Figure 5. There are now two points of commonality. In addition to the common dollar value of consumption goods, the amount of (exogenous) investment in the Keynesian model corresponds in the Austrian model to the

amount of (endogenous) investment brought about by a shift in
the demand for present goods. Again, the problems created by
expressing the Keynesian model in dollar terms rather than real
terms are overlooked.

MONETARY DISTURBANCES

To this point it has been implicitly assumed that the economy
is free from monetary disturbances. Changes in the endogenous
variables were brought about only by actual changes in the
preferences of laborers and capitalists, by shifts in the supply
and demand for present goods reflecting changes in time (or
liquidity) preferences. In this section the supply of money will be
introduced as an exogenous variable in the Austrian model, and
its effects on the intertemporal market and the structure of
production will be analyzed. To facilitate this analysis the actual
time and liquidity preferences will be assumed to remain unchanged. The supply and demand for present goods as represented in Figure 3 will be fixed in place throughout the remaining discussion.

In analyzing the effects of monetary disturbances Austrian
macroeconomics is not concerned with increases in the quantity
of money *per se*, but rather with the process by which the new
money enters the economy. According to Hayek: "[E]verything
depends on the point where the additional money is injected into
circulation."[43] Thus, when Hayek begins his investigation of the
" . . . effects of a change in the amount of money in circulation
. . .", he immediately turns his attention to the " . . . case most
frequently encountered in practice: the case of an increase of
money in the form of credits granted to producers."[44] The
primary effect of a monetary expansion in the Austrian view
stems from the fact that newly created money (credit) tends to
fall disproportionately into the hands of producers.

By way of contrast the analysis of a monetary expansion in
orthodox macroeconomics is generally begun by assuming that
the new money is injected uniformly throughout the economy. A

familiar assumption, for instance, is that a helicopter dispenses the newly created money and that individuals dash out into the streets gathering up the new money in direct proportion to the amount they already had.[45] In this sort of highly artificial scenario it can easily be shown that money is neutral. No real magnitudes are changed—apart from a temporary increase in cash holdings that causes *all* prices to be bid up. The only consequence of an increase in the monetary stock, then, is an equi-proportional increase in the general price level. Consequences of a nonuniform injection of newly created money, that is, of the fact that some individuals receive a greater share of the new money than others, are categorized as "distribution effects." These effects are considered to be of second-order (or nth order) importance and are generally assumed away in order to get at the "more fundamental" aspects of an increase in the stock of money.[46]

But money in the Austrian view should not be assumed to be neutral and cannot be shown to be neutral in any relevant sense. "The notion of neutral money," according to Mises, is a contradiction in terms: "Money without a driving force of its own would not, as people assume, be a perfect money; it would not be money at all."[47] The relevant question, then, is not whether a monetary expansion is neutral or non-neutral, but rather how the non-neutrality manifests itself in a market economy. The Austrian theorists have focused their attention on this question and have been critical of other monetary theorists for ignoring it. Hayek, for instance, criticized them for focusing " . . . either exclusively or predominantly [on] the superficial phenomenon of changes in the value of money, while failing to pursue the far more profound and fundamental effects of the process by which money is introduced into the economic system, as distinct from its effects on prices in general."[48]

A "neutral" monetary expansion is represented diagrammatically in Figure 9. The vertical axis represents the nominal magnitude of the original stock of money (M_0), i.e., the stock in existence prior to the monetary expansion. The horizontal axis represents the nominal magnitude of the expanded stock of money (M_e), i.e., the stock in existence after the expansion has occurred. The 45° line, representing the equality $M_0 = M_e$, serves as a reference. A neutral expansion can be shown, then, by rotating a line clockwise from the reference line.

But if the expansion is achieved by extending newly created credit to producers, it is not a neutral expansion. In the terminology of the present model the newly created money falls disproportionately into the hands of capitalists (as opposed to laborers). This can be represented diagrammatically by showing separately the increase in the quantity of money in the hands of capitalists and the increase in the quantity of money in the hands of laborers. In Figure 10 it is assumed for the sake of simplicity that *all* of the newly created money takes the form of credit extended to capitalists. Initially, then, the laborers are completely unaffected by the monetary expansion. This is represented in Figure 10 by M'_L, which is coincident with the 45° reference line. Capitalists, on the other hand, experience an initially amplified monetary expansion as indicated by M'_c. But

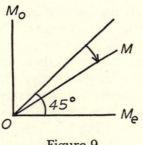

Figure 9

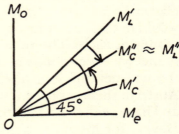

Figure 10

as the capitalists purchase additional quantities of labor services, the new money filters through the economy such that eventually the expansion experienced by the laborers is approximately the same as the expansion experienced by the capitalists. This is indicated by the expansion line $M''_c \approx M''_L$. The arrows indicate the dynamics of the expansion as it appears to the capitalists and to the laborers.

This non-neutral monetary expansion manifests itself as a

temporary distortion in the intertemporal market. In terms of the Austrian model the expansion experienced by the capitalists affects the supply-of-present-goods curve, while the expansion experienced by the laborers affects the demand-for-present-goods curve. These two asymmetrical effects can be traced out by the apparatus of Figure 11. The upper panels represent the

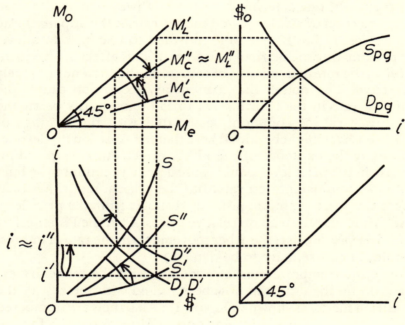

Figure 11

monetary expansion of Figure 10 and the intertemporal market of Figure 3. The southeast panel is a dummy diagram that facilitates the construction of the remaining panel. The southwest panel, then, shows the effect of the monetary expansion on the supply and demand for present goods. The supply curve, reflecting the behavior of capitalists, initially rotates clockwise from S to S^1, while the demand curve, reflecting the behavior of laborers, initially remains in place ($D = D^1$). Eventually, though, as the new money becomes more evenly distributed, the supply curve retracts to S'' and the demand curve rotates out to D''. These final positions of the two curves correspond to the expansion line labeled $M''_c \approx M''_L$ in the northwest panel.

Figure 11 illustrates that the rate of interest associated with the "real" parameters remains unchanged, i.e., that the supply and demand curves in the northeast panel remain in place throughout the monetary expansion, while the apparent rate of interest—the rate determined by the southwest panel—does not. The injection of newly created money causes the apparent rate of interest to fall from i to i' and then to rise back to a level approximating the original rate $(i'' \approx i)$. This effect of an expansion on the rate of interest is, of course, neither new nor uniquely Austrian. The notion that a monetary expansion causes the interest rate in the loan market to fall temporarily below the "natural" rate is commonly associated with the writings of Wicksell.[49] (It might be added here that the Austrian model does not deny the existence of the Fisher effect. An anticipated increase in the price level would cause a price premium to be built into the nominal interest rate. But the present model abstracts from this price premium just as it abstracts from the price level itself. It focuses instead on relative prices. That the Fisher effect could *completely* offset the other movements in the rate of interest would, of course, have to be denied.)

The intertemporal market, together with the monetary expansion mechanism, can now be reunited with the rest of the Austrian model as shown in Figure 12. All panels are numbered to facilitate the discussion. The only new one is panel VI which simply shows the monetary expansion independent of the process by which the newly created money is injected into the economy. This allows us to express the changes that occur in panels II and III in terms consistent with the original monetary stock, that is, it allows us to focus on relative rather than absolute changes.

The monetary expansion shown in Figure 12 is a neutral one—at least neutral with respect to capitalists and laborers—as indicated by the single expansion line in panel IV. As might be expected this neutral expansion has no effect on the structure of

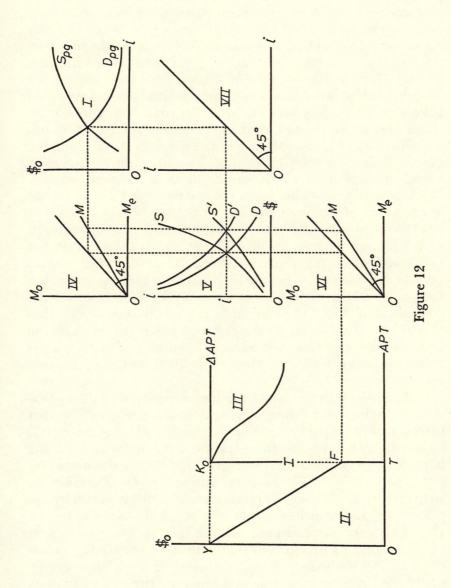

Figure 12

production (panel II). Such an "expansion" could be achieved by renaming the monetary unit: From this day on "one Dollar" will be known as "ten Burns." No real changes would result. The only consequence would be the fundamentally uninteresting one (not even shown in Figure 12) that the price level would increase tenfold. The expansion could be achieved instead by using the notorious monetary helicopter. There seems to be no reason to believe that the capitalists would gather up a disproportionate share of the new money. And so, as before, the primary consequence would be an increase in the price level reflecting the extent of the monetary expansion. Two differences, however, make this expansion a little less sterile than the previous one. Firstly, the price level increases not as a matter of definition but as the result of a market process. Prices are bid up to the new level as individuals attempt to draw down their newly acquired cash holdings.[50] Secondly, distribution effects *among* capitalists and *among* laborers are not ruled out. Thus, the consumption goods are valued at OY both before and after the expansion, but they are likely to be different consumption goods and to be consumed by different individuals as a result of these distribution effects. That this is the only change in panel II rests on the heroic assumption that the real-world structure of production is in fact suitable for producing these different consumption goods.

If the increase in the stock of money is achieved by the expansion of credit, there will be a systematic distribution effect that can be accounted for in the Austrian model. The expansion will be experienced first by the capitalists and only later by the laborers. This is illustrated in Figure 13. Unlike the monetary expansion of Figure 12, credit expansion has real effects on the structure of production. Diagrammatically, this is shown by the prime and double-prime notation in panel II. As the apparent rate of interest falls from i to i', the capitalists begin construction of a structure of production that is to have the configuration $OY'F'T'$. But as the newly created money becomes more evenly distributed among capitalists and laborers, the rate of interest rises to i'' ($\approx i$). The beginnings of the longer structure are then

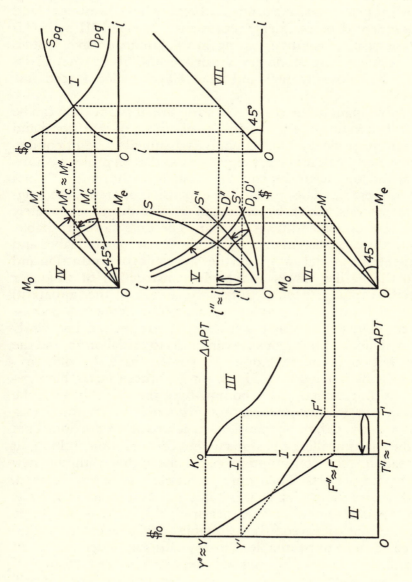

Figure 13

liquidated or abandoned in favor of the configuration $OY''F''T''$ which approximates the original structure. The investment (and subsequent dis-investment) represented in panel III by K_0I' is not the result of voluntary saving (and voluntary dissaving) but is the result of the monetary disturbance. This is what Mises termed malinvestment[51] and what Hayek called forced savings.[52]

The changes in the real-world structure of production can be described in terms of the relative profitability of short-term and long-term projects. The economy is assumed to be in equilibrium prior to the monetary expansion so that all projects (short-term and long-term) are equally profitable at the margin. When the interest rate falls, due to the expansion of credit, the long-term projects, which by definition involve disproportionately high interest expenditures, appear to become more profitable. Thus, the capitalists in their entrepreneurial roles bid labor and non-specific capital away from the later stages of production and into the earlier stages and begin construction of whatever specific capital is needed to take advantage of the (apparent) profitability of these long-term projects. But in the very process of constructing the new structure of production the newly created money flows from the capitalists to the laborers, and the distribution of money comes to approximate the old, pre-expansion, distribution. The laborers, whose tastes have remained unchanged, and who now have their full share of the new money, will bid for consumption goods in an amount consistent with the old, pre-expansion, structure of production. That is, they are unwilling to forgo current consumption and to wait instead for the consumption goods associated with the new long-term projects. Their time preferences have not changed. With their bidding for consumption goods the rate of interest rises back to somewhere near its original level. The long-term projects that appeared to be profitable during the expansion are revealed to be unprofitable. The capitalists must act now to cut their losses. The minimizing of losses may require that some of the new long-term projects be completed. Others, however, will have to be liquidated. The specific capital associated with them will have to be abandoned. The laborers and non-specific capital can eventually be reabsorbed in the reconstruction of the original structure of production. But the transition back to the old structure is bound to involve abnormally high levels of unemployed labor and capital.[53]

The two phases of the process that are initiated by a monetary expansion (the first phase corresponding to the prime notation; the second phase to the double-prime notation) should be recognized as the expansion and contraction phases of the business cycle. The above discussion and the diagrammatics of Figure 13 are faithful to Rothbard's capsulization of the cyclical boom and bust:

> The "boom" . . . is actually a period of wasteful misinvestment. It is the time when errors are made, due to the bank credit's tampering with the free market. The "crisis" arrives when the consumers come to reestablish their desired proportions. The "depression" is actually the process by which the economy adjusts to the wastes and errors of the boom, and reestablishes efficient service of consumer desires. The adjustment process consists in the . . . liquidation of wasteful investments. Some of these will be abandoned altogether . . .; others will be shifted to other uses . . . .
>
> In sum, the free market tends to satisfy voluntarily-expressed consumer desires with maximum efficiency, and this includes the public's relative desire for present and future consumption. The inflationary boom hobbles this efficiency, and distorts the structure of production, which no longer serves consumers properly. The crisis signals the end of the inflationary distortion, and the depression is the process by which the economy returns to the efficient service of consumers.[54]

And finally, it should be mentioned that to the extent that the malinvestment cannot be recovered there has been a net decrease in the economy's wealth. This can cause real changes in time and liquidity preferences (capitalists' and laborers') resulting in shifts in the supply and demand curves of panel I. To this extent a monetary expansion is not neutral even in the long run.

The Austrian model can be summarized in terms of the diagrammatics of Figure 13. Panels I, II, and III are the basic components of the model. Panel I describes the tastes that are relevant to the macroeconomic variables, i.e., the time and

liquidity preferences of capitalists and laborers. Panel II depicts
the structure of production that is consistent with the tastes
described in panel I. Changes in these tastes will cause the
structure of production to undergo a corresponding change
subject to the relationship between capital and production time
as indicated in panel III. The remaining panels deal with the
monetary linkages that translate the individuals' tastes into a
corresponding structure of production. In the absence of
monetary disturbances the structure of production can be expected to accurately reflect the tastes described in panel I. The
presence of a monetary disturbance, however, will prevent these
tastes from being accurately reflected in the structure of production. More specifically, an increase in the monetary stock by
means of credit expansion will mislead the capitalists into making an (ultimately unsuccessful) attempt to lengthen the structure of production.

FURTHER STUDY

Further development of the Austrian model outlined in this
paper could take any of several directions. The effects of various
institutional rigidities could be analyzed in terms of the model,
for instance, or the model could be modified to take explicit
account of expectations of one sort or another. Discussion will be
confined here, however, to one particular direction that appears
to be potentially fruitful. At the conclusions of earlier sections of
this paper the Austrian model was contrasted diagrammatically
with the Keynesian model, but no such contrast has been made
since the introduction of monetary considerations. The appropriate comparison, then, is one between Figure 13 and some
version of the *IS-LM* model. A few comments are in order about
how such a comparison might be made.

The key to the comparison of the two models is panel V of
Figure 13. The movements of the curves in this panel are sus-
piciously similar to the movements of the *IS* and *LM* curves. The
axes in panel V and in the *IS-LM* diagram measure the same or

similar magnitudes, and the conceptualization of the curves in the two models bears a certain resemblance.

In both models the vertical axis measures virtually the same magnitude: *IS-LM* is concerned with the interest rate in the loan market, while panel V measures the apparent rate of interest, which encompasses the loan rate. Where the *IS-LM* diagram measures (real) total income on the horizontal axis, panel V measures (nominal) income of laborers, that is, it excludes interest income. (It is not altogether clear, though, that interest income is actually included in the *IS-LM* diagram in that the Keynesian full-employment income *Y* is the income of *N* workers reckoned in "wage units.")

Further, in elementary formulations of the *IS-LM* model the *IS* curve is frequently conceptualized in a manner consistent with the conceptualization of the corresponding curve in panel V. Dernburg and McDougal, for instance, tell us that " . . . we may . . . interpret the *IS* schedule as the schedule of aggregate demand for goods and services with respect to the interest rate."[55] The rate of interest referred to is clearly the rate in the loan market. It is somewhat less clear, though, whether "goods and services" refers to present (consumption) goods or to all (consumption and investment) goods. If the former interpretation is adopted, the corresponding curves in the two models are very similar indeed. If the latter interpretation is adopted, the actual meaning of the conceptualization is called into question: If the *IS* curve is the demand for all goods, who are the suppliers of all goods, and what are they receiving in exchange for the quantity supplied? (!) The less-elementary macroeconomics texts do not clear up the problem. They usually avoid it by abstaining from any attempt to conceptualize the *IS-LM* curves. They are viewed instead as simply an outgrowth of the graphics that describe the real and monetary sectors of the economy. In a prelude to his discussion of the *IS-LM* diagram Ackley tells us that "[w]e must now throw all these elements into a single pot, stir well, and taste the resulting stew."[56]

Viewing the supply and demand curves of panel V as *LM* and *IS*, respectively, a number of familiar movements of the curves

can be described. A (non-neutral) increase in liquidity preferences, for instance, can shift the *LM* curve up and to the left,
causing the interest rate to rise; or a (non-neutral) increase in the
willingness to save (decrease in time preference) can shift the *IS*
curve down and to the left, causing the interest to fall. Changes
in taste will cause real and lasting changes in the *IS* and *LM*
curves, but changes in the nominal stock of money will not. A
monetary expansion will shift the *LM* curve to the right, driving
the rate of interest down, but the monetary stimulation will only
have a temporary effect because the real sector will soon adjust to
the larger monetary stock. The *IS* curve will also shift rightward,
returning the rate of interest to its original level. A change in the
nominal monetary stock does not cause a real and lasting change
in the rate of interest.

This is not to say that the Austrian model and the *IS-LM* model
yield the same or similar conclusions or have the same or similar
implications. Quite to the contrary. Equilibrium conditions cannot be defined in terms of panel V of the Austrian model. This
panel shows the movements of the apparent rate of interest and
of the nominal income to laborers during the period that the
economy is experiencing a monetary disturbance. Equilibrium
must be defined in terms of panels I and II, i.e., in terms of the
relevant tastes (time and liquidity preferences) and the structure
of production corresponding to those tastes. It cannot be defined in terms of *IS-LM* stew. Panel V does open the door,
however, to a thorough comparison of the two models and their
implications.

NOTES

1. Ludwig von Mises, *Human Action: A Treatise on Economics*, 3rd
revised ed. (Chicago: Henry Regnery Co., 1966), pp. 538–86. Also see
Mises, *The Theory of Money and Credit*, trans. by H. E. Batson (New
Haven: Yale University Press, 1953), pp. 339–66. And Mises, "Money,
Inflation and the Trade Cycle: Three Theoretical Studies," trans. by
Bettina Bien Greaves, ed. by Percy T. Greaves Jr. (Unpublished pa-
pers, 1923, 1928, and 1931).

2. Friedrich A. von Hayek, *Prices and Production* (New York: Augustus M. Kelley, 1967). Also see Hayek, *Monetary Theory and the Trade*

Cycle, trans. by N. Kaldor and H. M. Croome (New York: Augustus M. Kelley, 1966).

3. Murray N. Rothbard, *Man, Economy, and State: A Treatise on Economics*, 2 vols. (Los Angeles: Nash Publishing Co., 1970), pp. 273–501, 850–81. Also see Rothbard, *America's Great Depression* (Los Angeles: Nash Publishing Co., 1972), pp. 11–38.

4. See, for instance, Don Patinkin, *Money, Interest, and Prices*, 2nd ed. (New York: Harper and Row, Inc., 1965), p. 200.

5. Hayek, *Prices and Production*, p. 34.

6. Gerald P. O'Driscoll, Jr., *Economics as a Coordination Problem: The Contributions of Friedrich A. Hayek* (Kansas City: Sheed Andrews and McMeel, Inc., 1977).

7. Hayek, *Prices and Production*, p. 38.

8. *Ibid.*, p. 36.

9. W. Stanley Jevons, *The Theory of Political Economy*, ed. by R. D. Collison Black (Middlesex: Penguin Books, Inc., 1970), pp. 225–53.

10. Gustav Cassel, *The Nature and Necessity of Interest* (London: MacMillan and Co., Ltd., 1903), pp. 96–157.

11. Eugen von Böhm-Bawerk, *Capital and Interest*, trans. by George D. Huncke and Hans F. Sennholz, 3 vols. (South Holland, Ill.: Libertarian Press, 1959), vol. 2., pp. 10–15 and *passim*.

12. Mises, *Human Action*, pp. 493–503 and *passim*.

13. Hayek, *Prices and Production*, pp. 36–68. Also, see Hayek, *The Price Theory of Capital* (Chicago: University of Chicago Press, 1941), pp. 193–201 and *passim*.

14. Rothbard, *Man, Economy, and State*, pp. 486–92 and *passim*.

15. Jevons, *Theory of Political Economy*, pp. 229–30.

16. *Ibid.*, p. 230.

17. Cassel, *Nature and Necessity of Interest*, p. 54.

18. Rothbard refers to this concept using the term "aggregate production structure." Rothbard, *Man, Economy, and State*, p. 491.

19. Jevons, *Theory of Political Economy*, p. 231.

20. Böhm-Bawerk, *Capital and Interest*, p. 312ff.

21. Mises, *Human Action*, pp. 488–89.

22. Hayek, *Pure Theory of Capital*, p. 140ff. Hayek rejected the notion of aggregate as well as average production time except as the term might be used in a very loose sense. See *Ibid.*, p. 70.

23. Rothbard, *Man, Economy, and State*, p. 412.

24. Hayek, *Prices and Production*, p. 39.

25. *Ibid.*, p. 40.

26. Hayek, *Pure Theory of Capital*, p. 113ff.

27. Mises, *Human Action*, p. 244ff.

28. Rothbard, *Man, Economy, and State*, p. 332.

29. Jevons, *Theory of Political Economy*, p. 227.

30. *Ibid.*, p. 229.

31. See footnotes 20 through 23.

32. Mises, *Human Action*, p. 495.

33. *Ibid.*

34. Rothbard, *Man, Economy, and State*, p. 487.

35. Hayek, *Pure Theory of Capital*, p. 70.

36. G. C. Harcourt and N. F. Laing, eds., *Capital and Growth* (Middlesex: Penguin Books Ltd., 1971), p. 211. Also see G. C. Harcourt, *Some Cambridge Controversies in the Theory of Capital* (Cambridge, England: The Cambridge University Press, 1972), pp. 118–76.

37. John R. Hicks, *Capital and Time* (Oxford: The Clarendon Press, 1973), p. 44.

38. Hayek, *Prices and Production*, pp. 49–54.

39. *Ibid.*, p. 53. Also see Rothbard, *Man, Economy, and State*, pp. 470–79 where similar diagrammatics are used to depict changes in the structure of production brought about by changes in time preferences.

40. Patinkin, *Money, Interest, and Prices*, p. 205.

41. *Ibid.*, pp. 17–21 and *passim*.

42. Friedrich A. von Hayek, *Profits, Interest and Investment* (London: George Routledge and Sons, Ltd., 1939), p. 177.

43. Hayek, *Prices and Production*, p. 11. Hayek reaffirmed this position in his Nobel lecture. See Hayek, *Full Employment at Any Price?* (London: Institute for Economic Affairs, 1975), pp. 23ff. and 37.

44. Hayek, *Prices and Production*, p. 54. See also Mises, *Human Action*, p. 556 and Rothbard, *Man, Economy, and State*, p. 885.

45. Milton Friedman, *The Optimum Quantity of Money and Other Essays* (Chicago: Aldine Publishing Co., 1969), p. 4ff.

46. Patinkin, *Money, Interest, and Prices*, p. 200 and *passim*.

47. Mises, *Human Action*, p. 418.

48. Hayek, *Monetary Theory and the Trade Cycle*, p. 46.

49. It should be pointed out, however, that the Wicksellian "natural" rate is the rate corresponding to a constant price level, while the Austrian "natural" rate is the rate corresponding to the absence of money creation via credit expansion. See Hayek, *Monetary Theory and the Trade Cycle*, pp. 109–16. Also see Rothbard, *Man, Economy, and State*, p. 940.

50. This is the market process that captures Patinkin's attention. Patinkin, *Money, Interest, and Prices*, pp. 236–44.

51. Mises, *Human Action*, pp. 559–61.

52. Hayek, *Prices and Production*, pp. 18–31, and Hayek, *Profits, Interest and Investment*, pp. 183–97.

53. Hayek accounts for this unsuccessful attempt to lengthen the structure of production in terms of the Ricardo effect. See Hayek, *Profits, Interest and Investment*, pp. 8–15. Also see Hayek, "The Ricardo

Effect," *Economica*, IX, No. 34 (new ser.; May 1942): pp. 127–52 reprinted in Hayek, *Individualism and Economic Order* (Chicago: Henry Regnery Co., 1972) pp. 220–54, and Hayek, "Three Elucidations of the Ricardo Effect," *Journal of Political Economy*, 77 (March/April 1969): pp. 274–85.

54. Rothbard, *America's Great Depression*, p. 19. Also see Lionel Robbins, *The Great Depression* (London: The MacMillan Co., Ltd., 1934), pp. 30–54.

55. Thomas F. Dernburg and Duncan M. McDougal, *Macroeconomics* (New York: McGraw-Hill Book Co., 1968), p. 161.

56. Gardner Ackley, *Macroeconomic Theory* (Toronto: The Macmillan Co., 1969), p. 347.

BIBLIOGRAPHY

Ackley, Gardner. *Macroeconomic Theory*. Toronto: The MacMillan Co., 1969.

Böhm-Bawerk, Eugen von. *Capital and Interest*. Translated by George D. Huncke and Hans F. Sennholz. 3 vols. South Holland, Ill.: Libertarian Press, 1959.

Cassel, Gustav. *The Nature and Necessity of Interest*. London: MacMillan and Co., Ltd., 1903.

Dernburg, Thomas F. and McDougal, Duncan M. *Macroeconomics*. New York: McGraw-Hill Book Co., 1968.

Friedman, Milton. *The Optimum Quantity of Money and Other Essays*. Chicago: Aldine Publishing Co., 1969.

Harcourt, G. C. and Laing, N. F., editors. *Capital and Growth*. Middlesex: Penguin Books Ltd., 1971.

Harcourt, G. C. *Some Cambridge Controversies in the Theory of Capital*. Cambridge, England: The Cambridge University Press, 1972.

Hayek, Friedrich A. von. *Full Employment at Any Price?* London: Institute of Economic Affairs, 1975.

Hayek, Friedrich A. von. *Monetary Theory and the Trade Cycle*. Translated by N. Kaldor and H. M. Croome. New York: Augustus M. Kelley, 1966. (First published in 1933.)

Hayek, Friedrich A. von. *Prices and Production*. New York: Augustus M. Kelley, 1967. (First published in 1935.)

Hayek, Friedrich A. von. *Profits, Interest and Investment*. London: George Routledge and Sons, Ltd., 1939.

Hayek, Friedrich A. von. *The Price Theory of Capital*. Chicago: University of Chicago Press, 1941.

Hayek, Friedrich A. von. "The Ricardo Effect," *Economica*, IX, No. 34

(new ser.; May, 1942) 127–52 reprinted in *Individualism and Economic Order*. Chicago: Henry Regnery Co., 1972.

Hayek, Friedrich A. von. "Three Elucidations of the Ricardo Effect," *Journal of Political Economy*, 77 (March/April, 1969): 274–85.

Hicks, John R. *Capital and Time*. The Clarendon Press, 1973.

Jevons, W. Stanley. *The Theory of Political Economy*. Edited by R.D. Collison Black. Middlesex: Penguin Books, Inc., 1970.

Mises, Ludwig von. *Human Action: A Treatise on Economics*, 3rd rev. ed. Chicago: Henry Regnery Co., 1966.

Mises, Ludwig von. "Money, Inflation, and the Trade Cycle: Three Theoretical Studies." Translated by Bettina Bien Greaves, edited by Percy L. Greaves, Jr., unpublished papers, 1923, 1928, and 1931.

Mises, Ludwig von. *The Theory of Money and Credit*. Translated by H. E. Batson. New Haven: Yale University Press, 1953. (First published in 1911.)

O'Driscoll, Gerald P., Jr. *Economics as a Coordination Problem: The Contributions of Friedrich A. Hayek*. Kansas City: Sheed Andrews and McMeel, Inc., 1977.

Patinkin, Don. *Money, Interest, and Prices*. 2nd ed. New York: Harper and Row, Inc., 1965.

Robbins, Lionel. *The Great Depression*. London: The MacMillan Co., Ltd., 1934.

Rothbard, Murray N. *America's Great Depression*. Los Angeles: Nash Publishing Co., 1972. (First published in 1963.)

Rothbard, Murray N. *Man, Economy, and State: A Treatise on Economic Principles*. 2 vols. Los Angeles: Nash Publishing Co., 1970. (First published in 1962.)

Toward a Program of Research and Development for Austrian Economics

Louis M. Spadaro

Fordham University

I.

Now that Austrian economics has entered its second century, it is both natural and useful—as the subject of the present conference implies—to look to the future and to try to discern, as far as is possible, the most promising directions along which our discipline might develop further. Of course, the anniversary customarily also invites review and evaluation of past experience; it is, in fact, as the result of some reflection on the latter that I venture to make the single underlying suggestion which will be seen to be the point of the present paper.

While the centenary we are celebrating will be thought by many to be that of the start of the "marginalist revolution," the fact is that the truly seminal insight was not the marginal analysis—valuable as that analytical device admittedly was, and continues to be—but, rather, the strangely belated recognition of the subjective nature of economic value and even of human action in general. It is the special merit of Austrian economics that, while it shares the concept of the margin with its simultaneous[1] co-discoverers elsewhere, its distinctive and characteristic contribution has been its insistence on the explanatory power of subjectivism.

For one thing, unlike either of the other branches of marginalism, the Austrians put forward a complete *alternative* to the cost-of-production concept of economic value which permeated classical analysis (and also its derivatives, including Marxism) and not just the second half of a dualistic explanation.

Moreover, it was precisely this role of subjectivism that caused the early, and subsequently widening, divergences in both theory and policy among the "marginalisms." The failure on the part of the non-Austrian marginalists to perceive the full explanatory power of the subjective theory of value is, I believe, what led them—each in its own way—away from economic reality and into an increasingly vacuous formalism. On the one hand, English marginalism, perhaps because it was unable to turn its back on its own Classical heritage, chose to supplement rather than supplant it. The result was a "neo-classical synthesis"[2] of supply and demand—best illustrated by the Marshallian "scissors" and progressively refined by an almost obsessive preoccupation with the geometry of intersections, which continues unabated—in class and textbook—to the present time.

The French marginalists, on the other hand, misled by both the pretensions of the Enlightenment and their own mathematical prowess—and also lacking the corrective force of a fully subjectivist view—were led to conceive of the economic process as a general equilibrium system (expressible by the algebra of simultaneous equations)—grander, more inclusive (and, alas, more illusory) than the "partial" equilibrium of the English economists. Both have spawned a numerous progeny who have labored mightily, if single-mindedly, in exploring the theoretical and policy implications of their respective paradigms; and though their results have shown more elegance than usefulness, they have given only cursory—and often contemptuous—attention to the Austrian tradition.

Austrians, on the contrary, have spent an inordinately large part of their talents and resources in efforts to deal with the errors of others, including some frivolous and some highly repetitive ones, and correspondingly less on the development and extension of their special insight. It is to this misallocation of our resources that my central suggestion is addressed, as we shall presently see.

Before proceeding, let me hasten to say that there is, of course, no denying the fact that individual Austrian economists have continued to make contributions of great power, clarity, and depth—and this is increasingly recognized outside their own membership. But those of us who are a little older must, I think, also be sadder to realize how much of the efforts of so many of our people—never a numerous company—has gone into encounters with an endless series of egregious errors, and to speculate on what might have been accomplished had all this investment been directed, instead, to refining and extending our own analysis.

For, we have allowed ourselves, time and again, to become embroiled in time-consuming and largely inconclusive controversies: with Marxism, macroeconomics, mathematical economics, and monetary medicine men—just to name an alliterative few. And the end is nowhere in sight, since most of these exhibit the sort of imperviousness that led the scholastic philosophers to coin the term "invincible error."

Out of many, let us consider briefly two examples, which not only illustrate this resource misallocation, but also serve as reference points later on in our discussion.[3] The first concerns the important Austrian insight that a centrally directed economy cannot, of itself, provide the data necessary for effective decision-making (*i.e.*, consistent with the preferences of consumers). Immediately after Mises had called attention to this defect, socialists and other interventionists trained their heaviest analytical artillery on the idea. There ensued a very long and involuted discussion of "shadow-pricing" and other devices, including not a few mathematical models, which would allegedly enable the ministry of production in a socialist economy to allocate resources efficiently.

It is fair to say, I believe, that all the strenuous rebuttals failed to blunt the force of the original criticism of *dirigiste* planning, though they may have served to obfuscate it somewhat in the minds of the faithful and of the unwary. But the debate engaged a good deal of time and effort by the then relatively few, highly competent advocates of the market system—time and effort which doubtless would have been better spent on refining and extending their own analysis.[4] In short, instead of trying to show the inadequacies of every surrogate for calculation that the advocates of central planning saw fit to come up with, our people might have been better advised to stop after one or two of them and devote the time saved to exploring the agencies, channels, and forms through which a market system conveys and utilizes information—and thus how it *does* calculate. There is reason to believe that if this had been done successfully, some of our present tasks (*e.g.*, the "rehabilitation" of the entrepreneur as an active, motive force) could have advanced earlier and further.

The second instance is the latest—most certainly not the last—resurgence of the advocacy of national economic planning, one of those imperishable errors we mentioned a little earlier. Although Hayek and others had long ago carefully and definitively shown that the real issue is not planning versus chaos, but rather who is to plan and for whom, the current proposal seems to be proceeding as if the earlier corrective work had never been done at all. Already, Hayek has found it necessary to write in reply,[5] repeating the distinction, though with a shade less of the "politeness to a fault" noted by Schumpeter and characteristic of this civilized man.

Though it is undoubtedly presumptuous, one cannot resist expressing the hope that no further time be taken from other, more deserving tasks, in order to beat this recycled dead horse. I feel certain that Professor Hayek would be forgiven—even applauded by many—if he decided to limit himself, on this question, to sending to two senators and to a select group of academicians and others simply a card inscribed with the French saying: "On ne dit pas la Messe deux fois pour les sourds," together with an order blank for *The Road to Serfdom*.

If there is a lesson in all this, it is that we ought to scale down very sharply the extent to which our future efforts—and especially those of our best young people—are devoted to the refutation of any and every fallacy which others choose to propose. Instead, increased investment should be made in efforts to work out further the implications of subjectivism—the distinctively Austrian contribution—and to increase its impact on contemporary thought and action. It will be the task of much of the rest of the present paper to show that a good deal of this work is still to be done.

There is, then, much more than a simple anniversary occasion to counsel the value of pursuing our own analysis. Furthermore, political and economic developments during the last decade have created a climate in which subjectivist analysis can expect—temporarily, at least—to get a wider and fairer hearing than before. Though one is tempted to think otherwise, the present temper, and opportunity, may be attributable more to the manifest failure of policies based on non-Austrian economic reasoning than to any sudden persuasiveness of our own. In any event, the increasing number of talented young scholars attracted to the Austrian approach deserve, and probably prefer, a more challenging and productive objective than putting out small and recurrent brush fires.

By now, the central suggestion of this paper—that we concentrate our resources on perfecting and extending subjectivism—hardly needs to be stated explicitly. But its implementation is very far from being obvious. Along what lines is further research in Austrian economics needed? In which of these is there more urgency? Are any of these most effectively pursued by enlisting participation and contribution from specialists or practitioners in other disciplines or activities? Answers to such questions probably can emerge only from a continuing, frank, and critical discussion of points of obscurity, difficulty, or controversy among Austrian economists. The present conference promises to give significant initial impetus in this direction.

The contribution of this paper, if any, is the modest one of setting out a few of the possibilities—as a tentative frame of reference—and thus getting the discussion under way. It is expected that some (or all) of these will be rejected and that others will be proposed. These possible "new directions" will be listed and discussed very briefly under two headings: The next section will offer a small sampling of theoretical (*i.e.*, analytical, methodological) questions. The final section presents an even smaller sample of interaction between Austrian economics and operations-oriented and other "outside" fields. These two types are treated separately largely for convenience and clarity; it will be obvious that they are ultimately interdependent and mutually reinforcing.

II.

As new implications of subjectivism unfold, the conceptual-analytical-methodological framework of Austrian theory may require extensions, and even revisions, for purposes of consistency and coordination. While the bulk of such changes will almost certainly be made by Austrian economists themselves, others may properly come from people not now considered to be Austrian economists—or even economists at all.

Inasmuch as attempts at discovery are mere gropings, and therefore always run high risk of failure, it is perhaps worth pausing to reflect that—even when they fail—explorations may have useful residue in the form of fresh insights, or in other ways. In the present case, it is highly probable that such efforts will produce—at the very least—a deeper understanding on the part of more people as to just what human action is (and, especially, what it is not).

1. The most obvious and urgent areas needing our attention are those which are causing some disagreement among competent Austrians themselves or those in which theorists, individually or in consensus, feel there is a need for additional analytical support. Since each of us is doubtless aware of a number of such problem areas, a single illustration will suffice.

Some time ago, notice began to be taken of the fact that standard economic analysis tended to make, of the entrepreneurial function, something bloodless—rigid, automatic, and unreal. The present writer, for instance, found it necessary to deplore the fact while received theory had gradually relieved everyone else from the despicable role of "economic man," the technical requirements of its own equilibrium paradigm led to imposing precisely this role on the entrepreneur.[6]

Since then, in one of the more exciting recent developments of Austrian analysis—notably in work done by Kirzner[7]—the function of the enterpriser in a market system is being reformulated and refined in a manner that is both more realistic and more consistent with individual freedom of choice than ever before.

The present case is also useful in demonstrating how, typically, answering one question raises others that need to be dealt with next. There is some difference of opinion as to whether—given uncertainty—this new, much more active concept of entrepreneurship is stabilizing or not. This question, which will be seen as an aspect of the more general problem of convergence[8] in a free market system, has already begun to be discussed among a group of Austrian economists from the New York metropolitan area who now meet regularly.

Once the specification of the new entrepreneurial concept has been completed, and its implications worked out, there will still remain the task of getting non-Austrian theorists to take it into account. This will, of course, be difficult; resistance will be all the greater because, as we noted earlier, the new formulation removes an important element in the neatness and automaticity of their models. But any success at all in this direction may ultimately lead to wider recognition of the power and potential of a free market to operate without outside direction.

Accumulating evidence of the failure of recent interventions may, in any event, make others a bit more receptive. Samuelson, for example, in a recent piece[9] devoted to Adam Smith on the occasion of the bicentennial of the *Wealth of Nations*, after quoting two of its best-known passages (one on the self-interest of " ... butcher, the brewer. ... "; the other the passage mentioning the "invisible hand"), says, in conclusion:

To know the truth—and the limitations!—of these passages is the *ultima Thule* of economic wisdom.

There is reason to hope that our efforts, together with the force of events, may eventually persuade him to reduce the qualification.

2. Admittedly, the class of further explorations in subjectivist theory just illustrated have a legitimate first claim in any systematic reallocation of our resources. Beyond these, however, there is another group of needs, whose immediacy is less apparent, but whose ultimate contributions to subjective economic theory might prove to be of considerable importance. As a group, these are indirect—theoretic goods of "higher order," so to speak—and involve inputs from a wide variety of disciplines different from, but often bordering on, economic theory itself. Let us consider, briefly, a small sample of these possibilities.

(a) Statistical inference, in the form it eventually took and as currently understood and applied, is fundamentally incongruent with subjectivity and therefore of little, if any, use in the treatment of most of the phenomena with which Austrian economics is concerned. The conceptual (even the axiomatic) basis of contemporary statistical theory—and, derivatively, of all of its calculations—is admittedly that of "objective" probability (*i.e.*, the observed, or observable, frequency of independent and random events). It is therefore really inapplicable to any phenomena that are unique, or interactive, or subjective—and inapplicable *a fortiori* to those that are all three, as is the case with human action, in the sense understood by Austrian analysis. Instead of refraining from such phenomena, objectively derived statistical analysis and inference are applied to them widely—at a very high cost in both realism and validity—on the (largely implicit) assumption that such events are somehow amenable to the same "law of large numbers" applicable to independent, random events.

To this writer's knowledge, there has been virtually no systematic effort to develop alternative inferential systems more consistent with the inescapable subjectivity of human events, despite the fact that the clear inadequacy of received statistical theory in this connection has been recognized for some time.[10] It is the more puzzling in that the possibility and feasibility—if not the primacy—of subjective probability were discussed very early[11] in the development of statistical thought and have continued to be mentioned.[12]

Despite these and other insights concerning the essentially subjective element in probability statements,[13] the almost irresistible urge to assign cardinal numbers to degrees of belief has led to the arbitrary restatement (and distortion) of subjective probability in objective terms—to the consequent neglect of the need to search for a viable alternative. What is currently referred to as "subjective probability" is thus nothing more than the usual objective probability analysis broken down into segments: an antecedent (or "prior") probability and a consequent ("posterior") one[14]—a process for which subjective is a manifest misnomer; it is more properly designated as "conditional" or "sequential" probability.

Even here, the crucial problem—and the subject of continuing controversy—is the assignment of some weight to the antecedent (prior) probability segment in the many instances where occurrences are too few to justify reliance on the law of large numbers, which underlies the usual statistical apparatus. The facile device for skirting this difficulty—that of arbitrarily assigning equal probabilities to such events—is disputed, as one might easily guess. Some alternative approaches,[15] involving the concept of learning by experience, should be of some interest to subjective theorists in a number of respects, including information theory (to be mentioned briefly below) and the analysis of entrepreneurial decision-making.

(b) The advocacy of a free-market system (as clearly superior to one run by central direction) relies, to an important degree, on the assertion that decentralized (*i.e.*, individual) decisions are made on the basis of much more realistic and accurate information available at the source of human decisions: individual valuations and preferences. But in any complex economy, these elemental (*e.g.*, consumer) choices trigger long sequences of derivative decisions by producers and by suppliers of attendant services (*e.g.*, financial, distributive, etc.) at every level and stage of production. The capability of the market process to transmit highly reliable information along networks of such bewildering complexity—and to do so without undue distortion or loss of information—is impressive and a standing rebuke to the aspirations of central planners. That the process works is evident; but precisely *how* is only dimly and intuitively understood, though the importance of information in the economic process is recognized.[16] More detailed understanding of its operation (*e.g.*, the location and role of linkages, the localization [decentralization] of decision-making through subnetworks of information flow, etc.) could help substantially in validating and extending our theories—and might even cause some rethinking by interventionists.

It happens that—in connection with problems different from, but ultimately not unrelated to, economics—the technical analysis of information processing has made significant strides in the last quarter century.[17] The results of studies in "communications theory" (or "information theory") have proven value in the communications industry and in business management in general. And it is not unlikely that this field may have contributions to make to market theory. For one thing, it may help us understand and explain in a much more precise way how the transmission of information facilitates the convergence of the plans and decisions of large numbers of independent individuals and firms. For another, the basic concepts of this analysis—*e.g.*, the minimum amount of information (a binary unit or "bit") needed to distinguish between two alternatives (binary choice)—might prove to be as suggestive for the development of new approaches to subjective-choice analysis as they were in the early design of electronic computers.[18]

Again, it seems unfortunate that no serious attempt has been made to invite the attention—and contribution—of these specialists in the explication of the market system. Although these are primarily engineers, there is reason to believe that more than a few of them would respond to the challenge of adapting portions of their analysis to the needs of economic theory. At the very least, some dialogue with them would not leave the field open for advocates of a contrary economic philosophy to bend communication theory to their purposes.[19]

(c) One aspect of the above—the concept of entropy— deserves brief, separate mention for at least two reasons. The first is related to the special (technical) use made of this concept in communication theory. "Entropy" in this adaptation is very different from the concept of entropy as employed in physics (though possibly ultimately reducible to it). Here, the term is used to mean a measure of the amount of information that a theory provides and is understood to vary directly with the degree of freedom of choice (or "uncertainty") on the part of recipients of information[20]—again, there may be interesting insights and implications here for subjective theory.

The second point is that entropy in its more general sense (*i.e.*, the one more directly consistent with its traditional use in physics) seems to offer a viable alternative to the equilibrium paradigm so pervasive in contemporary economic theory—and one seemingly more adaptive to the analysis of economic activities as *processes*. It also touches conceptually on a number of questions which should be of some heuristic interest to our theorists. Space here will not permit more than the mere mention of some of these: purposive activity, order and probability, partial processes, irreversibility, etc.[21] Some investment in exploring the potentialities, possibly in consultation with specialists in that field, would appear to be worthwhile.

(d) It is apparent that some explorations of the sort touched upon in this section imply that at least some of our students have, or acquire, the ability to follow mathematical argument— perhaps even to initiate it. Many of us who have been involved in the theoretical wars for some time will—quite understandably—be skeptical of any such involvement. For, we are all too familiar with mathematical models of high elegance and small economic content; and with countless instances of the

Procrustean torturing of economic reality to make it fit the mathematical bed. It is, moreover, notoriously true that mathematical formulation is often made the end, rather than a means, of economic reasoning; and that (especially graduate) students are coerced into this mode of argument by a labor-intensive route which tends to render them the locked-in victims of their over-investment.

But all these are, after all, outrageous abuses of an essentially formal discipline which, like logic, cannot be presumed in advance to be either wrong or useless. Each of the abuses mentioned can easily be avoided; indeed, all of them are attributable to dilettantes rather than to competent mathematicians—and it is to the latter that reference is made here.

Several considerations deserve attention in this connection. First, the summary rejection of mathematics—root and branch—acts to exclude all mathematicians from our company. Yet, it should be possible for a mathematician to be a libertarian, too—and without schizophrenia. Secondly, it is a fact, however regrettable, that arguments in symbolic form—even when invalid—are held in awe by many. There is no good reason for those who have something valid to say to cede this advantage to their opponents. Thirdly, and more important, the scope of mathematics—as understood by its most able practitioners—is far broader, more humane, and more flexible than it appears to be to others. What Boulding[22] calls "the puritanism of mathematics" is likely to be merely in the eye of the casual observer.

This brings us at last to the suggestion of this subsection: that we explore the usefulness, for our purposes, of less numerical and more purely relational branches of mathematics.[23] One of these—topology—which seems to have special applicability to discontinuous phenomena (and should therefore have interested us long ago), is currently being utilized by a different group, in conjunction with so-called "catastrophe theory."[24] It is also interesting to note that this branch of mathematics, which is relatively neglected in our general treatises, is given more space in the Soviet texts.[25]

3. The final point of this section is a suggestion for the implementation of our central recommendation on the allocation of our resources with respect to controversies like those mentioned earlier as examples of "malinvestment" on our part. It is unrealistic—and perhaps unwise—to expect that we shall be able to avoid any involvement at all in recurrent and provocative fallacies. But we can—and should—determine to deal with them *on our terms* rather than on those of others.

This implies not only setting quantitative limits on our engagement in controversies of high (and increasing) marginal futility, but also on two qualitative ones. The first is that we act to set the conditions and the form of the discourse in which we consent to participate, for the purpose of eliminating both sheer repetition and all the small-minded, often demagogic, stratagems and posturings that one would expect, if at all, of secondary school debates and not of mature academic discourse. The second is that we insist on a fairly frank and clear specification of the context (usually a complex of tacit assumptions and esoteric definitions) of the discussion, since the failure to do so often artificially restricts the full scope of the discussion or otherwise puts one group of discussants, from the start, under unfair burden. It is only prudent to ensure that the terms of discourse, like the terms of trade, are not always unfavorable to the same people.

Let us try to illustrate, briefly, with reference to several of the controversial perennials. The issues of economic planning and mathematical economics have already been discussed and will be passed over here, except to say that we ought to insist at the outset of any further discussion of these that (1) it be recognized that we are not opposed to planning, but only to a special form of it; (2) we reject not mathematics per se, but its irrelevant or distortive application to economic analysis; and (3) we shall not continue in any discussion which does not accept these distinctions.

(a) Although discussion of socialism and capitalism as alternative economic systems long ago ran into diminishing returns, very little has been done about changing the context. From the start, Marxism restricted itself to a detailed exposition of the inner stresses expected to emerge within capitalist systems, which would eventually bring about their collapse and replacement by socialist regimes. Now, over a century later, the latter half of which has seen one major such state in actual operation, together with a number of satellites, expositions of the contradictions of capitalism continue,[26] while those of socialism are either very lightly touched upon or are allowed to be buried with obfuscation.

Despite the fact that many crucial predictions of Marxism have failed (*e.g.*, the theory of immiserization, the industrial reserve army, the absorption of the middle class, the withering of the state, etc.), we are still largely defending (or criticizing) the operation of capitalism only. On a more theoretical level, both the "transformation problem" and the calculation critique will illustrate clearly the obfuscation mentioned above.

We should therefore cease acceding to discussions of the problems of one system only, or those which compare the actual operation of one with only putative weaknesses in the other. Instead, there ought to be some insistence on the use of some common denominator for comparison—preferably a set of performance standards capable of empirical verification. The designing of such standards admittedly would be difficult—given the incommensurabilities of economic organization and, in particular, the differing degrees of coyness with which data are made available—but the task is far from an impossible one with which to challenge young scholars.

In fine, the burden of proof should shift in part, so that socialists, too, would have to defend their system against the charge that it is failing. Nor should an ideological "détente" be permitted to take the place of the rapidly evanescing political-military one; their "drift" toward capitalism is not on the same road as ours toward socialism—so we may never meet. They are backing slightly away from socialist arrangements which did not work; while in the West we never really got to trying a really free market system.

(b) In our differences with macroeconomic analysis, we have been once again too accommodating in our willingness to accept its context and definitions. By this context, macroeconomics is taken to be a system of causal and other relationships among aggregative economic entities and consequently an alternative to microeconomics—and, indeed, often in sharp conflict with it. As such, it has been vigorously resisted and opposed by free-market economists. But suppose this conception of macroeconomics is neither the only—or correct—one?

It is by now virtually forgotten that it was the intention of the pioneers of national income estimates to set up the equivalent of a profit-and-loss statement for the whole economy—like its prototype, *ex post* and evaluative. Indeed, Kuznets (a founder and leading architect of national income statistics) states this fact unequivocally:[27]

... national income is the end product of a country's economic activity, reflecting the combined play of economic forces and serving to appraise the prevailing economic organization in terms of its returns. Being thus *a summary and appraisal notion rather than an analytical entity*, national income demands statistical measurement. [Emphasis added.]

In this case, as before, we can insist on the recognition of the distinction between macroeconomics as a set of *ex post* data on the outcomes in the economy and as a distinct explanatory theory— emphasizing that taken in the former sense we accept, and even welcome, it as a valuable supplement to any explanation of the working of the market economy. If this is done, we may be able to avoid becoming enmeshed in a host of wasteful efforts of which the following are illustrations.

One is the frequently-heard wish that some way be sought to coordinate macro- and micro-models of analysis—presumably as separate parts of an even grander, more inclusive explanatory model. This appears to be at least improbable, given their mutually contradictory explanations, and would comprise an inexcusable waste of time and talent if the correct disposition of the conflict turns out to be not the coordination of the two, but the subordination of one to the other as serving very different but complementary functions.[28]

Another is the interesting—and generous—offer recently voiced by Lachmann:[29] that we undertake to "subjectivize" the macro-entities by some process of disaggregation until they are consistent with subjective choice. One suspects that this arduous effort will merely lead us back out of the looking glass and into the familiar micro-economic world. Fortunately, this travail will prove unnecessary if the subordination we have mentioned turns out to be the correct relation between micro- and macro-economics.

III.

If it is to be taken seriously, any body of theories about the real world must eventually take its own measure against that reality. To fail to do so may avoid, for a time, the risk of disconfirmation, but also forgoes the opportunity for potent reinforcement.

It is often claimed, in defense of delay, that the particular and accidental forms in which actual events present themselves are different and incongruent with those of abstract, systematic thought—and this, of course, is true in part. But, while the most general propositions of a theory may not lend themselves to direct observation, the deductive working out of their implications should tend to produce subsidiary statements whose form and content lend themselves to some form of comparison with empirical reality—if not by the structured methods of positivistic "science," then by informed subjective judgment ("verstehen").

The need for some sort of outside confirmation is especially important for those theoretical systems which, like Austrian economics, make the claim that they are axiomatic and apodictically true—and are therefore open to the facile criticism that they are purely formal (*i.e.*, devoid of real content) and are merely internally consistent circularities.

When, in addition to all this, the central propositions of a theory have great generality in their frame of reference, they "vector" out to touch hands with other areas of analysis or of activity not normally subsumed within the domain of the theory itself. This certainly appears to be the case with Austrian economics on at least two grounds: (1) it purports to deal with all human action and not just one aspect or subset (economic activity); and (2) it insists on the categorical primacy of individual choice.

In turn, this generality of Austrian theory implies both an obligation and an opportunity; the obligation, on the one hand, to make whatever contributions it can to other areas to which its principles apply, and, on the other, the opportunity to invite and receive contributions from people with special competence in such areas.

The "field" for such mutuality of interest extends not only to other theoretical disciplines, but also to "applied" areas. Several examples of the former have already been mentioned in another connection (*i.e.*, statistics and mathematics); others will readily occur to the reader (consider, for example, the continuing interest in Austrian theory on the part of philosophers, political theorists, legal scholars, *et al.*) and will not be discussed here.

The specific task of the final section of this paper will be to offer illustrations of more practical, operational areas which bear this sort of interface with Austrian analysis. Space—and the patience of the reader—will permit only a very small sampling of these; their selection should not be taken to indicate their importance relative to the many omitted, but merely as an attempt to show range and diversity.

A. Business operations and management should be the most obvious—and easiest—of the applied areas with which to establish the sort of two-way communication we are discussing. Yet, the exchange between economists and businessmen continues to be very disappointing both in extent and quality. (The many historical, institutional, and other factors behind this puzzling and complex state of affairs—and the possibilities for changing it—are clearly beyond the scope of this paper.)[30] Nevertheless, the relatively realistic nature of its concept of the economic process, together with its emphasis on the power of individual action, gives Austrian economics a special opportunity to explore some proximate and straightforward possibilities for mutual contributions.

(1) Business organizations offer a vast theater for testing the advantages of reliance on the motivation and responsibility of individuals. Indeed, management theorists[31] have presented a compelling case for moving away from traditional centralized and authoritarian organizational designs of decision-making responsibility ("Theory X") and toward more reliance on decentralized, individually oriented initiatives ("Theory Y"). Experimentation with changes along these lines has had to be cautious and marginal (since firms must operate within the constraints of the cost-recouping "imperative"), and the results thus far have not been uniformly conclusive. Detailed and frank analysis of instances of success and failure in such experiments would appear to offer interesting opportunities for practitioners to confer with theorists, to the benefit of both.

(2) Regular consultation with businessmen would not only acquaint the latter with the often esoteric language and concepts of economic theory, it would also tend to reduce the risks that theorists run when they depart from realism. To use one of the points already familiar to the reader as illustration: It is inconceivable that the prevailing conception of the entrepreneurial function in traditional economic theory would appear to actual entrepreneurs as accurate. If this conception is in serious error, a very long sequence of theorizing—as well as costly policies deriving from it—could have been averted by the simple process of identifying the picture of the entrepreneur which was implicit in the early analysis and making it explicit so that experienced practitioners could evaluate it.

Even now, it would be useful to do this. For any revision of the role of the enterpriser will involve radical changes in the traditional models of the operation of the economy and will therefore not be embraced immediately or with enthusiasm. The cooperation of businessmen will not only help confirm that the revision is realistic, but they can help flesh it out further.

(3) The subjective view of human action necessarily puts a great deal of reliance on the concept of "verstehen"—a composite of experience, intuition, and other qualities not adequately conveyed by the word "understanding." The prevailing positivist temper of our age is apt to dismiss so subjective a notion as being simply vague (if not worse) unless it is buttressed by practical and highly realistic examples. These are best and most influentially to be provided by those experienced in a variety of management decisions in which the "objective" data had to be evaluated and supplemented by human judgment.

(4) Finally, this very subjectivity has important implications for the proper role of present managers in the education of those who will follow them.[32] For, if the essence of what they do is subjective, it cannot be conveyed adequately either by rigid sets of rules or by abstract models devised largely without reference to the realities of actual performance. There is reason to think that just such a deficiency now exists and is being dealt with by on-the-job remedial action. The prevalence and extent of management training programs in so many of our large corporations may thus be a tacit—and very costly—criticism of the adequacy of programs in the formal education of young business managers.

B. This brings us to the second illustrative area—and one very close to home. Quite apart from its content—one aspect of which we have just now touched on—the organization of formal education on the collegiate and even on the graduate level is deeply inconsistent with subjectivism. In this respect, we in education have lagged far behind industry, where, as we saw a little earlier, there has been at least some attempt to give greater scope to individual initiative and provision. But where, in our own house, is the application of the same "Theory *Y*" which we have been urging on others? The fact is that education remains—as it has long been—essentially paternalistic and authoritarian. Persisting patterns of sanctions and rewards are hardly conducive to—or even tolerant of—the exercise of independent judgments and valuations by the individual student. True academic freedom (that is, in its original meaning and intent) has more the appearance of a class privilege reserved to the faculty than an intellectual right that extends to students—or even to applicants for faculty positions.

A little reflection by anyone who has attended college, and especially graduate school, will suggest many examples of this perverse state of academic affairs—and the point will not be pursued here. But it should be obvious that subjective theorists have here a special obligation to establish a dialogue with educational administrators and others and to seek ways in which students can be encouraged—certainly not discouraged—in the exercise of independent judgment.

C. The third and final example, literature, is illustrative of a large class of pursuits or professions whose essence and practice depend significantly on individual effort and on subjective values. The history of literatures from Milton to Solzhenitsyn exhibits real concern for individual freedom of expression and of action[33]—often defended courageously and at great personal cost. Moreover, as the case of the Fabian Society illustrates all too well, it is possible for people of great literary talent to become interested in social and economic issues and to present these to the reading public with great potency and effect. Here, again, Austrian theorists would seem to have the opportunity and the obligation to establish and maintain communication with all those—however distant from strict economy theory—who share their insight on the nature and significance of human action.

REFERENCES

1. Although it was published three years after the others, the work of Leon Walras (*Éléments d'économie politique pure*, 1874) is now generally accepted as independently developed.

2. Unfortunately, this term is currently being used for things very different from this, its original meaning, resulting in unnecessary confusion. Cf., *e.g.*, P. A. Samuelson, *Economics: An Introductory Analysis*,

7th ed. (New York, 1967), pp. 351–52; and also, *Newsweek*, May 12, 1975.

3. Were it not for this double purpose and the related need to save space, an excellent example would be provided by the extended discussion by so many Marxists and their opponents of the so-called "transformation problem" since Böhm-Bawerk (*Karl Marx and the Close of His System*, London, 1898).

4. This may also apply to extended discussions with less antagonistic critics. For example, as Ludwig Lachmann observed at a recent conference on Austrian economics (Milwaukee, March 1976), the long discussions following Knight's criticism of Austrian capital theory took time which was needed elsewhere.

5. F. A. Hayek, "The New Confusion about Planning," *Morgan Guaranty Survey*, January 1976.

6. L. M. Spadaro, *The Present State of Profit Theory: Asset or Liability?* (Philadelphia, 1963).

7. I. M. Kirzner, *Competition and Entrepreneurship* (Chicago, 1973).

8. See Gerald O'Driscoll, "Spontaneous Order and the Coordination of Economic Activities," elsewhere in this volume.

9. *Newsweek*, March 15, 1976.

10. Cf., *e.g.*, L. J. Savage, *The Foundations of Statistics* (New York, 1954); also, L. M. Spadaro, "Averages and Aggregates in Economics," in M. Sennholz, ed., *On Freedom and Free Enterprise* (Princeton, 1956).

11. Both Laplace (*Théorie analytique des probabilités*, Paris, 1814) and De Morgan (*An Essay on Probability*, London, 1838) regarded probability as the degree of belief in a proposition and as referring to a state of mind.

12. Cf., *e.g.*, E. Nagel, "The Meaning of Probability," in J. R. Newman, ed., *The World of Mathematics* (New York, 1956), vol. 2, pp. 1398–1414; F. J. Anscombe and R. J. Aumann, "A Definition of Subjective Probability," *Annals of Math. Stat.*, vol. 34 (1963), pp. 199–205. It is interesting, too, to note that J. M. Keynes, in an early work on this subject (*A Treatise on Probability*, London, 1921), treats probability as a directly intuitable relation which, while capable of varying in degree, is not analyzable by the calculus of probability.

13. One of the earliest and most able of those interested initially in the truly subjective aspect of probability, Thomas Bayes, also emphasized its relation to degrees of belief (cf., his two memoirs in *Philosophical Transactions*, 1763 and 1764). Nowadays, however, his name is almost exclusively associated—because of a theorem of his (Bayes's Theorem)—with conditional probability.

14. *E.g.*, S. B. Richmond, *Operations Research for Management Decisions* (New York, 1968), *passim*, espec. pp. 129–33, 148–52, and 541–47.

15. Cf., *e.g.*, R. Carnap, "What is Probability," *Scientific American* (September 1953), pp. 128–36.

16. Cf. F. A. Hayek, "Economics and Knowledge," in *Individualism and Economic Order* (Chicago, 1948), pp. 33–56; also, G. J. Stigler, "The Economics of Information," *Jour. Pol. Econ.* (June 1961), pp. 213–25.

17. The modern resurgence of interest in the analysis of information begins with a seminal paper by Claude Shannon (C. E. Shannon, "A Mathematical Theory of Communication," *Bell Syst. Tech. Jour.* [1948]. For more general implications, see N. Wiener, *Cybernetics* [New York, 1948]).

18. For comprehension of various aspects of this area, see: C. Cherry, *On Human Communication*, 2nd ed. (Cambridge, Mass., 1966); J. R. Pierce, *Symbols, Signals and Noise: The Nature and Process of Communication* (New York, 1961); and espec. H. Theil, *Economics and Information Theory* (Chicago, 1967).

19. One interesting example is an attempt to use communication theory to buttress what is essentially a variant of many inflationist schemes: S. Bagno, *The Angel and the Wheat: Communication Theory and Economics* (New York, 1963). Unfortunately, space does not permit an extended analysis of the inflationism involved, but its dedication is revealing:

"Dedicated to
Claude Shannon and Norbert Wiener
Whose Theorems are the Foundations of a Consistent Economic Doctrine
and to
John Law
Whose Methods Enabled Us to Learn Our True Potential"

20. Cf., *e.g.*, Pierce, *op. cit.*, chap. 5.

21. For a detailed exposition, see N. Georgescu-Roegen, *The Entropy Law and the Economic Process* (Cambridge, Mass., 1971).

22. K. E. Boulding, *Economics As a Science* (New York, 1970), p. 101.

23. The writer had occasion to make this same suggestion some time ago in another context: L. M. Spadaro, "The Heuristic Value of Simulation in Business and Economic Research," *Proceedings, Amer. Stat. Assoc.*, 1966, pp. 73–79.

24. *Newsweek*, January 19, 1976.

25. Cf., *e.g.*, A. D. Aleksandrov, A. N. Kolmogorov, and M. A. Lavrent'ev, eds., *Mathematics: Its Content, Methods, and Meaning*, Eng. transl., 2nd ed. (Cambridge, Mass., 1969), espec. vol. 3, chap. 18.

26. The most recent example known to the writer is D. P. Bell, *The Cultural Contradictions of Capitalism* (New York, 1975).

27. S. S. Kuznets, "National Income," *Encycl. Soc. Sci.* (1933) and reprinted in Amer. Econ. Assoc., *Readings in the Theory of Income Dis-*

tribution (Philadelphia, 1949), pp. 3–43. The quotation here is from p. 3.

28. For discussion of some of the difficulties and errors resulting from attempts to establish causal relationships among macro-quantities directly, cf., H. Theil, "Alternative Approaches to the Aggregation Problem," in E. Nagle, P. Suppes, and A. Tarski, eds., *Logic, Methodology, and Philosophy of Science* (Stanford, 1962).

29. Also in his remarks at the Milwaukee conference cited in note 4.

30. The writer is planning a monograph which is expected to include a detailed analysis of this situation.

31. Cf., *e.g.*, D. McGregor, *The Human Side of Enterprise* (New York, 1960); A. H. Maslow, *Eupsychian Management* (Homewood, Ill., 1965); and P. F. Drucker, *Management: Tasks, Responsibilities, Practices* (New York, 1973).

32. For a literate and cogent discussion of this role, cf., H. M. Boettinger, "Is Management Really an Art?" *Harvard Bus. Rev.*, (January–February 1975), pp. 54–63.

33. For one suggestive example from literary criticism, cf., L. Trilling, *The Liberal Imagination* (New York, 1950).

INDEX

Ackley, Gardner, *Macroeconomic Theory*, 203 n56
Action: in Austrian theory, 24; axiom of, 50–52; conceptualization and, 25–36; erroneous, 61–63; praxeology and, 50, 54; probability in, 31–32
Alchian, Armen A., 88, 91
Aleksandrov, A. D., *et al.*, eds., *Mathematics*, 226 n25
Alertness, 68–69
Anscombe, F. J., and R. J. Aumann, "A Definition of Subjective Probability," 225 n12
Antitrust approaches, erroneous, 98
Application of theory, 220–224
A priorism, 19–20, 49–52
Armentano, D. T., ix, 94–110; *The Myths of Antitrust*, 109 nn4,5
Arrow, K. J.: "Limited Knowledge and Economic Analysis," 18 n8; on market economy, 12–15
Asset markets, 3–4; volatility of, 4–6
Aumann, R. J., *see* Anscombe, F. J.
Austrian differentia, 23–24
Austrian economics, vii–x, 1 *et passim*; future development, x, 205–227
Austrian method, 32–35
Austrian School: Chicago School and, 122–124; coordination and, 128–135; on equilibrium, 129–134; money-supply definitions, 143–156; planning in, 127, 128–134; spontaneous order and, 128–134
"Autonomy of the human mind," 129–130

Ayer, A. J., *Language, Truth, and Logic*, 55 n2

Bagno, S., *The Angel and the Wheat*, 226 n19
Bailey, Martin J., "Review of *Capital and Its Structure*," 139 n31
Barriers to entry, 97–99; legal, 102, 108–109; monopoly and, 95, 96
Bayes, Thomas, 225 n12
Becker, Gary S.: on time preference, 161; *also see* Ghez, Gilbert
Bell, D. P., *The Cultural Contradictions of Capitalism*, 226 n26
Blanshard, Brand, *Reason and Analysis*, 55 nn7,8
Boettinger, H. M., "Is Management Really an Art?" 227 n32
Böhm-Bawerk, Eugen von: capital dimensions, 169; *Capital and Interest*, 166 n17, 201 nn11,19, 202 n31; on capital/production time, 179; capital theory, 1–2; interest theory, 158; *Karl Marx and the Close of His System*, 225 n3; "Positive Theory of Capital," 166 n17; on production time, 170–171
Bond market, 162–163
Boulding, K. E., *Economics as a Science*, 226 n22
Buchanan, James M.: on the Chicago School, 137 n19; *Cost and Choice*, 92 n1; "The Justice of Natural Liberty," 135 n1; on the London School of Economics, 81–82; "Public Goods and Natural Liberty," 137

Louis M. Spadaro was born in New York City in 1913 and holds the A.B. and M.S. degrees from the City University of New York. He received his doctorate in economics from New York University in 1955.

A member of the faculty of Fordham University since 1938, Spadaro has also served in various administrative posts, including Dean of the Graduate School of Business Administration and Chairman of the Department of Economics.

He is the author of numerous articles in economics and the textbook *Economics: An Introductory View* (New York: Macmillan, 1969).

Spadaro is President of the Institute for Humane Studies. He is a member of and has held office in both Beta Gamma Sigma and Omicron Delta Epsilon. His other memberships include the Mont Pelerin Society, the American Economic Association, and the American Statistical Association.